ONE STEP AHEAD

ONE STEP AHEAD

THE LEGAL ASPECTS OF BUSINESS GROWTH

ANDREW J. SHERMAN

amacom

AMERICAN MANAGEMENT ASSOCIATION

Library of Congress Cataloging-in-Publication Data
Sherman, Andrew J.
    One step ahead : the legal aspects of business growth / Andrew J.
Sherman.
        p.   cm.
    ISBN 0-8144-5962-5
    1. Corporation law—United States.   2. Corporations—United
States—Growth.   I. Title.
KF1414.S44   1989
346.73'066—dc20
[347.30666]   89-45456
                                                               CIP

Printing number

10   9   8   7   6   5   4   3   2   1

*Inspiration and support
for the publication of this book
was provided by
clients, friends, and family,
and especially by my wife, Judy.
I am grateful to them all.*

Acknowledgments

It seems as though there are always more people to thank than time and space ever permit. And such is the case with the publication of this book. Nevertheless, there are certain individuals to whom I am deeply indebted: Ripley Hotch of *Nation's Business* and Julie Sobieski of *Business Age,* for their early support of my writing; Acquisitions Editor Andrea Pedolsky, Associate Editor Barbara Horowitz, and Periodicals Group Editor Florence Stone of the American Management Association, for their guidance in and support of this project; the entire staff of McVey & Sherman and particularly my partner, Tom McVey, for putting up with me on a daily basis; and finally Maggie Coffey and Cathy Jo Caseman, for their word processing magic and patience.

I am especially grateful to my wife, Judy, who endured countless lonely nights and weekends, watching me hovering over my notes, reference materials, and legal pads at our dining room table.

Contents

PART IV
Staying One Step Ahead

Exhibits

Preface

Of the hundreds of entrepreneurs and small companies over the years for whom I have had the pleasure (and displeasure) of serving as legal counsel, no two have been exactly alike. Each company had different management teams, financial problems, marketing challenges, and business objectives, with one notable exception: the desire to grow.

I have never met an entrepreneur who started a business, regardless of the person's specific industry or experience, who did not identify growth as the top priority. Nor have I met an entrepreneur who did not initially underestimate the severity of the challenges that growing a business would present. The men and women who succeed in building their companies are often the first to admit that business growth brings with it a wide variety of management, financial, marketing, and legal problems. This book is a pragmatic resource that discusses the legal problems and issues that a typical company faces as it grows.

One Step Ahead examines business growth and organizational change from a legal perspective. Its primary objective is to provide owners and managers of growing companies, as well as professional advisers, management consultants, investors, bankers, and all others who may work with emerging businesses, with a resource for understanding the fundamental legal issues and hurdles that affect the short-, medium-, and long-term business objectives of rapidly growing organizations. Basic principles of corporate, securities, intellectual property, antitrust and trade regulation, employment, and contract law have a tremendous impact on the transactions, financing, goal setting, and day-to-day operations of a growing company. Yet few entrepreneurs or their advisers truly understand the basic legal issues that affect the planning and decision-making process. And many more fail to take the steps to help control their own legal destiny.

This book is not a substitute for the advice and guidance of qualified legal counsel. Instead it is designed to provide readers with a core knowledge of the legal issues affecting corporate development and business growth, which ultimately will make the relationship with legal counsel more effective and efficient. Owners and managers who understand these legal issues will be able to (1)

manage and control legal problems and disputes before they mature into litigation or business failure (known as *preventive law*); (2) take legal considerations
and hurdles into account before engaging in a particular transaction or implementing a particular strategy; (3) reduce legal costs by avoiding the need to turn
to legal counsel for answers to basic questions and problems; (4) identify the
optimal structure, method, or alternative for accomplishing specific business
objectives; and (5) protect the company's tangible and intangible assets and intellectual property.

The chapters that follow provide an overview of the legal issues owners and
managers of rapidly growing companies most often face. Virtually all of the
issues are applicable to growing companies regardless of the specific industry or
territory in which they operate and compete.

The body of the book has been divided into four major parts. Each of the first
three addresses the legal issues raised by the three principal components necessary to foster and sustain the growth of a business: *management*, i.e., internal
managers and external advisers whose expertise and energy are harnessed to fuel
the growth; *money*, i.e., capital needed to acquire and exploit assets required for
growth; and *markets*, i.e., methods for reaching customers and clients more
effectively and efficiently than competitors. The fourth part discusses legal audits, the management of business conflict, and the management of financial distress.

Different types of companies will face different types of legal problems raised
by growth that will affect all aspects of corporate planning and decision making.
For example, manufacturing companies may be more concerned than others with
zoning, environmental, safety, health, and labor laws, whereas a consulting services company may be concerned with protecting its trade secrets and the development of employment contracts. Industry-specific laws, however, such as
transportation, pharmaceuticals, or admiralty laws, will not be discussed, nor
will laws affecting personal affairs, such as wills, trusts, or matrimony. Readers
are strongly encouraged to seek qualified attorneys whose practices include these
areas if assistance is needed.

Virtually every aspect of business growth and organizational development is
directly or indirectly affected in some manner by legal issues and problems.
Owners and managers at all levels in the company must be familiar with the
applicable legal constraints, as well as the legal protections, that may be relevant
to the particular transaction, strategy, or venture under consideration. An awareness and basic understanding of these legal issues and the situations where legal
counsel should be retained, *well before* the actual event occurs or strategy is
implemented, will help save a growing company precious time, trouble, and
valuable resources.

Andrew J. Sherman
Washington, D.C.

CHAPTER

1

Legal Aspects of
Managing Growth

The 1980s were hailed by politicians, academics, and business leaders as the "decade of the entrepreneur." During that decade a record number of businesses were started by Americans whose thirst for financial gain, independence, and leadership were unmatched by any other nation. But as we enter the 1990s, the emphasis has shifted from small business to business growth because many companies that were at the start-up stage in the mid-1980s have (1) failed (often due to an inability to manage growth properly, as a result of a lack of capital, inadequate business and strategic planning, or an inability to manage resources); (2) remained stagnant (small businesses that will always be small, usually due to some external or internal limitation on growth, ability, or targeted marketplace); or (3) positioned themselves for growth.

It is the companies in this third category that will dominate the next decade. The efforts and accomplishments of the business survivors of the 1980s will be of economic significance in the 1990s. The challenges and problems associated with building a company beyond the start-up phase have certainly taken a toll on the many entrepreneurs who began new businesses in the 1980s. Growth has traditionally been regarded by academics as the stage of the business life cycle that follows market entry. Many small companies that were founded during the "decade of the entrepreneur" never made it to this stage, instead stagnating or failing. To advance to the growth stage—and stay there—all of the challenges and changes resulting from sustained growth must be well managed—no easy task.

Growth leads to a wide variety of changes that present management, legal, and financial challenges. Growth means that new employees will be hired, who will be looking to the top management of the company for leadership. Growth means that the company's management will become increasingly more decentralized, perhaps creating greater levels of internal politics, protectionism, and dissension over the goals and projects that the company should pursue. Growth

1

means that market share will expand, calling for new strategies for dealing with larger competitors. Growth means that additional capital will be required, creating new responsibilities to shareholders, investors, and institutional lenders.

The plans and strategies that management develops in response to the various changes caused by rapid growth cannot be made in a vacuum. Management must understand the legal implications, costs, benefits, and risks of each proposed decision, transaction, plan, or strategy in order to manage the organization effectively and to ensure its long-term success and continued profitability.

The Dilemma of Business Growth

Business growth is truly a two-edged sword. When it is controlled and well managed, it has the potential of providing tremendous rewards to the managers and shareholders of the company. When it is poorly planned and uncontrolled, it often leads to financial distress and failure.

Rapid growth for many companies is the only way to survive in highly competitive industries. These companies face the choice of acting quickly to capture additional market share or sitting on the sidelines and watching others play the game. These competitive conditions do not justify unplanned and unbridled growth, where sound management, legal, and accounting principles can be disregarded. Instead the organization must understand that profitable long-term growth is the by-product of effective management and planning. A strategy that focuses on sensible and logical growth dictates that a balance is created between the need for organizational flexibility in order to be able to seize market opportunities, adapt to changes in the marketplace, and develop creative solutions for problems that arise versus the need for controlled and well-managed expansion. Organizations that fail to create this balance will be vulnerable to attack by competitors, creditors, and creative takeover specialists.

Management that is committed to well-planned expansion will invariably undertake risks necessary to achieve specific growth objectives. These risks must be managed from a legal perspective, as must the changes that the organization will experience during growth. Accelerated growth will mean that these risks and changes will occur with greater frequency and with more serious implications. The requirements and restrictions imposed by the law that affect most business objectives and transactions will typically retard the rate at which a company can grow. The delays caused by legal drafting and negotiation of documents, filings with regulators, and meeting statutory requirements, however, are inevitable setbacks and costs of doing business. Prudent owners and managers of growing companies should take the time to learn the fundamental legal issues that govern their plans and strategies.

Some Model Companies

In order to understand better how the law affects the management of business growth, consider the following examples.

In Search of the Better Mousetrap

Impasse, Inc., a West Coast manufacturer of consumer electronics products, has reached a crossroads in its growth and development. Under the leadership of George Eightrack, the company became a leading producer of portable stereo systems in the late 1970s and enjoyed steady increases in revenues and profits. Increasing international competition, however, has caused Impasse to lose a substantial portion of its market share. In addition, its product lines are rapidly becoming obsolete. As a result of these product development and competitive problems, its earnings are decreasing, and the company's shareholders are losing confidence in Eightrack's strategies and management team. Eightrack has decided to bring in a well-known industry consulting firm, Phyllis Compactdisc & Associates, in order to develop a long-range growth strategy. Compactdisc has identified three alternatives in its report:

1. Raise additional capital in order to fund new product research and development.
2. Position the company for a sale to either a current competitor or a disinterested third party.
3. Use retained earnings and the company's available lines of credit to identify and acquire smaller manufacturers or complementary product lines in order to diversify in the marketplace.

Recognizing that these three alternatives raise a wide range of legal issues in areas such as corporate structure, capital formation, antitrust, and mergers and acquisitions, Eightrack immediately contacted legal counsel in order to understand the legal implications of the three growth alternatives.

The New Discovery

The Sweet-Tooth Bakery Products Company has been baking doughnuts for nearly 40 years in New England. Its bavarian creme, glazed, and chocolate-topped treats are well known to and liked by consumers, who purchase them in local supermarkets. Bob Middleman, the founder and chairman of the board, has a strong bias toward wholesale distribution and has never considered establishing a retail location to compete with the national franchised chains. But late last year, Bill Eatalot, an aggressive and innovative employee, developed a recipe for a new bakery product. His doughnut/bagel hybrid, the BagDough, is popular for breakfast with the company employees. Eatalot is anxious to bring this new product to the marketplace and is insistent that the BagDough would serve as an excellent showcase product for the establishment of retail shops. In addition, Eatalot has threatened that if action is not taken by Middleman and his board in the near future, he will take his recipes elsewhere. At Sweet-Tooth's next board of directors meeting, the following issues were discussed:

- What is the most efficient and effective method of exploring this new recipe? Should company-owned retail locations, business format franchises, distributorships, or licensing programs be considered? What are the costs and benefits of each method of distribution?
- Can Eatalot take the recipes elsewhere? What are the company's legal rights and remedies in connection with these trade secrets? In what manner can the recipes and proprietary production processes be protected if Eatalot is convinced to remain with the company?
- How can the company structure a stock ownership and compensation package that will be sufficient incentive for Eatalot to stay?
- How will the project be financed if the company pursues it?

Because of the complex franchising and licensing, intellectual property, labor and employment, and capital formation issues raised by Eatalot's invention, the company has begun to assemble a management team that will explore these issues in greater detail, and corporate counsel has been asked to serve as a key member.

The Need for Fresh Talent

HighTech Corporation was started three years ago by a group of software engineers who had become frustrated with the bureaucracy of the very large corporations where they were employed. The engineers had originally met at a software conference where they discovered a wide range of mutual interests. In particular, all had an interest in the newspaper and magazine publishing industry and had observed that no software company had introduced a program that could assist smaller publications with financial and circulation management.

The founders settled on the suburbs of Chicago for the company's corporate headquarters and quickly began to recruit management, financial, technical, and sales personnel. Although the development of the company's two principal software products for the publishing industry was progressing ahead of schedule, qualified staff were becoming more difficult to recruit because of the aggressive recruiting efforts and compensation offered by larger competitors. In addition, many of the current personnel, who had been hastily hired, lacked the skills and knowledge necessary to enable the company to achieve its next level of growth.

Roger Hardrive, the company's president, asked HighTech's director of personnel, Lionel Cutthroat, to "get rid of the deadwood" immediately and aggressively recruit the software team currently in place at the company where Roger was previously employed, a direct competitor. The director of personnel, recognizing the problems with Roger's strategy, contacted legal counsel in order to discuss the following problems:

- What are the legal risks of soliciting the employees of a competitor?
- What is the safest and most effective manner of screening unqualified applicants without triggering discrimination claims?
- How should employment agreements be structured for those key staff members whom HighTech wants to retain?
- What is the safest and most effective manner of firing an unproductive or technically deficient employee?

From Rags to Riches

When Jim Cleansoil and Barbara Pureair were students at a small college in upstate New York during the early 1970s, they began publishing a newsletter, *EcoNews*, which covered a wide range of topics of interest to supporters of the ecological movement. Deeply committed to making the planet a safer place to live, Cleansoil and Pureair began consulting work after graduation to supplement subscription revenues. In 1974 they organized CleanWorld Consulting Company as a closely held corporation.

The company grew steadily for eight years, primarily due to contracts and grants awarded by federal, state, and local governments. As environmental legal issues and regulations grew in importance in the early 1980s, Pureair urged the board of directors to consider entry into the hazardous and toxic waste disposal and consulting market. Up to this point, CleanWorld had been financed entirely by internal means, but this shift in the company's marketing strategy would require an infusion of significant equity capital. CleanWorld therefore retained a financial consultant and an investment banker to assist it in developing a capital formation strategy. They determined that a business plan would need to be prepared and that the necessary capital would be raised in two stages: first, a private placement of convertible preferred stock in the aggregate amount of $2 million and then an initial public offering within 18 months for $5 million. Before implementing this plan, the board of CleanWorld wanted to understand the answers to the following questions:

1. What changes in the corporate structure will be necessary to implement these strategies? Will amendments to the corporation charter be necessary? How are these amendments adopted?

2. What are the advantages and disadvantages of a private placement of the company's securities? What documents must be prepared for investors? How is the offering regulated at the federal and state level?

3. What are the advantages and disadvantages of an initial public offering? What business and legal procedures must be followed prior to the offering? How will life be different as a publicly held corporation?

Haste Makes Waste

David Decor's passion for ceramic and porcelain home furnishings created in the Far East began during his service with the U.S. Army during the Korean and Vietnam wars. Following his retirement from the military, Decor formed Far East Imports Company, a small retail store in Atlanta, Georgia. Retail sales grew steadily, and he opened several additional stores throughout the Southeast in the early 1980s. When he reached $12 million in sales and was employing nearly 200 employees, Decor began to explore new markets.

Sarah Thinkbig, director of purchasing for Far East, proposed expanding into the wholesale market. She had noticed many national chains taking an interest in the inventory carried by the stores and was confident that these chains would be persuaded to purchase large quantities of merchandise from Far East at the wholesale level. Decor trusted Thinkbig's instincts but was hesitant about the large amounts of commercial debt financing required to finance the larger purchases, as well as to establish larger warehousing and distribution facilities. Nevertheless, he accepted her plan. It was a disaster. Changes in the international economy, inadequate market research, and insufficient capital caused the launch into wholesaling to be a huge failure. Trade creditors, landlords, and bankers began to threaten to take action if various defaults were not cured. Decor called upon legal counsel to address the following issues:

1. Should Far East Imports Company consider bankruptcy? What are the legal and business consequences of bankruptcy? What alternatives are available?

2. If disputes cannot be resolved, is litigation inevitable? What alternatives to litigation are available?

In the scenarios discussed above, each emerging-growth company, by understanding and analyzing the legal aspects of the proposed act, strategy, or transaction, will be better able to

• Protect its tangible and intangible assets.
• Enhance the value of the company in an effective and efficient manner.
• Manage the risk of business failure or litigation.
• Reduce its business transactional costs and professional fees.

- Identify the optimal structures, methods, and alternatives for accomplishing its business objectives.
- Understand the regulations at a federal and state level that affect these strategies and decisions.

The legal issues surrounding and implications of the problems these companies face, as well as other examples, case studies, and hypothetical companies, will be explored in greater detail in the chapters that follow.

PART

I

Management

In analyzing a candidate for a loan or equity investment, virtually all sophis-ticated lenders and investors agree that the management team of the entity is of the utmost importance. A strong team of executives and outside advisers with only a mediocre concept is far more likely to attract funding than an entity with a strong concept and a weak team.

As a result, Part I focuses on legal aspects of managing people and organiza-tions. Chapter 2 presents an overview of the legal aspects of hiring and firing. Chapter 3 discusses the management of professional relationships. Chapter 4 focuses on the legal aspects of managing a corporation.

These three chapters are not a crash course on either all of the legal or all of the business aspects of *managing* a growing corporation and the people who make it tick. Rather, they are intended to introduce and remind the reader of the many legal issues triggered each time a new employee, consultant, director, or shareholder is added as the corporation grows.

Managing Human Resources Within the Bounds of Labor and Employment Laws

The management of human resources plays a key role in the growth of all business organizations. Recruitment, selection, training, compensation, and promotion of key personnel are at the heart of any emerging-growth company's ability to meet its short- and long-term strategic goals. As a company grows, its original owners must be prepared to part with certain responsibilities and find employees with the skills and abilities necessary to manage various operating divisions within the company. Effective management teams made up of qualified, loyal, creative, and hardworking people whose blended skills and expertise allow the company to achieve new levels of growth and achievement must be established.

Human resources management means that an efficient organizational structure has been developed for the company to meet its objectives and that individuals have been selected to fill the various slots on the organizational chart. Human resources management also requires effective management of employees. For example, a decision to modify existing distribution channels requires either recruiting new workers or retraining current employees. For a rapidly growing company, managing employees is especially important, since the lack of one key person or the presence of an extra person on the payroll could be the difference between a net profit and a net loss for any given fiscal year. A company that ignores human resources management is likely to begin losing one of its most important assets: the people who are required to establish and meet the company's business objectives.

Growing companies face especially difficult challenges in recruiting and retaining key employees. Many growing businesses do not yet have a formal personnel department or a recruitment program because they lack the time or the capital to spend searching for qualified workers. Often they cannot afford to pay the commissions charged by expensive executive recruitment and placement agencies. Thus, their hiring decisions are often made hastily—especially damaging to a small company where most employees at almost every level are often immediately given significant responsibilities. Capital-poor companies that put off hiring new employees find that current staff are overloaded, a situation that usually leads to disenchantment and loss of morale.

Recruitment is competitive, and many small businesses cannot match the compensation packages their larger competitors can offer. Similarly, once a key employee is finally recruited and trained, he or she may be hired away by a competitor offering more significant pay, growth potential, and employee benefits. Clearly employers must be careful to protect key assets with employment agreements and creative compensation and stock ownership plans.

The systems and procedures for hiring and firing personnel trigger a host of federal and state labor and employment laws that owners and managers of businesses of all sizes must understand. But small companies that fail to understand these laws can be especially damaged by extensive litigation costs incurred as the result of an employment-related dispute. Suits under federal employment laws currently comprise the largest group of civil filings in the federal court system. Federal and state legislatures have been equally active in designing new laws in the labor and employment arena, and small-business groups have been quick to respond to the adverse impact of these laws.

Understanding the Fundamentals

The growing body of employment law encompasses employment discrimination, comparable worth, unjust dismissal, affirmative action programs, job classification, workers' compensation, performance appraisal, employee discipline and demotion, maternity policies and benefits, employee recruitment techniques and procedures, employment policy manuals and agreements, age and retirement, plant closings and layoffs, sexual harassment and discrimination, occupational health and safety standards, laws protecting the handicapped, and mandated employment practices for government contractors. A comprehensive discussion of all of these topics would require several volumes. This chapter focuses on employment and labor laws as they affect employee selection, the preparation of employment agreements, and the procedure for terminating an unproductive worker.

A large body of federal law prohibits employment discrimination based on race, color, religion, national origin, gender, and age. The most comprehensive federal statutes and regulations affecting employment practices are listed in Exhibit 2-1.

In addition to these federal laws, many state legislatures have enacted antidis-

Exhibit 2-1.   Federal employment laws.

- Equal Pay Act of 1963. Prohibits pay differentials based on gender.
- Title VII of the Civil Rights Act of 1964 (Title VII). Prohibits discrimination based on race, color, religion, sex, or national origin.
- Age Discrimination in Employment Act of 1967 (ADEA). Prohibits discrimination against individuals age 40 or older.
- Vocational Rehabilitation Act of 1973. Requires government contractors to take affirmative action in hiring qualified handicapped individuals.
- Vietnam Era Veteran's Readjustment Assistance Act of 1974. Requires government contractors to take affirmative action to recruit, hire, and promote qualified disabled veterans and veterans of the Vietnam era.
- Immigration and Nationality Act. Prohibits employers from discriminating on the basis of citizenship or national origin. The Immigration Reform and Control Act of 1986 contains similar nondiscrimination provisions and also makes it unlawful for employers to recruit, hire, or continue to employ illegal immigrants to the United States.
- Pregnancy Discrimination Act of 1978. Prohibits discrimination against women affected by pregnancy or related conditions.

---

crimination laws that go beyond the protection afforded at the federal level. Companies must carefully review these state laws in order to ensure that employment practices comply.

Most litigation involving claims of discrimination has arisen under Title VII, enforced by the Equal Employment Opportunity Commission (EEOC), which makes it unlawful for an employer to fail or refuse to hire, decide to fire, or practice any other kind of discrimination with respect to terms and conditions of employment against any person on the basis of race, color, religion, sex, or national origin. Under limited circumstances, the EEOC will tolerate discriminatory practices in the recruitment process but only if the criteria for making the determination are based on a "bona fide occupational qualification" (BFOQ). A BFOQ is a job requirement that is both reasonable and necessary in the light of the normal operation of the business, even if the practice has a discriminatory impact. For example, the job of a towel clerk in an all-women's fitness facility might be justifiably limited to female candidates, despite its impact on male prospects. In reality, BFOQ criteria have been limited to very specific circumstances by the courts when applied to hiring decisions based on sex, religion, or national origin. Race, however, is rarely an acceptable basis for a BFOQ.

U.S. Supreme Court cases over the years have recognized that hiring policies that have a discriminatory impact may be practically justified by a business necessity. The business necessity must be related to job performance, however, and not encompass matters such as cost or inconvenience. Rather, the business necessity must be essential to the safe and efficient operation of the company so as to override any racial impact.

The broad scope of federal and state antidiscrimination laws makes it imperative that owners and managers of emerging-growth companies understand their obligations in structuring employee recruitment, selection, training, compensation, reward, employee testing, and seniority programs.

When we last discussed the hiring and firing requirements of HighTech Corporation, company president Hardrive had instructed its personnel director, Cutthroat, to recruit the personnel necessary to achieve the next level of growth and to get rid of the "deadwood." Cutthroat must now develop a basic recruitment and selection procedure that does not intentionally or inadvertently operate to screen out any particular minority group members, discourage them from applying for the position, or treat a candidate differently solely due to race, religion, sex, citizenship, or national origin.

Structuring a Recruitment and Selection Program

The equal opportunity laws do not require a company to recruit actively or maintain a designated quota of members of minority groups. These laws do, however, prohibit companies from developing recruitment and selection procedures that treat an applicant differently due to race, sex, age, religion, or national origin. In determining whether a particular company's recruitment policies have resulted in disparate treatment of minorities, the courts and the EEOC would look closely at

- The nature of the position and the objective education, training, and skill level required to fill the position
- The minority composition of the company's current work force and its relationship to local demographic statistics
- Prior hiring practices
- The recruitment channels, such as newspapers, agencies, industry publications, and universities, that were selected to attract candidates for the position
- The information requested of the candidate through the job application and interview

- Any selection criteria, testing, or related performance measure implemented in the decision-making process
- Any differences in the terms and conditions of employment offered to the applicant and to the successful candidate for the position

An individual alleging discrimination in the hiring process would need to demonstrate that the following key facts were present:

1. The applicant was a member of a protected minority class;
2. The individual was qualified for the job that was open;
3. The individual was denied the position; *and*
4. The advertised position remained open after the individual was rejected and the company continued to interview applicants with the same qualifications as the rejected candidate.

If the applicant could successfully demonstrate these facts, then the burden would shift to the company, which would have to present legitimate business reasons for not having hired the particular applicant.

There are several preventive measures that Cutthroat can implement to protect HighTech against such claims and ultimately to prevail when and if a disgruntled applicant files a discrimination charge.

1. *Prepare a well-drafted job description prior to any public advertising for the position.* The description should accurately reflect the duties of the position, the skills, ability, and knowledge needed to perform the position competently, the compensation and related terms and conditions of employment, and the education, training, prior work experience, or professional certification, if any, required for the position. A well-prepared job description will not only assist HighTech in developing a set of objective criteria that an applicant needs and aid in selecting and retaining qualified people from a business perspective but will also serve as protection against a claim that the standards for the position were developed arbitrarily or in violation of applicable antidiscrimination laws.

2. *Develop an advertising and recruitment program that meets EEOC standards.* The phrase *equal opportunity employer* must appear in advertisements. The context of the advertisement should not indicate any preference toward race, sex, religion, national origin, or age unless it meets the requirements of a BFOQ for the particular position. If HighTech uses employment agencies for recruiting, it must inform them in writing of the company's nondiscrimination policy. If HighTech plans to recruit applicants from universities or trade schools, it must visit minority institutions also. In selecting publications for the placement of advertisements for the positions, HighTech should target all potential job applicants and advertise in minority publications where possible.

3. *Develop a job application form that is limited to job-related questions and meets all federal, state, and local legal requirements.* It should contain no questions regarding an individual's race or religion. HighTech will generally bear the

burden to prove that any question on the application, especially one relating to handicap, marital status, age, height or weight, criminal record, military status, or citizenship, is genuinely related to the applicant's ability to meet the requirements of the position. Even questions regarding date of birth or who to contact in the event of an emergency should be reserved for posthiring information gathering.

4. *Designate one of its employees as the equal employment opportunity compliance officer, charged with monitoring employment practices.* His or her responsibilities will include structuring position descriptions, job applications, and advertisements; collecting and maintaining applicant and employee files; meeting with interviewers to review employment laws that affect the questions that may be asked of the applicant; and working with legal counsel to ensure that the company's employment policies, as well as recent developments in the law, are adequately communicated to all employees.

Interviewing Prospective Candidates

From a business perspective, the interviewing process should consist of an honest and open exchange of information between the candidate for the position and the management team responsible for the hiring decision. Both the positive and negative aspects of the position should be discussed. The interviewer should ask questions based on the job description prepared for the position and information gathered from conversations with references given by the candidate and from the candidate's employment application. The flow of conversation should be directed by the interviewer but dominated by the applicant. Careful notes the interviewer takes during the meeting prevent claims of misrepresentation or discrimination, as well as aid in making a more informed decision regarding the applicant.

From a legal perspective, the questions asked during an interview must substantially be job related and asked on a uniform basis of all candidates for the position. The exact types of questions vary depending on applicable state laws; therefore, owners and managers should carefully consult the applicable employment laws for guidance. As a general rule, however, the following types of questions *should be avoided.*

- What is your marital status? How many children do you have? How do your family responsibilities affect your ability to meet work-related obligations?
- What is your religious affiliation? What religious holidays do you expect will interfere with work-related obligations?
- What is your national origin? Where are your parents from? What is your native language?

- Do you have any specific disabilities? Have you ever been treated for any diseases?
- Does your husband [or wife] object to your traveling or to your anticipated relocation? Will you be able to make arrangements for child care given the long hours of this job?

In addition, there are several topic areas for which questions are not necessarily prohibited but nevertheless should be asked carefully to avoid an indirect claim of discrimination. Questions regarding the applicant's prior or current drug history or social clubs and hobbies, or even a woman's maiden name, should be structured carefully.

Notwithstanding these somewhat draconian guidelines, there are still several types of questions legally available to the management team responsible for screening candidates, such as:

- Why are you leaving your current position? How does the position we are offering resolve some of those problems?
- What was the most challenging project that you were responsible for in your last position?
- Do you have any physical or mental impairments that will restrict your ability to perform the responsibilities of this position?
- Are any criminal indictments currently pending against you? What is the nature of these charges?
- What are your expectations regarding this position? How do these expectations influence your short- and long-term career goals?
- How would your former co-workers and supervisors assess your strengths and weaknesses?

Employment Agreements for the Growing Company

The ability of a small business to grow and prosper largely depends on the strength of its foundation and internal framework. At the heart of this foundation are two of the company's most important assets: human resources and intellectual property. (Intellectual property is defined and considered further in chapter 13.) The loss of either of these two key assets is likely to lead to the rapid decline of the business.

Small-business owners especially will have difficulty protecting these assets. The smaller company, for example, often serves as a training ground for new entrants into the work force, who are later attracted to the prestige, salary, growth opportunities, and other benefits offered by larger employers. The costs of high turnover affect the bottom line when precious time must be devoted to training new employees. Financing this learning curve, rather than enjoying the economy of scale offered by an experienced worker, will greatly affect revenues and profits.

Protection of intellectual property is also especially difficult for the small-business owner. Increasing entrepreneurialism and high employee turnover increases business vulnerability to trade secret theft. Internally trade secret pilferage is difficult to monitor because security measures may be too costly, divisions between departments are loosely defined, and financial and customer information may be stored on a single data base that lacks encryption or a restricted access system.

An *employment agreement* serves as an important and cost-effective way of safeguarding confidential business information and preserving valuable human resources. These agreements, when combined with a well-developed compensation plan, provide an economic and legal foundation for long-term employee loyalty.

Employment agreements may be fundamental to a growing company's existence and expansion for other reasons. For example, venture capital investors often insist on employment agreements between the company and its founders and key employees in order to protect their investment. Individuals with special management or technical expertise may insist on an employment agreement as a condition to joining the enterprise. Such agreements serve as an important human resources management tool in terms of description of duties, the basis for reward, and the grounds for termination.

Employers should carefully consider the long-term implications of the terms and conditions contained in the employment agreement. Once these promises are made to an employee in written form, the expectation is created that any special benefits will be available throughout the term of the agreement. A company that fails to meet these obligations will expose itself to the risk of litigation for breach of contract.

Drafting the Employment Agreement

Once the recruitment and selection process has been completed, the business should prepare employment agreements for the candidates who have been hired. It is generally more effective to enter into the contract at the commencement of the relationship rather than in midstream in order to avoid claims of coercion or duress. An exception to this rule, however, would be an agreement between Sweet-Tooth Bakery Products Company and Bill Eatalot, where the facts and circumstances of the relationship have substantially changed as a result of Eatalot's invention of the BagDough.

An agreement with a key employee should include the following provisions:

- Duration
- Duties and obligations of the employee
- Base salary arrangements
- Grounds for special compensation, such as profit sharing, rewards, and bonuses
- Provisions for reimbursement of expenses, vacations, and benefits
- Nondisclosure clauses
- Covenants against competition
- Provisions defining rights to inventions and "shop rights"
- Arrangements in the event of illness, disability, or death
- Grounds for termination, including the employee's obligations upon departure

Duration

The key issue in determining the duration of the employment agreement is whether the arrangement is best for the employer as a trial marriage or as a long-term commitment. If HighTech, for example, is unsure of the skills or qualifications of a possible new employee, a short-term contract with an option to renew may be more desirable. Conversely, if a candidate has an established reputation and is likely to be in high demand, HighTech's agreement should lock in the employee for as long as possible with incentives that will foster his or her long-term loyalty to the company.

Other factors that should influence duration are the nature of the assignment, the growth potential of the candidate, the company's business plans, and any relevant economic cycles or business trends. A separate section related to the duration of the contract should address the effect a subsequent merger or acquisition by HighTech would have on the agreement. The provisions discussing duration should also specify the exact commencement and expiration dates and the terms and procedures for tenure or renewal and refer to the grounds for early termination.

Duties and Obligations of the Employee

The description of the nature of the employment and the employee's duties should contain

- The exact title, if any, of the position
- A statement of the exact tasks and responsibilities the employee will perform and a description of how these tasks and duties relate to the objectives of other employees, departments, and the company overall

- The amount of time to be devoted to the position and to individual tasks (e.g., "Mr. Staff Member shall devote his entire time, attention, and energies at least 40 hours per week to the development of improved software products, including at least 6 hours per week to meetings with the market research department to gain a greater understanding of consumer demand.")
- Where appropriate, whether the employee will serve on HighTech's board of directors, and if so, whether any additional compensation will be paid for serving on the board

In certain circumstances, such as executive and managerial positions, the statement of duties should be defined as broadly as possible (e.g., "as directed by the board") so that the employer has the right to change duties and title if human resources are needed elsewhere, with a statement merely limiting the scope of the employee's authority or ability to incur obligations on behalf of the company. This will protect HighTech, to a limited extent, against unauthorized acts by the employee, unless apparent or implied authority can be established by a third party.

Compensation Arrangements

The type of compensation plan HighTech offers will vary depending on the nature of the employee's duties (e.g., sales representative versus software engineer), industry practice and custom, compensation offered by competitors, the stage of the company's growth market conditions, tax ramifications, and the employee's skill level. The agreement must state clearly the schedule of payment, calculation of income, and conditions for bonuses and rewards.

The tax ramifications of the compensation arrangement should be carefully examined by a qualified accountant in order to determine the impact of the clause on the company. Key operative terms, such as *sales* or *net income*, should be defined in some detail, especially if the employee will receive a bonus or share in the profits based on the definition and outcome of these terms. For example, suppose Sweet-Tooth, in order to retain Eatalot as a key employee and motivate him to develop a market for BagDough, ties part of Eatalot's compensation to the company's profitability. The exact definition of *profits* is vital here. Does *profits* include sales of company assets? investment income? before or after taxes? Similarly, if Eatalot's compensation will include a stock bonus, issues of valuation, classes of stock, vesting, purchase price, and any restrictions on transferability must be addressed. If the exact definitions of these terms and conditions are not clear, disputes are likely to arise, causing unhappy employees who, like Eatalot, are generally more prone to walk away with the company's intellectual property in order to join the competition or start their company, in part, because they feel that their employer still "owes" them something.

A sample base salary and incentive compensation clause might look like the following:

During the Term of this Agreement, Employee shall:

(a) Receive base compensation of $150,000 a year, payable in equal monthly installments for the period of time during which Employee is employed on a full-time basis.

(b) Receive incentive compensation for each full calendar year if employed by the Company on a full-time basis on the last day of such calendar year, beginning January 1, 1990 (Incentive Bonus), in an amount determined by multiplying the Incentive Bonus Percentage set forth below by the pretax net profits realized by the Company in excess of $500,000, determined after deducting all proper charges and expenses, including corporate, general, and administrative expense allocated to said operations, but excluding any nonrecurring gains or losses or other extraordinary charges or credits, all determined in accordance with generally accepted accounting principles applied on a consistent basis.

The Incentive Bonus Percentage shall be:

1990	10%
1991	5%
1992	3%

If the employee's compensation is to be based on a commission, as with the sales force hired by HighTech, it is especially important that key terms relating to the sale of the product are set forth in a detailed fashion. The percentage, sliding scale, or fixed amount for each item or class of items sold must be determined, with any applicable ceilings or floors established (e.g., 10 percent on all orders up to $100,000, and 8 percent on all orders over $100,000, so long as gross sales exceed $250,000 each quarter). The exact time when HighTech must award the commission to the employee should also be included, such as whether the company has a right to reject orders and when payment to sales personnel will be made (when the order is taken, when goods are shipped or sources provided, or when payment is received).

Any limitations on commissions must be specified in the agreement, such as a description of any geographic exclusivity or limitations, provisions for adjustments in the event of refunds, bad debts, or rejected orders, reimbursement of expenses, entitlement to a drawing account or some other advance on future commissions, or the effect of an employer's insolvency. In the section that addresses termination, the agreement should discuss who is entitled to commissions for efforts performed by the employee prior to termination.

Generally a small, growing company will have difficulty structuring a compensation and benefits package that will allow it to compete for qualified personnel. When a company starts up, it must invest precious cash in the growth of the company, leaving little money for large officer salaries or fancy company cars. Therefore the compensation package often includes equity or the right to acquire equity through an employee stock option plan. As the company grows, additional cash may become available for larger salaries, cash bonuses, and incentive pay plans to reward key employees. Naturally, the lion's share of the available capital will still go to internal growth and investment. As the company matures and/or experiences financial distress or business decline, key employees will be far less willing to take a long-term view and be more concerned about immediate cash reward through salary, bonuses, and executive perquisites.

Employee benefit plans range from income-replacement programs (retirement and disability plans) to equity-oriented incentive compensation (stock option plans and stock appreciation rights) to fringe benefit programs (automobiles, club memberships, or even group legal services). These types of compensation plans are heavily regulated by the Internal Revenue Service and the Department of Labor, and, in certain cases, the Securities and Exchange Commission and Pension Benefit Guaranty Corporation. The development and structuring of employee benefit plans has become a dynamic and specialized field dominated by compensation and benefits consultants who work closely with accountants and attorneys in order to ensure that the program meets corporate objectives and complies with applicable laws.

Protecting Intellectual Property and Restrictive Covenants

For growing companies such as HighTech and Sweet-Tooth, the provisions in the employment agreement regarding protection of intellectual property are clearly vital. Three key categories of covenants must be included in the employment agreement: (1) Covenants of Nondisclosure, (2) Covenants of Noncompetition (both during and after the term of the agreement), and (3) Covenants Regarding Ownership of Inventions.

1. *Covenants of Nondisclosure.* Trade secrets the growing company owns may be protected with covenants in the employment agreement that impose obligations on the employee not to disclose, in any form and to any unauthorized party, any information the company regards as confidential and proprietary. This includes, but is not limited to, customer lists, formulas and processes, financial and sales data, agreements with customers and suppliers, business and strategic plans, marketing strategies and advertising materials, or anything else that gives the employer an advantage over its competitors. This covenant should apply to pre-employment (interview or training period), during the term of the agreement, and post-termination. The scope, conditions regarding use and disclosure, sources and forms of information, and geographic limitations described in the covenant should be broadly in favor of the employer; however, the covenant will be enforceable only to the extent necessary to reasonably protect the nature of the intellectual property at stake.

2. *Covenants of Noncompetition.* Naturally, growing companies like to be able to impose a restriction on key employees that should any one of them ever leave the company, he or she will be absolutely prohibited from working for a competitor in any way, shape, or manner. Courts, however, have not looked

favorably on such attempts to deprive individuals of their livelihood and have required that any covenants against competition be reasonable as to scope, time, territory, and remedy for noncompliance. An unreasonable restriction runs the risk of being completely set aside by the court, unless the jurisdiction applies the "blue pencil" rule, under which only the offensive and unreasonable language is struck by the judge.

The types of covenants against competition that the courts tolerate vary from state to state and from industry to industry, but they must always be reasonable under the circumstances. An attorney with a background in this area must be consulted when drafting these provisions of the employment agreement. (For example, at least 14 states have enacted statutes that regulate the use of covenants not to compete and provide that an agreement prohibiting a person from practicing a lawful profession, trade, or business is void and unenforceable.)

To be enforceable, the covenant against competition must be supported by some form of legal consideration such as money or the offer of employment. An offer of paid employment will usually suffice; however, additional consideration might be necessary to support an unusually long period of time or large territory under which the employee agrees not to compete after the term of the agreement. The covenant should be no broader than is necessary to protect the legitimate business interests of the employer, and its terms should be reasonable as to duration, territory, activity, remedy, and its relation to other provisions in the employment agreement.

3. *Covenants Regarding Ownership of Inventions.* Eatalot's development of BagDough raises a host of legal issues for Sweet-Tooth. Must Eatalot disclose the discovery to the company's management at all? Who will own the trade secret or patent on the discovery? Must Sweet-Tooth pay Eatalot a fee or royalty if it commercially exploits the discovery? Is Eatalot entitled to share in the proceeds if his employer licenses or sells the discovery?

All of these questions must be expressly addressed in the employment agreement; otherwise, basic common-law rules regarding ownership of an employee's ideas, inventions, and discoveries will govern. These rules do not necessarily favor the employer, especially if the discovery was made while working outside the scope of the employment or if the employee did not utilize the employer's resources in connection with the invention. For example, the common-law principle of "shop rights" dictates that if an invention is made by an employee that is outside the scope of the employment but utilizes the resources of the employer, then ownership is vested in the employee, subject to a nonexclusive, royalty-free, irrevocable license to the employer.

A sample clause for such a situation is

Work Made for Hire. If any inventions or discoveries of Employee are protectible by definition of "work made for hire," as such term is defined in 17 USC § 101, such work shall be considered a "work made for hire," the copyright of which shall be owned solely, completely, and exclusively by Employer. If any one or more of the aforementioned items are protectible by copyright and are not considered to be included in the categories of work covered by the "work made for hire" definition contained in 17 USC § 101, such items shall be deemed to be assigned and transferred completely and exclusively to Employer by virtue of the execution of this Agreement.

Sweet-Tooth can limit the reward for an invention to Eatalot's basic salary if express provisions regarding ownership of inventions were included in his employment agreement. Naturally, this clause must be balanced against business considerations such as Sweet-Tooth's ability to attract and retain key employees with such a limited reward for innovation. The provision should insist on prompt and full disclosure of any inventions, as well as full cooperation in any subsequent attempt by the company to obtain a patent, copyright, or trademark on the discovery.

Protection of Intellectual Property Upon Termination

When an employee leaves the company, such as the HighTech employees whom Cutthroat has been designated to fire, the obligations of nondisclosure and noncompetition should be reaffirmed with an exit interview. The applicable provisions of the employment agreement should be reviewed with the departing employee with at least one witness present. Cutthroat should apprise each employee of his or her continuing duty to preserve the confidentiality of trade secrets and reiterate what information is regarded as confidential. He should obtain assurances and evidence (including a written acknowledgment) that the employee has returned all confidential and proprietary documents and retains no copies. He should obtain the name of the new employer or future activity and, under certain circumstances, even notify the new employer of the prior employment relationship and its scope. This disclosure will put the new employer-competitor on notice and prevent it from claiming that it was unaware that its new employee had revealed trade secrets. Finally, the employer should insist that the employee covenant not to hire co-workers, such as:

Covenants Not to Hire Employees. It is recognized and understood by the parties hereto that the employees of Employer are an integral part of Employer's business and that it is extremely important for Employer to use its maximum efforts to prevent Employer from losing such employees. It is, therefore, understood and agreed by the parties hereto that, because of the nature of the business of Employer, it is necessary to afford fair protection to Employer from the loss of any such employees. Consequently, as a material inducement to Employer to employ (or to continue to employ) Employee, Employee covenants and agrees that, for the period commencing on the date of Employee's termination of employment for any reason whatsoever and ending two (2) years after Employee's termination of employment with Employer, Employee shall not, directly or indirectly, hire or engage or attempt to hire or engage any individual who shall have been an employee of Employer at any time during the one (1)-year period prior to the date of Employee's termination of employment with Employer, whether for or on behalf of Employee or for any entity in which Employee shall have a direct or indirect interest (or any subsidiary or affiliate of any such entity), whether as a proprietor, partner, coventurer, financier, investor or stockholder, director, officer, employer, employee, servant, agent, representative, or otherwise.

Expense Reimbursement

The employment agreement should clearly define the types of business expenses the employer will reimburse the employee for when incurred on behalf of the company. The employee should be required to keep detailed expense reimbursement records and be prepared to demonstrate that such expenses were incurred to further the purposes of the company.

Employee Benefits

All employee benefits and perquisites should be clearly defined in the employment agreement, such as health insurance, company cars, education and training, death, disability or retirement benefits, defined compensation plans, and pension or profit-sharing plans. In addition, any vacation or sick leave policies should be included in either the employment agreement or the employee manual, or both.

Preparing Employment Manuals

Even the most comprehensive employment agreement will not address certain key issues and company policies that govern the rights and obligations of employer and employee during the term of their relationship. In addition, it would be overkill to enter into a formal employment agreement with each employee of the growing company. Instead, it is the responsibility of owners and managers to develop employee manuals and handbooks for the purposes of communicating to all employees applicable management procedures and guidelines.

A well-drafted employment manual can serve as a personnel training program, a management tool for improving the efficiency of the organization, an employee morale builder, and a guardian against excessive litigation. The manual should be sufficiently detailed so as to provide guidance to employees on all key company policies; however, overly complex manuals tend to restrict management flexibility and lead to employee confusion and uncertainty.

Legal counsel must be retained to review the manual before distribution to the company's staff. Although the manual is *not* a binding contract, it nevertheless serves as a written record of the company's hiring, compensation, promotion, and termination policies, which could be offered as evidence in litigation. Courts increasingly seem willing to look at statements made in the employment manual, or even unwritten employment policies of the company, in disputes between employer and employee. Although the exact contents of the manual will vary depending on the nature and size of the company, as well as its management philosophies and objectives, all employee handbooks should contain the categories of information listed in Exhibit 2-2.

Developing Employee Termination Procedures

One of the most difficult tasks for managers of growing companies is terminating an unproductive worker. Many small-business owners have described the employee termination dilemma in this way: "The only thing more expensive than having deadwood on the payroll is the cost of hiring and training fresh lumber."

Notwithstanding these expensive replacement costs, once all methods to make an employee more effective have been exhausted, the decision to terminate the employment relationship should be made and swiftly implemented. Until recently most courts and state legislatures refused to tamper with an employer's right to rid itself of an unproductive resource at its discretion. Known as the *employment-at-will doctrine*, such a policy had been supported by a judicial reluctance to interfere with principles of freedom of contract in an employment setting.

A sample employment-at-will clause in an agreement follows:

> *Employee's Status.* Nothing in this Agreement shall be construed as constituting a commitment, guarantee, agreement, or understanding of any kind or nature that Employer shall continue to employ Employee, nor shall this Agreement affect in any way the right of Employer to terminate the employment of Employee at any time and for any reason whatsoever. By Employee's execution of this Agreement, Employer acknowledges and agrees that Employee's employment is "at will." No change of Employee's duties as an employee of Employer shall result in, or be deemed to be, a modification of the terms of this Agreement.

Several recent theories have emerged to erode the employment-at-will doctrine, however, and courts have been willing to entertain claims of unjust dismissal by employees who allege theories such as:

Exhibit 2-2. Essential subject areas for employee handbooks.

A. Key goals and objectives of the company
B. Background of the company and its founders
C. Description of the company's products and services
D. Current organizational chart of the company and brief position descriptions
E. Compensation and benefits
  1. Hours of operation
  2. Overtime policies
  3. Vacation, maternity, sick leave, and holidays
  4. Overview of employee benefits (health, dental, disability, etc.)
  5. Performance review, raises, and promotions
  6. Pension, profit-sharing, and retirement plans
  7. Eligibility for fringe benefits
  8. Rewards, employee discounts, and bonuses
  9. Expense reimbursement policies
F. Standards for employee conduct
  1. Dress code and personal hygiene
  2. Courtesy to customers, vendors, and fellow employees
  3. Smoking, drug use, and gum chewing
  4. Jury duty and medical absences
  5. Personal telephone calls and visits
  6. Training and educational responsibilities
  7. Employee use of company facilities and resources
  8. Employee meals and breaks
G. Safety regulations and emergency procedures
H. Procedures for handling employee grievances, disputes, and conflicts
I. Employee duties to protect intellectual property
J. Term and termination of the employment relationship
  1. Probationary period
  2. Grounds for discharge (immediate versus notice)
  3. Employee termination and resignation
  4. Severance pay
  5. Exit interviews   *(continued)*

Exhibit 2-2. (continued).

K. Maintenance of employee records
   1. Job application
   2. Social security and birth information
   3. Federal and state tax, immigration, and labor/employment law documentation
   4. Performance review and evaluation report
   5. Benefit plan information
   6. Exit interview information
L. Special legal concerns
   1. Equal employment opportunity
   2. Sexual harassment
   3. Career advancement opportunities
   4. Charitable and political contributions
   5. Garnishment of employee wages
M. Dealing with the news media and distribution of press releases
N. Summary and reiteration of the role and purpose of the employment manual
O. Employee acknowledgment of receipt of manual (to be signed by the employee and placed in his or her permanent file)

- Implied contract (based upon some statement in the employee handbook or on a representation made by the employer)
- Public policy (such as terminating an employee due to whistle-blowing or jury duty)
- An implied covenant of good faith and fair dealing between employer and employee

Remedies for unjust dismissal have ranged from simple reinstatement to back pay and actual damages, and even to punitive damages for certain cases.

In order to avoid any potential unjust-dismissal litigation or in order to prevail if a matter is filed by a disgruntled ex-employee, the following practices and procedures should be implemented. They will be helpful in determining that the employer had bona fide reasons for its decision to terminate the particular employee.

Record keeping. Keep comprehensive records on each employee, including any formal performance appraisal or informal warnings, comments, or memos prepared by a supervisor to demonstrate the employee's poor work or misconduct. If a case ever reaches litigation, these documents and records may be the only evidence available as support for valid reasons for terminating the employee.

Employment policy audit and monitoring. Carefully review and monitor employee manuals, policy statements, memoranda, and related documentation to ensure that no implied representation or agreement has been made regarding the term of employment, severance pay, or grounds for termination that may be inconsistent with the intent of the company. The various grounds for termination should be clearly set forth in the employment manual; they should include but not be limited to

- Discriminatory acts toward employees or hiring candidates
- Physical or sexual abuse
- Falsifying time records or other key documents
- Willful or negligent violation of safety or security rules
- Violation of company policies
- Unauthorized disclosure of the company's confidential information
- Refusal to perform work assigned by a supervisor
- Destroying or damaging company property
- Misappropriation or embezzlement
- Drug abuse or gambling on company premises

Avoidance of hasty decisions. An employee who has been performing poorly should be provided with plenty of advance notice of management's disappointment with his or her performance through personal and written evaluations, warning notices, and published employment policies. Where the cause for termination is an act of insubordination, improper conduct, or related incidents, the witness statements, accident reports, customer complaints, and related documentation should be collected and reviewed. Once a termination decision has been made by the immediate supervisor and the evidence supporting the cause collected, a member of management at least one level above the direct supervisor of the employee should review the proposed dismissal.

The reviewer should consider offering the employee an opportunity to cure the defect in performance. He or she should hear the employee's side of the story prior to making the final dismissal decision and should place written records of these meetings in the employee's file. The reviewer should question the employee's supervisor and coworkers to gather additional facts and to ensure that all company policies and procedures have been followed, especially those regarding performance appraisal and employee discipline.

Exit interviews. After the final decision to terminate the employee has been made, the company must explain the reasons for the discharge during the employee's exit interview. The explanation should be candid and concise, in accordance with all available evidence, and consistent with any explanation of the termination that will be provided to the employee. The employer should emphasize to the employee that the reasons for termination are legitimate and are consistent with the employer's past practices under similar circumstances. The employee should also be advised what will be told to prospective employers and reminded of any covenants not to compete and of his or her continuing obligation to protect the trade secrets of the company.

Release and termination agreements. When an employee is terminated, the company should prepare a comprehensive release and termination agreement to protect itself against subsequent litigation and recommend that the employee engage counsel to review this agreement. The release and termination agreement should

1. Be supported by valid consideration (e.g., some form of severance pay or covenants)
2. Be signed by the employee knowingly and voluntarily
3. Include the grounds for termination in the recitals
4. Contain covenants against competition, disclosure, and litigation
5. Include all possible defendants in an employment action (company, officers, directors, subsidiaries)
6. Avoid commitments regarding references to future employers
7. Be checked carefully against all applicable federal and state laws

Employers have faced charges of discrimination or violation of federal statutes in connection with the termination of an employee. Federal statutes prohibit termination based on race, religion, sex, handicap, age, or national origin. The National Labor Relations Act prohibits the termination of employees for belonging to a union or even acting in attempt to prevent the formation of a union. The Fair Labor Standards Act prohibits the termination of employees for filing claims of wage and overtime violations.

In order to defend against these types of claims, the employer must be prepared to demonstrate that employee performance evaluations, policies contained in employment manuals, and grounds for termination were implemented and enforced in a nondiscriminatory fashion and not as a result of any act contrary to applicable federal law. Specific, clear, and uniform guidelines should be developed for probation periods, opportunities to improve job performance, availability of training, and termination procedures.

The company may defeat any charges of discrimination if it has maintained proper documentation. This documentation should include a complete personnel file of the former employee, detailed records of complaints of supervisors and coworkers related to the cause of termination, copies of work produced by the employee that was considered unsatisfactory, a written record reflecting the race and sex of other persons dismissed or disciplined for the same or similar purposes, and the name, race, and sex of the individual replacing the discharged employee.

3

Managing Relationships
With
Professional Advisers

Every growing business relies on key advisers to foster development and expansion. They make up part of the management team and are hired to assist the organization in developing, implementing, and monitoring its key goals and objectives, as well as to manage risk. These advisers are attorneys, accountants, and consultants from a wide variety of business disciplines: marketing, sales, finance, administrative management, strategic planning, office automation, manufacturing, production, advertising, operations, and personnel. To ensure cost efficiency and compatibility among management team members, the advisers must be *managed* by the company. It is important that the tasks and problems assigned to them are appropriate to their background and expertise.

A lot of mystery, confusion, and disenchantment taints the relationships that develop between entrepreneurs and their advisers. Professional service providers constantly complain about small-business clients who never pay their bills, never listen to their advice, and always wait until the last minute to discuss a task or problem. And entrepreneurs can tell countless horror stories about inferior work product, high fees, slow response time, projects assigned to incompetent junior associates, a lack of expertise or understanding of the company's products and markets, an insensitivity to the business objectives of the client or in a particular transaction, an inability to communicate in "plain English," a lax attitude toward conflicts of interest, and a greater concern over the client's golf handicap than his competitive handicap.

Somewhere in between all of this finger pointing is the utopian entrepreneur-adviser relationship, toward which owners and managers of growing companies must strive. The first step in understanding and improving relationships with outside advisers is to comprehend why the adviser is needed in the first place.

Why Are Professional Advisers Hired?

Professional service providers and business consultants are hired to fill particular needs of the emerging-growth company, such as:

- Expert advice in a particular field of knowledge
- A readily available pool of human resources (in lieu of hiring a full-time employee)
- An objective evaluation of a particular problem or proposed project
- Stimulation or implementation of new ideas, technology, or programs
- Identification and solution of problems or barriers to growth

Once a company determines a need for an outside adviser, selecting the right person is paramount. Certain key questions must be addressed, such as:

- How do the background, education, and experience of the adviser relate to the task or problem at hand?
- How does the adviser charge for the services rendered? What billing options are available? How do rates vary among various members of the adviser's firm? How much will it cost to resolve the problem?
- Which staff members will be assigned to this project? What is their expertise?
- What is the anticipated timetable for completing the work? What progress reports will be provided? What input will be required from the company's management team to the service provider?
- What is the service provider's representative client base? Can references be provided? Does the firm have any actual or potential conflicts of interest? How does the company compare to the firm's existing client base?

Many company owners and managers harbor misperceptions and myths regarding the use of outside advisers. These must be dispelled so companies and advisers can enter into the relationship with a positive attitude. The most common *myths* are

- The need for an outside consultant is a sign of your management team's inability, business weakness, or failure.
- Your internal management team is too busy to work with external advisers.
- Consultants never really understand the special demands and problems of a company.
- Consultants are just too expensive, especially for what you get in return . . . a lot of advice about things already known.
- If this consultant knows this industry so well, then why isn't he running his own company?

The discussion that follows is devoted to the relationships between owners and managers of growing companies and their legal counsel. These thoughts and comments, however, are for the most part equally applicable to relationships with accountants, business consultants, bankers, advertising agencies, and other key advisers.

Selecting and Working With Legal Counsel

A business is likely to undergo wide changes in its structure, products and services, markets, and capital requirements as it grows. Each change raises a host of legal issues that must be considered prior to implementing the growth strategy identified. That is why legal counsel must serve as a key member of the management team and as an active participant in the planning for the growth of the company. When an experienced business lawyer is made an integral part of the management team, the growing company enjoys several benefits, including an understanding of the legal hurdles and requirements raised by proposed strategies or transactions, *prior to* implementation or closing; identification of the optimal legal structure and alternatives for achieving the company's objectives; and cost savings resulting from the lawyer's grasp of the company's goals, internal politics, and trends affecting its industry. The costs of having legal counsel participate in the growth planning and decision-making process are far outweighed by these benefits.

Selecting Appropriate Legal Counsel

The process of selecting, retaining, and knowing how and when to use an attorney is one of the most important business decisions that the business owner will ever make. Yet most entrepreneurs are frustrated by, dissatisfied with, and confused by the law firm selection and retention process. They point to high fees, failure to meet deadlines, lack of business savvy, inaccessibility, inability to cut through red tape and mountains of paperwork, inexperienced staff, and a general inability to understand the business ramifications of legal decisions as the sources of their ongoing problems with attorneys. They view their attorneys as necessary evils. As a result, they tend to take matters into their own hands, only to have these "matters" backfire, creating even larger legal problems than they ever anticipated. Having an experienced business attorney as a key member of the management team does not mean that an attorney needs to be involved in every step of every transaction. The key to a prosperous and harmonious attorney-entrepreneur relationship is knowing how and when to seek advice from your attorney.

If your idea of an attorney with strong corporate legal skills and business acumen begins with the ability to keep your spouse away from key assets in a hotly contested marital dispute, think again. The days when your divorce lawyer could also handle a complicated corporate transaction are long gone. Due to the increasing complexity of the law and the ever-growing specialization of the legal profession, the division of assets in your family in a divorce or in estate planning and the division of assets in your corporation in a merger, acquisition, or share-holders' agreement must be handled by two very different types of lawyers. Although it is more than likely that the attorney who prepared your will could also assist you in the performance of routine corporate tasks during the forma-tion of your company, many business owners quickly outgrow their general prac-titioners as the business expands and legal needs become more complex. Small companies on a rapid-growth track must periodically assess whether their legal interests and requirements are best met by their current law firm.

Owners and managers of growing companies express varying preferences with respect to the age, experience, and interests of the lawyers whom they prefer to hire. Priority may be placed on experience and clout, which tends to favor an older, more seasoned lawyer—or on aggressiveness and cost, which tends to favor a younger lawyer. However, it is dangerous to place too great a priority on either experience or billing rates. For example, an older lawyer with time con-straints is likely to assign your project to a younger, less experienced attorney, and a younger lawyer who offers lower billable rates may take twice as long to complete the assigned project.

Age and reputation also should be viewed with a grain of salt. An attorney practicing for three years who has devoted all attention to a specific area of law will probably know more about a matter in that area than a general practitioner with 30 years' experience. Nonetheless, there are certain common denominators that a growing company should identify when selecting legal counsel:

Responsiveness. A law firm must meet a client's timetable for accomplishing a particular transaction or implementing a particular strategy. An attorney with wide expertise on a given legal topic is of no use to a growing company if he or she cannot communicate the knowledge to the client clearly and on time. Make sure that deadlines are discussed with counsel and that the law firm has adequate resources set aside to meet those requirements in accordance with the schedule established.

Business acumen. Clients often complain that their attorneys do not under-stand the impact of their legal advice on the client's business goals and objec-tives. An attorney who is advising growing companies needs business acumen, management and marketing skills, and a genuine understanding of the industry in which the company operates, in addition to strong legal skills.

Reputation. A growing company will want to hire a law firm with a good reputation and contacts in the business community. Its managers, however, should look closely at the *foundation* of that reputation. Is it based on the accomplishments of named partners who have been dead for over 20 years? Or perhaps a recommended lawyer enjoys a fine reputation as a golfer and a philanthropist, but nobody can really give you an opinion as to the quality of his legal documentation. Rather, the firm's reputation should have been built by its accomplishments, client base, legal skills, and its ability to provide quality advice in an efficient manner to growing companies.

Representative client base. It is often said, "A small business is not a little big business," yet many corporate lawyers assume that because they have handled a $500 million acquisition, they automatically understand the legal needs of the parties to a $500,000 transaction. Although some of the legal planning and documentation may be similar, the business goals and philosophies of the parties are likely to be very different. Small-business managers should also evaluate a prospective law firm's client base to determine whether there are any actual or potential conflicts of interest or complementary resources or whether the firm has experience in matters similar to those their company faces.

Billing rates and policies. Legal costs are of great concern to companies of all sizes, but especially to smaller businesses with few resources. One way in which lawyers compete for small-business clients demonstrating growth potential is by flexibility in billing policies. Nevertheless, the small business must clearly understand the firm's billing rates and policies before any legal work is begun.

A retainer agreement is one way to control billing rates and policies; it also defines related rights and obligations of attorney and client. The agreement protects both attorney and client because it sets out the terms of the relationship before any work begins. The components of a well-drafted retainer agreement are included in Exhibit 3-1.

Attorneys at firms of all sizes expect to be paid for quality services that have been rendered within a client's deadline. There is nothing more frustrating or offensive to any professional service provider than to work nights and weekends for a client who does not pay its bills.

Efficiency. Growing companies should quickly get out of the habit of relying on legal counsel for basic tasks, such as routine corporate, securities, or tax filings, which can be performed in-house at a far lower cost. Counsel can train a legal compliance officer within the growing company who will be responsible for routine legal and administrative tasks.

The growing company should ensure that the law firm is completing assignments in an efficient and cost-effective manner. For example, tasks that an experienced attorney who charges $150 and up per hour can complete in a day should not be assigned to a junior associate who will take three days at $75 per hour.

Exhibit 3-1.   Outline of retainer agreement.

- Nature of the services to be provided
- Compensation for services rendered
- The use of initial retainers or contingent fees
- Reimbursement of fees and expenses
- Conditions for withdrawal of counsel or termination of the relationship
- Counsel's duty to provide status reports
- Time limitations or timetables for completion of work
- Ceilings or budgets, if any, that have been set for legal fees
- Any special provisions needed in the contract as a result of the nature of the project (e.g., rules governing media relations, protection of intellectual property, court appearances, protocol, etc.)

Knowledge and skills. The type of knowledge and skills that should be sought in selecting legal counsel will be influenced by the specific tasks, assignment, or transaction at hand. If the task involves an adversarial dispute, a skilled litigator will be more useful than an experienced transactional attorney. Conversely, a litigator may be inappropriate for a complex business deal where the skills of a seasoned corporate attorney would be more effective in negotiating and closing the transaction.

A good lawyer will be the first to tell you when a matter is outside his or her area of expertise or jurisdiction and should be the first to assist in identifying co-counsel or special counsel for the project.

Creativity. The identification and analysis of alternative methods of structuring a particular transaction or achieving a particular objective are among the most important tasks that a business attorney performs for the emerging-growth company. This ability to develop creative legal solutions to a client's problems or disputes is clearly one trait to seek in legal counsel.

Controlling the Costs of Legal Services

As a company grows, an increasingly larger portion of its annual budget must be allocated for legal services. In reaction to this, many owners and managers of growing companies attempt to control the expense either by avoiding lawyers—or by avoiding the invoices sent by lawyers. Neither strategy is effective.

Completely ignoring lawyers is likely to result in problems that far outweigh the cost of retaining competent counsel. Ignoring the invoices sent by lawyers will lead to tension in the relationship, a resentment by counsel toward tasks assigned by the client, and even litigation.

The most constructive way to control the cost of legal services is to work with legal counsel in an efficient and effective manner.

- Remember that time is money. Be prepared before you call or meet with your attorney. Gather all facts, review all documents, and develop a specific agenda and list of questions.

- Do not rely on your attorney for basic tasks that you or your staff can perform more quickly and cheaply—basic forms, correspondence, renewal filings, and so on.

- Do not let executed contracts collect dust. Most contracts are living, breathing documents that must be consulted periodically. If you fail to understand or perform your obligations under a contract, you may find yourself in expensive litigation.

- Do not be reluctant to give your attorney a ceiling on fees for a given project or transaction. Experienced attorneys should be able to predict the amount of time they will take to accomplish a specific task, absent any special problems, facts, or circumstances.

- Monitor administrative and incidental expenses: travel, photocopying, postage, and related expenses. If these extra fees are too steep for your budget, ask your lawyer to make alternative arrangements for these services.

- Review all bills and invoices carefully so that your company pays for services that were truly necessary and actually rendered. Insist on an itemized account that explains the nature of the services rendered or out-of-pocket expenses incurred. If unfamiliar names or charges are on it, the firm's billing system may not be functioning properly or perhaps the attorney primarily responsible for the matter is not carefully reviewing it.

- Do not tolerate paying for the training of an inexperienced attorney. Although virtually every legal matter will entail a certain amount of research, your company should not have to foot the entire bill to train a neophyte.

- Take a proactive, not a reactive, role in the preparation and negotiation of legal documents. Insist on participating in the process of identifying alternatives and developing solutions. Request periodic progress reports for managers within the company who are responsible for the given project or transaction.

- Establish controls within your company as to who may communicate with legal counsel and for what purposes. As the company grows, it is likely that a larger number of people will come into contact with legal counsel. If communication is not properly controlled, mixed signals may be given to counsel, unnecessary or duplicate tasks may be assigned, or personal matters may be handled at the company's expense.

Virtually every aspect of business development and growth is regulated or affected directly or indirectly by legal regulations and considerations. The variety of legal issues that the owner of an emerging business must confront is endless. The exact issues depend on the nature and size of the business, the company's goals and objectives, the extent of capitalization and rate of growth, the degree to which the particular industry is regulated, and numerous other factors. The best interests of the company—of its employees, shareholders, assets, products and services, and future—must have their place as the highest priority of legal counsel. And so the role of the attorney in protecting these interests must be clearly defined—there can be no mystery about the terms, parameters, and objectives of the relationship.

The relationship between entrepreneur and attorney must be synergistic, based on ongoing communication, mutual respect, and understanding, trust, and confidence. They must share the goal of planning, implementing, and monitoring actions to ensure that the company's business objectives come to fruition in a cost-effective and trouble-free manner.

4

Managing the Corporation

B usinesses of all sizes generally operate within the confines of one of four
available legal structures: sole proprietorships, partnerships, S corporations, or regular Chapter C corporations. The choice of structure is based on a
wide variety of factors—the company's anticipated sales growth, need for management flexibility, financing needs, level of interaction with the general public,
and the number of owners. Virtually all growing companies are organized as a
corporation, however, primarily owing to the management and financial flexibility offered by the corporate form.

Ironically, this choice of structure—one of the most important decisions the
founding owners of a company make—must be determined before operations
begin. This structure can be changed. In fact, it must be periodically examined
and analyzed to ensure that it still makes the most sense as the company grows.
Usually the structure is reconsidered from time to time for the following reasons:

- The need to raise additional capital for business expansion
- A change in applicable tax laws
- An increase in the level of risk due to additional dealings with creditors,
  suppliers, or consumers
- A shift in the company's business plans, which has an impact on the distri-
  bution and use of earnings and profits
- An opportunity to develop a new technology either in conjunction with oth-
  ers or under the umbrella of a separate but related subsidiary or research
  and development partnership
- The retirement, death, or departure of the company's original founders
- The need to attract and retain additional top management personnel
- Mergers, acquisitions, spinoffs, or an initial public offering planned in the
  near future

When the company reaches a new stage of growth or certain crossroads in its
development, its managers need to consider all available alternatives and combinations. Consider the following example:

Three entrepreneurs decide to combine their complementary talents and form a consulting business to be known as GovCo Associates and organized as a general partnership. As the company grows, a corporation, GovCo, Inc., is established in order to protect the three founders against personal liability to creditors, suppliers, and clients. Following the incorporation, the shareholders elect to be treated as an S corporation so that income and losses are passed directly through to the owners without the traditional double taxation. As GovCo continues to grow, the founders want to attract additional capital and reward key employees. They create a class of preferred stock with dividend preferences for new investors and a class of nonvoting common stock for the key employees. Because of these two additional classes of stock, GovCo must terminate its S corporation status.

Two years later, a consulting firm in a related field approaches GovCo to bid jointly on certain government and private contracts. They come to an agreement and create a joint venture in the form of a partnership agreement to manage the bid preparation. The joint venture, however, proves to be largely unsuccessful and becomes a significant drain on GovCo's resources. Several key employees leave the company, and all of the nonvoting common stock is repurchased and retired pursuant to the terms of an employee stock repurchase agreement. Following some financial difficulty, GovCo's current investors redeem their preferred stock, which is also retired. After the retirement of the two additional classes of stock, GovCo's board begins to take steps so that it once again is eligible for an election as an S corporation status under federal tax laws.

GovCo selected five different tax and legal structures over the course of its development in response to changes in liability exposure, capital requirements, human resource needs, new opportunities presented, and financial distress. Because its management understood the legal costs and benefits of each structural alternative, it could adapt its organization most advantageously.

Most businesses begin as a sole proprietorship or partnership, with little need for structured rules of operation and protocol. As the company grows, it will usually incorporate because of the limited liability, ease of transfer of ownership, and capital requirements. Yet many business owners lack an understanding of the legal obligations and responsibilities of managing a corporation and how the legal restrictions this structure imposes affect the growth and development of their company. Even upon incorporation, for example, the company is often initially closely held, which means that owners will usually wear so many hats that they do not appreciate the key legal differences between an officer, a director, a shareholder, and an employee. As the company grows, however, the distinctions among these four key roles become crucial internally—to avoid a claim for mismanagement or breach of fiduciary duty—and externally—to avoid an attempt by a creditor or customer to hold the owners and managers of the company personally responsible for the liabilities of the corporation or hold the company responsible for an act or transaction that the board of directors or officers did not authorize. Owners and managers of growing companies must understand the distribution of power and control contemplated by state corporate statutes.

Generally the management and control of any corporation, regardless of size, is vested in the board of directors, who are elected by the shareholders. In turn, the directors select the officers of the company, who are responsible for managing the day-to-day affairs of the business. Officers select and hire employees to help them manage and operate the company. As a result of the organizational structure established by state corporate law, the officers and directors owe a fiduciary duty to the corporation and to its shareholders; that is, each act they perform in furtherance of the company's business plans must be in good faith and for the benefit of the corporation. If they fail to exercise due care and diligence in managing the corporation or in selecting and supervising officers, a shareholder could initiate a civil suit for breach of this fiduciary duty. If they fail to respect corporate formalities (perhaps they do not hold regular and documented meetings or do not maintain separate business and personal bank accounts), a creditor or a person allegedly injured by the company's products can initiate a civil suit and attempt to impose personal liability on the owners or managers.

If fraud or inequity is demonstrated, a court will "pierce the corporate veil," thereby refusing to recognize the separate legal existence of the corporation. One of the most significant factors that a court will consider in this action is the *disregard by the shareholders for the formalities imposed by applicable corporate laws* (for example, if the owners or managers failed to incorporate properly or failed to engage in planning and decision making in accordance with the law's prescribed management structure). Growing companies must be especially mindful of liability to those individuals who would not be expected to have any familiarity with a company's workings who then engage in nonconsensual transactions with that company (for example, a person injured by a firm's product); typically courts are more willing to pierce the veil on their behalf than on behalf of creditors or others who may have had an opportunity to acquaint themselves with the internal affairs of the company and are dealing from a position of relatively equal strength. In addition, as the company grows and subsidiaries are created, a parent corporation may be held liable for the acts of its subsidiary if clear lines of demarcation are not drawn between the initial and ongoing business affairs and management of the companies as two distinct legal entities.

Legal Roles of Key Parties

Shareholders

The shareholders are the owners of the equity in the corporation, but they have only limited powers of management and control. These powers may vary slightly from state to state but generally include

- The power to select and remove directors
- The power to amend or repeal the by-laws (unless delegated to the board of directors in the charter)
- The power to approve fundamental changes in the corporation recommended by the board of directors, such as amendments to the charter, mergers and acquisitions, sale of key assets, and dissolution

In addition, management will often find it prudent to obtain shareholder approval for certain acts and transactions, even if not required by statute or by the company's charter, to reduce the chance of shareholder litigation.

Shareholders who disagree with the decisions of the board of directors may sell their stock or commence a direct action at law for mismanagement or breach of fiduciary duty. Among the more frequent improper actions that shareholders have successfully challenged in direct suits against boards of directors are failure to disclose material information on operating problems, improper loans or self-dealing, usurpation of a corporate opportunity, improper spending of corporate funds in connection with proxy contests or takeover bids, improper issuance of stock or declaration of dividends, and improperly entering into new lines of business without adequate market research or internal capability.

Managers responsible for growth planning within the company should be aware of these types of claims when formulating and implementing goals and objectives. Most of these decisions will fall under the umbrella of the well-known "business judgment rule." This rule, created by common law, operates on the basic presumption that directors of a company act in good faith and on an informed basis unless a shareholder or other interested party is able to demonstrate otherwise. Such a presumption essentially prevents the courts from second-guessing board decisions made in good faith and enforces the notion that although directors owe a high degree of loyalty and care to the shareholders, they are not guarantors of corporate success. Directors of growing companies should not rely too heavily on this doctrine, however, because recent cases have chipped away at its traditionally broad scope.

Directors

Subject to any legally permissible limitations in a company's articles or by-laws, the board of directors of a corporation is entrusted with the general power of management of the business and affairs of the entity. In most growth-oriented companies, however, the reality is that the board of directors is vested with the responsibility for formulating general policies, goals, and objectives. Once these strategic plans and objectives are established, it is the officers of the corporation, acting under the direction of the board, who are generally responsible for implementing plans and strategies to meet these goals and objectives. The board of directors has the power and responsibility to select officers who are best suited to implement these organizational goals, as well as to remove officers who act inconsistently with stated objectives.

Although the directors have delegated their authority to the officers, they are still responsible for the consequences of the general policies formulated. Therefore, it is crucial that they keep careful records of the deliberations that result in any particular board action and keep a careful watch over the officers.

As the corporation grows, the management of the company will become increasingly more decentralized and departmentalized, even at the highest level. In response, the board of directors may appoint committees with specific authority and responsibility. State corporation laws vary as to what duties and responsibilities may be so delegated. Among the various types of committees created by emerging-growth companies are executive, compensation, audit, shareholders' relations, employee relations, litigation, and an annual meeting and report committee. The company's bylaws will have to be amended to create these committees, with the amendments carefully delineating the criteria for membership, duties, and obligations and setting specific limitations and authority for reporting and record-keeping requirements. The bylaws and resolutions should also reflect the exact relationships among the committees, especially if there is any overlap in the authorities granted.

Officers

The officers of the corporation have limited authority and responsibilities under the traditional statutory approach to corporate governance and control. They cannot, for example, declare dividends or approve a merger with another company. Their role is restricted to *implementing* the policies and decisions of the board of directors. The functions that each officer is to perform are usually defined in the bylaws and modified or expanded by a specific resolution of the board. For example, typical bylaws will set out the following general responsibilities of the officers:

- *President.* This person supervises and controls the business and affairs of the corporation as directed by the board of directors. He or she should review, approve, and execute all material corporate contracts, stock certificates, and the hiring of key employees.
- *Vice-President.* This individual(s) performs the duties of the company's president when he or she is unable or refuses to act. Vice-presidents in growing companies are often granted specific responsibilities for key management disciplines, such as personnel, administration, finance, legal, sales, or marketing.
- *Secretary.* This person is primarily responsible for a variety of housekeeping functions, such as custodian of the corporate stock transfer books and

corporate minutes, cosignature of corporate documents and stock certificates, and keeper of the corporate records.

- *Treasurer.* This person is primarily responsible for the care and custody of the company's resources, including payment of accounts payable, collection of accounts receivable, and accurate management of the corporation's bank accounts and financial records.

Corporate officers may gain additional authority and responsibility from specific resolutions of the board, the terms of an employment contract, or based upon some implied authority granted by the board or by specific business circumstances. The concept of *implied authority* is governed by agency law principles under which the directors are essentially the principals (acting on behalf of the corporation) and the officers are the agents. This is especially important in situations where a third party is seeking to hold the corporation responsible for its obligations in a particular transaction that has been purportedly entered into by an officer on behalf of the company, such as a contract to purchase goods or services that the officer signed in his or her official capacity. Third parties seeking to hold the corporation liable under the transaction will generally allege one or more of the following theories:

- *Apparent Authority.* Some conduct or series of acts by the board of directors leads the third party to believe that the officer actually has the authority represented.
- *Implied Authority.* The board of directors has previously engaged in some conduct in which it appeared to have consented to the act by the officer in question.
- *Estoppel.* The board of directors has unjustly retained the benefits of the transaction or had reason to know that the third party would be relying on the power of the officer when entering into the transaction.
- *Ratification.* The board of directors, either by affirmative acts or by implied consent, subsequently accepts the benefits of an act by an officer who originally entered into a transaction without proper authority.

Guidelines for the Board of Directors of a Growing Company

The board of directors has broad responsibility for the management and control of the corporation. Each board member owes a fiduciary duty of care and loyalty to the corporation and its shareholders. Each act or decision of the board must be performed in good faith or for the benefit of the corporation.

As the company grows, it reaches a critical stage in its development where the need for knowledgeable, qualified, and willing people to serve on its board of directors becomes a priority. Initially the board is usually composed of insiders—shareholders wearing many hats—but as the company grows, outsiders are often recruited to bring diversity to the board. The use of outside directors may be necessary in order to bring additional credibility and expertise to the company for more effective growth planning and to provide management depth in connection with capital formation efforts; however, this generally increases the risk that the board will be subject to an attack for a breach of its fiduciary duties.

It is becoming increasingly difficult for many growing companies to attract qualified outsiders who are willing to sit on their board, usually because the prospective director is presented with an opportunity to serve what at least in the short term offers very little financial reward in exchange for a high degree of risk and responsibility. Director and officer liability insurance can protect against this risk, but it is often unavailable to or too costly for small companies. Therefore, in order to protect board members against personal liability and ensure that the board's decision making and growth planning are within the legal duties owed by directors, the various types of fiduciary duties owed by board members to the corporation are as follows:

1. *Duty of Care.* The test most often cited by the courts and statutes in defining a director's duty of care is that a director's duties must be discharged with the same degree of diligence, care, and skill "which ordinarily prudent men would exercise under similar circumstances in their own personal business affairs." This does not mean that a director must be an expert in every phase of the business conducted by the corporation. It does mean, however, that he or she must actively gather enough data to make an informed decision regarding company affairs and in formulating company strategies. In doing so, the board member is entitled to rely primarily on the data provided by officers and professional advisers provided that he or she has no knowledge of any irregularity or inaccuracy in the information. Board members have been held personally responsible in certain cases for misinformed or dishonest decisions made in bad faith, the failure to direct the corporation properly, the failure to enforce a litigation claim or otherwise act on behalf of the corporation, or knowingly authorizing a wrongful act.

2. *Duty of Fairness.* A director generally owes a duty of fairness in its dealings with the corporation. Issues over fairness usually arise in a self-dealing transaction where a board member or affiliate engages in a transaction with the corporation in a third-party capacity. The central legal concern here is that the director may be treating the corporation unfairly in the transaction since self-interest and gain could cloud his or her duty of loyalty to the company. When self-dealing is challenged, the director will have the burden of demonstrating the propriety and fairness of the transaction. If any component of the transaction involves fraud, undue overreaching, or waste of corporate assets, it is likely to be set aside by the courts. In order for the director's dealings with the corporation to be upheld, the interested director must demonstrate that the transaction

was approved or ratified by a disinterested majority of the company's board of directors.

3. *Duty of Loyalty.* A director owes a duty of loyalty to further the best interests of the corporation and, as a result, not to rob the corporation of an opportunity that belongs to it, secretly profit at the expense of the corporation, or unfairly compete with the business conducted by the corporation. Issues over loyalty usually arise when the director is accused of usurpation of a corporate opportunity. In most circumstances, if an opportunity arises for the corporation to engage in a new but related line of business, acquire a key asset, or bid on a new contract, the director must make the opportunity available to the corporation *first*, in order to determine whether the corporation will elect to take advantage of the particular opportunity. If the corporation declines or is unable to take advantage of the opportunity, then, in certain cases, the director may proceed to pursue the transaction.

The following general guidelines should be followed by the company in order to help board members meet their duties to the corporation:

- A booklet on the basic principles of corporate law should be prepared by legal counsel for all officers and directors. Ongoing management compliance seminars and bulletins issued periodically for the board should address the implications of recent cases or changes in the law.

- Work closely with a law firm experienced in corporate legal matters. If the board or an individual director is in doubt as to whether a proposed action is truly in the best interests of the corporation, consult a lawyer immediately, not after the transaction is consummated.

- Keep careful minutes of all meetings of the board of directors and comprehensive records of the information upon which board decisions are based. Be prepared to show financial data, business valuations, market research, opinion letters, and related documentation if the action is later challenged as being "uninformed" by a disgruntled shareholder. Well-prepared minutes will also serve a variety of other purposes, such as written proof of the directors' analysis and appraisal of a given situation, proof that parent and subsidiary operations are being conducted at arm's length and as two distinct entities, or proof that an officer did or did not have authority to engage in the specific transaction being questioned.

- Be selective in choosing candidates for the board of directors. Avoid considering or nominating someone who may offer credibility but is unlikely to attend any meetings or make any real contribution to the management and direction of the company. Such a passive relationship will only invite claims by shareholders for corporate mismanagement. Similarly, do not accept an invitation to sit on a board of directors unless you are ready to accept the responsibilities that go with it.

- In threatened takeover situations, be careful not to make decisions that will be in the best interests of only the board and the officers. Subject these defensive measures to the scrutiny of the courts and regulators. Board actions must be in the interest and protection of *all* shareholders, not just a select few, and any defensive measures adopted must be reasonable in relation to the threat.

- Any board member who independently supplies goods and services to the corporation should not participate in the board discussion or vote on any resolution relating to these dealings in order to avoid self-dealing or conflict-of-interest claims. Proposed actions must be approved by a disinterested board after the material facts of the transaction are disclosed and the nature and extent of the board member's involvement is known.

- Questionnaires should be issued periodically to officers and directors regarding possible self-dealing or conflicts of interest with the corporation with regard to required board duties. Incoming board members and newly appointed officers should be provided with a more detailed initial questionnaire. These questionnaires should also always be circulated among the board prior to any securities issuances, such as a private placement or a public offering.

- Corporate directors should be furnished with all appropriate background and financial information relating to proposed board actions well in advance of board meetings. An agenda, proper notice, and a mutually convenient time, place, and date will ensure good attendance records and compliance with applicable statutes regarding the notice of the meetings.

- A valid meeting of the board of directors may not be held unless a quorum is present. The number of directors needed to constitute a quorum may be fixed by the articles or bylaws but is generally a majority of board members.

- Board members who object to a proposed action or resolution should either vote in the negative and ask that such a vote be recorded in the minutes or abstain from voting and promptly file a written dissent with the secretary of the corporation.

Special Legal Issues for Closely Held Corporations and the Use of Shareholder Agreements

Emerging-growth companies whose progress and development are financed primarily with a combination of debt and retained earnings are likely to be closely held. Since there are only a few shareholders in most such companies, unique management problems arise; for example, there may be greater disregard of corporate formalities, an ignorance of the decision-making hierarchy imposed by corporate laws, and an especially difficult situation for minority shareholders who lack a secondary market in which to dispose of their shares in the event of dissension or a deadlock. These problems affecting management and control must be resolved within the bounds of the law. The instrument most often se-

Exhibit 4-1.   Shareholder agreement provisions.

1. Restrictions on the transfer of stock
2. Specific legends to be placed on certificates
3. Dispute-resolution procedures in the event of deadlock and related shareholder voting arrangements
4. The effect of death, disability, or retirement of a particular shareholder on the stock of the corporation
5. Procedures in the event that a shareholder's employment with the corporation is terminated
6. Pricing and buy-out formulas in the event of a mandatory or optional redemption
7. Preemptive rights for some or all of the shareholders
8. First-refusal rights in the event of a proposed transfer or sale of stock by a shareholder
9. The terms and use of installment payments, promissory notes, or insurance to fund a redemption or purchase of shares
10. Provisions for the management and control of the company that may be required by the founders or investors and that are consistent with applicable corporate law

lected to resolve these issues is a *shareholder agreement*, a contract among the owners of the securities issued by the company that specifies a wide variety of rights and obligations affecting the ownership and transfer of the stock. There are hundreds of different provisions that can be included in such an agreement (see Exhibit 4-1 for ten of them), depending on the purpose and intent of the document. Shareholder agreements can be very simple and straightforward, as in the case between two or three owners of a company, or very complex, such as shareholder agreements that are primarily designed to protect a minority investor.

The owners of a corporation should prepare a shareholder agreement upon the formation of the organization. Most new business owners, however, take a "honeymooner's" attitude, assuming that their decision making will always be in harmony. In most cases, the longer the founders wait to execute such an agreement, the more difficult it becomes to agree on certain provisions; if conflicts have already arisen, it may be too late. On the other hand, unduly restrictive shareholder agreements that are prepared too early in the company's development may become obsolete or overly prohibitive. For example, a shareholder agreement that includes favorable buy-out provisions may be rescinded or replaced as a condition to an investment by venture capitalists, who may have their own provisions in mind in order to protect their rights as minority share-holders. Therefore the terms of the shareholder agreements, as well as all other key corporate documents, should be evaluated as the company grows and changes.

Shareholder agreements are not the only way to allocate and balance management and control issues between majority and minority shareholders in a closely held corporation. Voting trusts or proxy agreements are often used to separate ownership rights from the voting rights of a particular security. Minority share-holder protective devices—such as cumulative voting rights, enhanced share-holder inspection rights, special antidilution provisions, and super-majority voting and quorum rights—can be built into the closely held company's character. Sophisticated investors and venture capitalists may demand these devices as a means of protecting their investments.

PART

II

Money

I have never worked with a business client whose corporation did not at some point need an infusion of capital to continue to fuel its growth. Be it debt or equity, from a venture capitalist or from a commercial lender, all growing companies eventually go through the frustrating process of raising capital.

There are many books available, some good and some not so good, on writing a business plan in preparation for the capital formation process. Chapter 5 is not a substitute for those books but is designed to introduce some basic principles of business and strategic planning that will be crucial as the company evolves and its capital needs change. Chapter 6 discusses capital structure and sources of capital. Chapters 7 through 10 discuss the legal aspects of the four most typical ways that a growing company raises capital: private placements, venture capital, commercial loans, and initial public offerings.

Chapters 11 and 12 are devoted to the mechanics of mergers and acquisition. Once capital is successfully raised by a growing company, it must be allocated to projects that will foster continued development and expansion of market share. One route available to the growing company is the acquisition of these resources, which is often more efficient than an attempt to develop them internally.

CHAPTER

5

Fundamentals of Business and Strategic Planning

Effective business and strategic planning is critical to the long-term success and viability of the enterprise and its ability to raise capital. In many ways, business planning should be viewed as a necessary prerequisite to ongoing strategic planning. The business plan is the foundation from which the process of strategic planning can be launched. If the principal purpose of business planning is viewed as the process of convincing investors why they should dedicate capital to your project, then strategic planning should be viewed as the process of managing the capital once it has been committed. Strategic planning becomes the process of analyzing trends and changes in the marketplace and adapting management and marketing strategies to this evolution for the principal purpose of maximizing the interests of those who have invested capital in the company as a result of the business plan.

Since business plans are typically prepared in order to raise capital, the key questions that must be addressed in it tend to be financial in nature, such as:

- What market niches and financial opportunities has the company identified?
- What services, products, and projects has the company planned to exploit these opportunities or solve these problems?
- How much capital will the company need to acquire the resources necessary to bring these projects to fruition?
- Exactly how will the capital be allocated?
- How will this infusion of capital increase the sales, profits, and overall value of the company?
- How will the company meet its debt-service obligations and/or provide a meaningful return on investment to its investors and lenders?
- How much equity in the company is being offered to investors, and how is it being valued?

• What exit strategies will be made available to the equity investors?

Business plans are used by both start-up companies and operating enterprises. CleanWorld Consulting Company has been in business for over 15 years and now requires a business plan in order to raise the necessary capital to reach the next stage in its development. The business plan will be prepared by Barbara Pureair, one of the two principals, with the assistance of a financial consultant, an investment banker, and her internal management team. Her attorneys and accountants will also provide advice and input on the plan. The seven topic areas her business plan should cover are outlined in Exhibit 5-1.

In preparing to draft a business plan for CCC, Pureair should be aware of some of the more common misperceptions regarding the preparation and use of business plans:

MYTH 1:
Business plans are only for start-up companies.

REALITY:
Businesses at all stages of development need to prepare business plans either for the planning and financing of a specific project or for general expansion financing, mergers or acquisitions, or overall improvement of financial and managerial performance of the company.

MYTH 2:
Business plans should be as detailed and slick as possible. The more that is spent preparing the plan, the better chance that the project will be financed.

REALITY:
Sophisticated investors will not have the time to review hundreds of pages of text. The plan must be concise, well written, and focused on the principal areas of concern to a lender or investor. Avoid overly technical descriptions of the company's processes or operations. Investors will commit funds based on the quality and clarity of the document, not its thickness. Although business plans ought to be presented professionally, an expensive binder or presentation will often demonstrate inefficient resources management.

MYTH 3:
Business plans should emphasize ideas and concepts, not people.

REALITY:
Many entrepreneurs fear that if the success of a company depends too heavily on a specific person, an investor will shy away. Although this is partially true, this concern can be easily quelled with "key man" life insurance. Venture capitalists ultimately prefer to invest in a company that has great people and only a good concept, rather than vice versa. Ultimately lenders and investors will commit funds based on the strength of the management team and the experience of the people who will make the company tick.

Exhibit 5-1. Business plan and financing proposal for CleanWorld Consulting Company (CCC).

I. Executive Summary

   A. Brief history of CCC
   B. Overview of CCC products and services
   C. Background of CCC management team (summary)
   D. Key features of CCC market
   E. Summary of CCC financial performance
   F. Brief discussion of capital required and anticipated allocation of proceeds

II. The Company: An Overview

   A. Organizational and management structure
   B. Operational and management policies
   C. Description of products and services offered (both current and anticipated)
   D. Overview of trends in the industry and marketplace in which CCC competes (or plans to compete)
   E. Key strengths and weaknesses of CCC

III. Products and Services Offered by CCC:
An Extended Discussion

   A. Key products and services offered
   B. Proprietary features, strengths, and weaknesses of each product and service
   C. Anticipated products and services to be offered (explain how these plans will be affected by the financing sought)

IV. Analysis of the Marketplace

   A. Extended description of the markets in which CCC competes (size, trends, growth, etc.)
   B. Analysis of key competitors
   C. Description and analysis of key customers/clients (current and anticipated)
   D. Market research (to support current and anticipated lines of products and services) *(continued)*

Exhibit 5-1. (continued).

V. Marketing and Advertising Strategy

    A. Strategies for reaching current and anticipated customers/clients

    B. Pricing policies and strategies

    C. Advertising and public relations plans and strategies

VI. Financial Plan and Strategies

    A. Summary of CCC financial performance for past three to five years

    B. Current financial condition of the company (include recent income statements and balance sheets as attachments)

    C. Projected financial condition of the company (forecasts for three to five years, assuming capital has been raised)

    D. Extended discussion of anticipated allocation of proceeds/budgets

VII. Suggested Exhibits and Attachments

    A. Current and projected financial statements (with detailed footnotes and assumptions)

    B. Resumes of key members of management team

    C. Timetables for completion of key goals and objectives

    D. Organizational chart for management

    E. Copies of key documents and contracts

    F. Copies of recent media coverage

    G. Pictures of key products or advertising materials for services offered

    H. List of customer and professional references

MYTH 4:

Business plans should be prepared only by the founding entrepreneur.

REALITY:

Most entrepreneurs are highly skilled in a particular profession or area of management, and they may not necessarily possess the ability to prepare a business plan. Ideally, the plan should be developed by a team of managers within the company and then be reviewed by qualified experts, including the company's accountants, attorneys, and board of directors. The plan should never be prepared solely by outside advisers without the input of internal management. A venture capitalist will be quick to recognize a "cooked" plan or one that reflects the views and efforts of the company's professional advisers rather than its management team, who will be responsible for running the company on a day-to-day basis.

MYTH 5:
Business plans should be distributed as widely as possible.

REALITY:
Business plans inevitably contain proprietary and confidential information. Therefore, distribution should be controlled and careful records kept as to who has been provided with copies of it. The cover sheet of the plan should contain a conspicuously positioned management disclaimer that these are only the *plans* of the company, the success of which cannot be assured, as well as a notice of proprietary information. All applicable federal and state securities laws must be carefully considered if the business plan is intended as a financing proposal. It should not be used in lieu of a formal private placement memorandum, however. Finally, certain institutional investors will consider investments only in certain kinds of companies or industries. Research these criteria before sending a business plan in order to save the time and resources of both the company and the prospective lender or investor.

MYTH 6:
A business plan should follow a specified format regardless of the industry in which the company operates.

REALITY:
Companies at different stages of growth facing different problems and operating in different industries will require a different set of topics that must be included in the business plan. For example, plans for a start-up manufacturing company may be far more concerned with financing of plant and equipment, patents, inventory, and production schedules than will an established service-oriented company, which may be more focused on personnel, marketing costs, and protection of trade secrets and goodwill.

MYTH 7:
Optimism should prevail over realism in the business plan.

REALITY:
Naturally any business plan should demonstrate the enthusiasm of the founders of the company and generate excitement in the reader. This should not, however, be an excuse for a business plan that lacks credibility and accuracy. Investors want to know all of the company's strengths *and* its weaknesses. In fact, a realistic discussion of the company's problems, along with a reasonable plan for dealing with these various risks and challenges, will have a much more positive impact on the prospective investor. Investors typically feel more comfortable investing in someone who has learned from previous business failures (commonly known as a degree from Hard Knocks University) rather than a person who has never managed an enterprise. In addition, investors expect a realistic assessment of the anticipated market. The "if we can capture

only 1 percent of the market" days are long gone. Rather, the investor wants to know *how* the market will be approached and *what* market share is likely to be obtained. Finally, any budgets, sales projections, business valuations, or related forecasts should be well substantiated, with accompanying footnotes, for both legal and business reasons. Unrealistic or unsubstantiated financial projections and budgets reveal inexperience or lack of attention to detail in the presentation to an interested investor.

MYTH 8:

A well-written business plan should contain an executive summary, which should be written before the full text of the document is prepared.

REALITY:

Institutional investors are exposed to hundreds of business plans each month and as a result initially devote only a few minutes to the review of the plan. It is true, therefore, that the executive summary, generally one to three pages in length, will be the first (and possibly the last) impression that the company makes on the investor. If the reader's attention is not captured in these first few minutes, he or she is not likely to complete the review of the plan. The summary should contain all of the information critical to the investment decision: the nature of the company and its founders, the amount of money sought, the allocation of the proceeds, a summary of key financial projections, and an overview of marketing considerations. The mistake often made in preparing the plan is writing the summary first, before the main components have been drafted. The main body of the plan should be prepared before the summary is drafted to ensure consistency.

MYTH 9:

Business plans are written only when a company needs to raise capital.

REALITY:

Although most business plans are written in connection with the search for capital, a well-written plan will serve a variety of beneficial purposes. It is a management tool that can serve as a road map for the company's growth and reflects a realistic self-appraisal of the company's progress to date, as well as its projected goals and objectives. The completed business plan serves as the foundation for the development of a more detailed strategic and growth management plan, especially after the proposed financing has been successfully completed.

Transition to Strategic Planning

The information presented to a prospective lender or investor in a business plan becomes the foundation from which the strategic planning process is launched.

The financial projections and management objectives set forth in it, however, will rarely be met in the exact manner and timetable in which they were predicted. The strategic planning process allows resources to be reallocated in accordance with the changes that inevitably take place between the time of preparation and implementation of the plan. Thus, the plan must be constantly reviewed and monitored. Its modification is an integral part of the strategic planning process. The ability to adapt to these changes and to exploit new opportunities is essential for measuring the performance of the company, as well as ensuring its survival.

The monitoring of the business plan encompasses both evaluation and reporting. Any departures from the original plan should be well documented in reports for internal management and outside investors that address such issues as the following ones:

- What types of changes have caused this variation from the original business plan (competition, product development, lack of personnel or capital)?
- Which key personnel are responsible for managing and adapting to these changes?
- What new resources are needed as a result of these changes?
- What is the impact of these changes on the overall plans and objectives of the organization?
- What legal issues must be considered as a result of these changes and deviations from the objectives set forth in the original business plan?

Traditionally the owners and managers of small and growing companies looked at strategic planning as a luxury reserved for large companies with the time to enjoy, or in some cases, the time to waste. These executives often argued instead that flexibility and "seat-of-the-pants" management were at the heart of their entrepreneurial credo.

But times are changing, and many entrepreneurs are realizing that failure to plan is planning to fail. Venture management principles dictate that entrepreneurship means not only taking risk but also managing risk—identifying and making the most effective use of all available resources, building a strong management team, and engaging in periodic strategic planning. Strategic planning thus becomes necessary to anticipating and managing change in order to ensure long-term success and continued growth.

The principles of strategic planning are also important to short-term management: Each business decision must have some relationship to the long-term goals and objectives of the organization. As difficult as it may be to turn away from an opportunity, the decision to pursue a particular project should be linked to the timetable set for the growth of the company and the achievement of its long-term plans. For example, bidding on a contract far beyond a company's current capabilities may at first seem to be an expedited method of growth. In reality, it is more likely to be an expedited route to business failure, since the company probably lacks the human and financial resources to meet the obligations under the contract if it is awarded, which not only may cripple the enterprise in the short term but is also likely to destroy its goodwill over the long term.

Strategic planning for a growing enterprise can best be understood as the process of *assessing* the current nature and status (strengths and weaknesses) of the enterprise; *identifying* methods for the efficient allocation and use of current resources; *establishing* medium- and long-range plans for the company; *under-standing* how short-term decision making affects these plans; *developing* strate-gies for taking advantage of opportunities and overcoming barriers and threats presented by the external operating environment (such as entry in new markets and dealing with changes in competition, law, and technology); *determining* methods for attracting, selecting, and using the resources needed to achieve these goals; and *monitoring* the results of the strategies selected, making adjust-ments to goals and objectives as may be necessary to keep the company on course toward its destination.

Strategic planning begins with a series of fundamental questions:

- Where are we, and how did we get here?
- What business are we really in? What business(es) should we be in?
- Where do we want to go? What will we need to get there?
- Does the company have a strategy for growth? How has it been implemented thus far? Is it still consistent with any changes in the company's competitive environment?
- What alternative methods and rates of growth are available?
- What is the company's competitive position within the industry?
- How are we viewed by our customers, employees, shareholders, suppliers, and competitors?
- What are the company's greatest strengths and weaknesses?
- What strategies can we adopt to allow the company to exploit its strengths and compensate for its weaknesses?
- What factors present the greatest risks of business failure? How is risk being managed?
- What is the company's capital structure? What additional financial resources will be needed to accomplish our plans and objectives?
- Once a strategic plan is developed and implemented, how can we best mon-itor and measure its results?

Although companies may leave the marketplace for a variety of reasons—merg-ers and acquisitions, owner retirement or death, or product or service obsoles-cence—many business declines and insolvencies can be traced to a failure by the owners and managers of the firm to come to grips with the answers to these questions and to plan for the company's future by adapting to changes in the law, technology, and the marketplace.

Periodic strategic planning helps mitigate but will not eliminate the risk of business failure or distress. Ultimately the success or failure of the strategies selected will be determined by the return on investment provided to the company's stockholders, in terms of both capital appreciation and current income. Effective strategic planning in a growing company requires the ability of management to make short-term decisions with a long-term view, so that such a return on capital invested is provided over an extended period of time, even in the face of unanticipated adversities.

Elements of a Formal Strategic Plan

Although strategic planning is an ongoing process, owners and managers of growing companies should periodically prepare a formal written strategic plan. The responsibility for preparing and monitoring specific components of the plan should be delegated to members of the management team according to their areas of expertise and levels of authority. The finished product is a formal strategic plan that contains the following components.

Statement of Goals and Corporate Mission

This introduction states the purpose of the organization, with a focus on the discussion of a basic question: "Why does the company exist, and what does it hope to achieve?" Any unique management philosophies, strategies, or objectives are set out in this section.

Analysis of Business and Economic Environment

This section provides an analysis of the external factors affecting the company's growth and development. It examines the company's present position and opportunities within its marketplace, trends and statistics affecting the marketplace, and the impact of these changes and trends on the company's products and services. Current and projected economic, political, and social trends relevant to the company are addressed, as are the market share, pricing policies, products and services, and strengths and weaknesses. Relevant changes in applicable laws, technology, or demographics are analyzed. This section should also contain a discussion of any market research conducted to assess consumer attributes, product or service recognition, and goodwill toward the company.

Assessment of Company Strengths and Weaknesses

This section focuses on the internal factors affecting the company's growth and development. It assesses how and why the company has achieved certain results (as well as experienced certain difficulties); challenges the validity of previously developed business and strategic plans and critically assesses progress to date; and appraises the company's current strategy. If pitfalls are found, the resources (and the cost of obtaining them) needed to fill the gaps need to be identified. The tendency to adopt an "if it ain't broke, don't fix it" philosophy should be replaced with an "are we really where we could be and should be?" approach. If the answer is no, plans and objectives for getting there should be identified, with a timetable and schedule of resources needed. The adequacy of the company's human resources, physical facilities, research and development, quality controls, and access to capital is also addressed in this section.

Statement of Key Objectives

The statement of key objectives contains clearly defined yet broad statements about how the company plans to achieve its goals. A timetable and a methodology capable of being monitored and assessed at a later date must be included. Consider the following example:

WRONG: The company plans to expand its market share through franchising.

This objective as stated fails to identify when the objective will be achieved, how it will be accomplished, who will be responsible, and what resources will be required.

CORRECT: The company plans to allocate sufficient capital to appoint a director of franchising who will be responsible for developing a sales and marketing program in order to sell 20 franchises in the mid-Atlantic region to expand the company's market share by at least 10 percent within 18 months.

Assumptions, Risks, and Alternatives

Here the key assumptions underlying the company's objectives are disclosed, with a candid assessment of the risks in the event that the assumptions are wrong. Alternatives are identified in the event that assumptions are found to be untrue or unstable and/or if risks cannot be managed.

Miscellaneous

Copies of any reports, studies, financial statements, and projections relevant to the objectives discussed in "Statement of Key Objectives" should be attached for review and assessment. Any capital or support requirements necessary to achieve these objectives should be discussed to the extent that they are not included in previous sections. A structural chart demonstrating the responsibilities within the organization from both an operational and strategic planning perspective should also be included.

Pitfalls of Strategic Planning

Small, growing companies that engage in ongoing strategic planning and in the periodic preparation of a formal written strategic plan should avoid:

Neglecting the operation of the company. Although the periodic preparation of a formal strategic plan is crucial to the ongoing viability of the company, it is likely to be a temporary significant drain on the resources of a smaller business. Careful planning and time management systems must be put into place so that the company's operations are not neglected when strategic plans are being prepared and developed.

The "not invented here" syndrome. Do not assume that only those individuals who are actually operating the company on a day-to-day basis are capable of assisting in the development of the strategic plan. Outside consultants and professional advisers can often offer a fresh and objective perspective and should be key members of the management team responsible for strategic planning. In fact, it is during the strategic planning process that the assistance of a management consultant should be strongly considered, if for no other reason than to have a new set of educated eyes take a look at the company's past performance and future plans.

The "if I want it done right, I'll do it myself" syndrome. Many chief executive officers of small companies fail to include key employees in the strategic planning process because either they believe that others are unqualified or they cannot afford to divert precious resources to the planning process. Both assumptions are mistakes that may be quite costly to the organization. Each department within the organization should participate in strategic planning, especially if members of the particular department will be responsible for implementing sections of the plan.

Internal policies and biases. It is only natural that each member of the management team will view his or her component of the strategic plan as the "most critical" to the long-term success and viability of the organization. The chief executive officer must ensure that all members understand the interrelationship of the various departments in developing, implementing, and monitoring the plan and ensuring that each manager understands that the whole is greater than the sum of its parts. Conversely, many members of the management team may be fearful that the strategic planning process will reveal inefficiencies within their department. Be sensitive to attempts to hide key details or inflate performance when the planning process begins.

The strategic plan as a work of art. Despite the many benefits to be enjoyed by an organization that takes the time to develop a formal strategic plan, the plan itself should not be viewed as the *Mona Lisa*. When a company falls into the "strategic plan as a work of art" syndrome, it is probably spending too much time and money on a plan that is likely to be overstated and inflexible.

The "burning need to expand" syndrome. Many strategic plans call for premature or unnecessary growth, often because of a perceived need to progress through expansion. A premature attempt to venture into new markets, enter into licensing or franchising agreements, or hire additional staff is contrary to the basic principle of "making sure that your own house is in order before inviting friends over."

Understanding the Big Picture

One of the key premises of this book is that it is important for managers of a growing company to understand the big picture in strategic planning and decision making. Therefore, one important component to such an approach is a fundamental understanding of the legal implications of any proposed business objective or transaction.

Effective big-picture strategic planning is accomplished through the team approach in which the disciplines of business, accounting, and the law are represented. A qualified business lawyer must be a key member of the group responsible for developing and implementing corporate plans and strategies. He or she must be recruited as a member of this team early on in order to ensure that

- Legal hurdles and requirements are understood and taken into account at the inception of venture or project as well as throughout its developmental life cycle.
- Tangible and intangible legal costs are factors in the analysis of a proposed transaction or project.
- The company takes full advantage of the protection, loopholes, and competitive advantages that may be offered by the law.
- The company properly assesses and manages the risk of litigation.
- The business lawyer understands the basic goals, philosophies, and objectives of the company.

The management team responsible for developing and implementing the strategic plan must understand the legal issues and hurdles raised when a set of strategies and alternatives is developed and implemented. Each manager must understand the costs and risks of making marketing, manufacturing, finance, or management decisions without the guidance of the company's attorney.

CHAPTER

6

Capital Structure and Capital Formation Strategies

One of the most difficult tasks faced by the management team of a growing company is the development and maintenance of an optimal capital structure for the organization. A corporation's capital structure has five central components: (1) long-term debt, (2) preferred stock, (3) common stock, (4) hybrid securities, and (5) retained earnings. Each component carries certain advantages and disadvantages to the growing company and certain direct and indirect costs. The management team must find the appropriate combination of these five components at any given time that will serve as an effective capital structure.

Before management establishes or modifies an existing capital structure or searches for funds, it needs to consider these important issues:

A. What are the immediate and projected capital needs of the corporation?

B. Who are the current stakeholders (e.g., creditors, bondholders, and stockholders) in the corporation, and what are their expectations with respect to ownership, control, and rate of return?*

C. Who are the projected stakeholders in the company, and what are their anticipated expectations with respect to rate of return?

D. How will the capital raised be allocated? How and when will the assets acquired begin to generate income to repay the costs of the capital utilized for the project?

E. If debt financing is selected:

1. What collateral is available to secure the loan?

---

*The answer to this question requires an analysis of the company's cost of capital, the discussion of which is beyond the scope of this book. From a financial manager's perspective, cost of capital decisions entail the deployment of corporate assets in such a manner as to yield the minimum rate of return expected by the company's stockholders (ability to pay dividends and appreciate in value) and its bondholders (ability to service the debt on a timely basis).

2. What assurances can be offered to the lender as to the company's ability to meet its debt-service obligations?

3. What additional risks of financial distress and/or failure have been placed on the corporation as a result of these debt-service obligations?

4. What are the direct (principal and interest) and indirect (restrictive covenants in loan agreements, failure to fit within average industry ratios) costs of this additional leverage?

F. If equity financing is selected:

1. What are the expectations of the current equity holders with respect to ownership and control? To what extent will current equity holders suffer dilution as a result of the offering? Are there any contractual restrictions on dilution?

2. What are the relative risks involved in the deployment of the capital to be raised? How will prospective investors assess this risk in determining their expected rates of return?

3. What are the projected profits to be generated by the deployment of the capital to be raised? How and when will these profits be divided and distributed among the holders of the company's equity securities?

4. What tax advantages are lost as a result of the choice of equity over debt? Do the benefits of not being obligated to repay the holders of the equity securities outweigh the deductibility of interest payments on the debt?

G. What are the industry norms and key industry ratios that the financial managers of the corporation should follow?

H. What methods of access to the capital markets are available to the corporation and what costs are attached to each method (loan brokerage fees, commissions to investment bankers, etc.)?

I. What impact will the choice of capital structure or the method of financing selected have on the company's:

1. Credit rating among lenders?
2. Bond rating among investment bankers?
3. Demand for the company's securities among stockholders?
4. Ability to raise additional capital?

The answers to these questions will help the company develop a sensible and efficient capital structure, as well as enable the founders to understand the costs, benefits, and risks of determining whether debt, equity, or a combination should be used in modifying the growing company's capital structure.

It is important to remember that no capital structure is perfect. The choice for any given company depends on the industry in which it operates, its stage of development, and the external factors affecting its ability to raise capital.

Capital Structure Decisions

A company's initial decision regarding the various components that should make up its optimal capital structure is likely to become obsolete as the organization grows. The management team must periodically assess and evaluate the structure as the company reaches various stages in its growth or in the developmental life cycles of its key products and services. In addition, changes in economic conditions, financial management philosophy, applicable tax and securities laws, and the company's production, distribution, or marketing strategies may require an analysis of the firm's capital structure.

Suppose, for example, that with the assistance of his management team, George Eightrack at Impasse, Inc., the manufacturer of consumer electronics products we met in chapter 1, sets its initial optimal capital structure at two-thirds long-term debt and one-third common stock equity. It will maintain this structure until changes in technology and increased competition cause Eightrack to acquire another company or restructure the existing manufacturing facility. Perhaps Compactdisc & Associates, its consulting firm, recommends retooling. Because this replacement of equipment comes at a time when interest rates are high, the company, which has been hampered by dropping sales, is unable to service any additional debt. Eightrack may decide to authorize a new class of preferred stock for sale to venture capitalists as the most prudent route from a strategic planning perspective. Prior to the offer or sale of these securities, however, the management team must address all of the issues set out previously and carefully consider the regulatory costs and implications of the creation and distribution of these new securities.

The effective management of the company's growth will encompass the consideration of all relevant factors in establishing the company's initial capital structure and the anticipation of change in periodically assessing and modifying the capital structure. The challenge for the company's owners and managers is to create a balance between the need for a secure capital foundation from which the company can be built and the need for enough flexibility in the capital structure to anticipate and adapt to changes in economic conditions, applicable laws, technology, and the marketplace.

Factors Affecting Capital Formation Strategies

The optimum source and type of financing available to a growing company will depend on a number of factors, including: current capital structure of the entity; nature of the entity's business and trends within that industry; short- and long-term capital needs; the costs and benefits of each alternative (legal, accounting, printing, registration and compliance fees, broker's commissions, etc.); projected income and anticipated return on investment; stage of development and business plans of the company; applicable securities and tax laws, such as whether the corporation has elected to be taxed as an S corporation under the Internal Revenue Code or whether the offering of securities will be exempt from registration under federal and state securities laws; present economic factors such as interest rates and performance of the stock market; and any restrictions contained in the company's articles of incorporation, by-laws, or shareholders' agreements, such as preemptive rights or restriction on transfer of the company's securities.

The type of security the company offers will also depend on a number of factors, such as the requirements and demands of the investor, the terms of the investment agreement, the current structure of the company, and applicable restrictions on the company to authorize the issuance of additional stock.

The most obvious and simplest way to raise equity is for the board of directors to adopt a resolution authorizing the sale of already available but unissued common stock. Negotiations with the investors, however, may trigger the need for authorizing and issuing additional classes of common stock, preferred stock, warrants, options or convertible hybrid securities such as convertible debentures (debt convertible into equity), or even preferred stock convertible into debt at the option of the company.

Types of Corporate Securities

There are essentially three types of securities that a corporation may issue: (1) debt securities, (2) equity securities, and (3) hybrid or convertible securities. Each type has certain fundamental characteristics, variable features, and attendant costs.

Debt Securities

A debt security is usually in the form of a bond—typically an obligation secured by a mortgage on some property of the company—or a debenture or note—an unsecured obligation issued on the strength of the company's reputation, projected earnings, and growth potential. Both bonds and debentures feature a maturity date, at which time the principal must be repaid. During the term of the instrument, a fixed amount of interest at regular intervals will be due to the holder. A company that fails to make timely payments of interest or to repay the principal at maturity will be in default, which will trigger certain rights of the holder against the company that may be defined in the instrument or the statute.

The terms of the debt security and the yield to the holder are determined by an evaluation of the level of the risk to the holder and the likelihood of default. For example, debentures usually carry a higher rate of interest because they are unsecured. Growing companies that lack a high bond or credit rating often face restrictive covenants in the debenture purchase agreement or in the bond's indenture that will govern its activities during the term of the instrument. For example, a restrictive covenant may state that no dividends can be declared that would jeopardize the ability of the company to meet its debt-secure payments. This type of covenant would create a conflict between debenture holders and common stockholders. The likely cost to the company of such a conflict could entail a reduced demand for its equity securities or a failure to meet the rates of return expected by its present equity holders.

One distinct advantage of a debenture offering is that since no specific collateral is earmarked to secure the obligations, the company keeps its assets available to pledge elsewhere if it subsequently requires additional debt financing. (The advantages and disadvantages of debt financing are discussed in greater detail in chapter 9.)

Equity Securities

Equity securities issued by a corporation can take many forms, including common stock, preferred stock, warrants, and options. Each carries a different set of rights, preferences, and potential rates of return in exchange for the capital contributed to the company. In planning the optimal capital structure of the company, the founders must determine the allocation of risk, return, and control among the various types of equity securities to be issued by the corporation. This allocation will be influenced by the true cost of the capital, as well as the expectations of the purchasers of the equity securities. Emerging-growth companies, whose value is usually attributed more toward intangible assets (patents, trade secrets, or goodwill) and projected earnings, will tend to issue equity securities before incurring additional debt, usually because they lack the assets to secure the debt and any additional debt increases their risk of business failure to unacceptably dangerous levels. Despite these risks and restrictions, many owners of growing companies seek to borrow funds in order to avoid dilution in control and ownership, which may lead to financial distress or failure if the company's finances are not well managed or the company fails to meet its growth potential.

An offering of common stock is often a traumatic experience for the owners of a closely held company who need additional capital for growth but lack the internal funds (e.g., personal savings or corporate retained earnings) to preserve the current capital structure and distribution of ownership and control. Certainly the offering of additional common stock will entail a surrender of some ownership and is generally regarded as the most costly form of financing, but it does provide the company an increased equity base and a more secure foundation upon which the company can be built and debt financing more easily and favorably obtained. Owners of closely held companies who are hesitant to offer additional common stock to new investors must remember that if their plans for growth are successful, their "smaller piece of a more valuable pie" will be worth considerably more than "a larger slice" of a company with minimal value and growth potential.

Preferred stock possesses certain features similar to debt securities. For example, a company that needs to raise additional capital could authorize the issuance of preferred stock, which would carry with it the right to receive dividends at a fixed or even an adjustable rate of return (similar to a debt instrument), with priority over dividends distributed to the holders of the common stock, as well as a preference on the distribution of assets in the event of a corporate liquidation. The preferred stock may or may not have certain rights with respect to voting, convertibility to common stock, antidilution rights, or redemption privileges that may be exercised by either the company or the holder. If redemption is by the company (generally known as a *call*), investors may want certain substituted benefits, such as a warrant in exchange for the early redemption. If the redemption is at the option of the investor (generally known as a *put*), the holders will want to know the terms and conditions of the repurchase by the company.

Although the fixed dividend payments are not tax deductible (as interest payments would be) and there is still a dilution of ownership of the company, the balance between risk and reward is achieved because the principal invested need not be returned (unless there are provisions for redemption), the preferred stockholders' return on investment is limited to a fixed rate of return (unless there are provisions for convertibility), and the claims of the preferred stockholders are subordinated to the claims of creditors and bondholders in the event of a failure to pay dividends upon the liquidation of the corporation. The use of convertible preferred stock is especially popular among venture capitalists (for reasons discussed in greater detail in chapter 8).

Equity securities also include warrants and options issued by the company that give the holder a right to buy a stated number of shares of common or preferred stock at a specified price and within a specific period of time. Generally warrants are used either as equity sweeteners when issued in connection with bonds or debentures in exchange for a lower rate of interest and more favorable terms to the company than would otherwise be provided or as payment to key advisers or consultants in lieu of fees or common stock. Warrants enable the holders to participate in the company's growth, assuming that they are happy with the progress of the company, by exercising their rights, usually at a purchase price lower than the fair market value of the stock at the time the warrant is exercised.

Convertible Securities

The typical convertible securities, such as convertible debentures or convertible preferred stock, are also forms of option securities in that they vest holders with an option to convert their current holdings, upon specified terms and conditions, into common stock of the issuer. The incentive for conversion is usually the same as for the exercise of a warrant: that the conversion price (e.g., the actual price the company will receive for the common stock when conversion occurs) is more favorable than the rate of return provided by the debenture or preferred stock currently held. In addition, the conversion price will be adjusted for any stock splits, stock dividends, offerings at a discount, or reorganizations by the company subsequent to the issuance of the convertible security.

Owners and managers considering the use of convertibles should remember that unlike the exercise of a warrant, which brings additional capital into the company, conversion brings only an adjustment to the balance sheet. It may improve the financial strength of the company and its ability to borrow from institutional sources, but it does not make any new capital directly available. Convertible debt securities nevertheless are attractive to investors because of the opportunity to hedge their capital. If the company is doing well, the investor usually converts in order to enjoy the appreciation in the equity. If the company is doing poorly, the investor can enjoy the preferred status as a creditor.

In sum, convertible securities offer several distinct advantages to the company:

- An opportunity to sell debt securities at lower interest rates and with less restrictive covenants in exchange for a chance to participate in the company's success if it meets its projections and objectives
- A means of selling common stock at prices 10 to 30 percent higher than those prevailing at the time the convertible security is issued
- A lower dilution in earnings per share, usually because the company can offer fewer shares when convertible securities are offered than in a straight debt or equity offering
- A broadened market of prospective purchasers for the company's securities since certain buyers may want to avoid a direct purchase of common stock but would consider an investment in convertible securities

Authorization and Issuance of Corporate Securities

Regardless of the type of corporate security deemed most appropriate, the company is required to follow certain legal steps and procedures when it authorizes and issues securities. These legal considerations generally fall into two categories: state corporation laws and federal and state regulation of the offer and sale of securities.

State Corporation Laws

We learned in chapter 4 that the board of directors owes certain fiduciary duties to the shareholders. The nature and type of securities to be offered by the company may be determined by the board of directors by virtue of its general managerial powers, *provided that* the board's resolutions are properly adopted and documented and the securities are authorized in the articles of incorporation. For example, the business plan for CleanWorld Consulting Company (CCC) calls for a private placement of convertible preferred stock and a subsequent public offering of the company's common stock. In order for these two offerings to be implemented, the corporate charter of CleanWorld will need to be amended or restated in order to authorize this new class of preferred stock (see Exhibit 6-1), as well as the additional shares of common stock required upon conversion of the preferred stock and upon registration of the shares of common stock when the company launches its public offering. Generally, unless otherwise provided in the by-laws or by statute, stockholder approval is required in order to implement these plans and strategies.

As with all other securities issued by a growing company, careful records should be kept with respect to ownership and transfer of the shares. It is also the

Exhibit 6-1. Steps for amending CCC's corporate charter.

1. Issue a resolution by the board of directors setting forth the rights and preferences of the new class of convertible preferred securities, as well as the additional shares of common stock, and a finding that the offer and sale of these securities is in the best interest of the corporation, and directing that the matter be submitted to stockholders of CCC for approval.

2. Notify the stockholders as provided by the by-laws or, if the by-laws are silent, in accordance with the statute, which includes a copy of the proposed amendment of the charter to be submitted for approval.

3. Hold a meeting of the stockholders (or written consents in lieu of such a meeting) at which the affirmative vote of 66 percent (or as otherwise provided in the charter) of the shares entitled to vote approve the amendment.

4. File the restated articles or the articles of amendment and applicable taxes and fees with the state corporate authority.

board's responsibility to ensure that proper payment for the securities has been fully received and that stock certificates are promptly and properly issued.

Federal and State Securities Laws

The basic federal statute governing the issuance of securities is the Securities Act of 1933, as amended, which is administered by the Securities and Exchange Commission (SEC). The act requires that all securities be registered with the SEC before they are offered or sold by any means of interstate commerce, *unless* the securities or the transactions in which they are sold fall within specified exemptions from registration. The two basic objectives of the act are to ensure that all investors are provided with all material investment information in connection with the sale and issuance of securities and to prevent fraud and misrepresentation in connection with the interstate sales of securities.

The 1933 Act generally requires issuers to file a registration statement with the SEC prior to issuing securities to the general public, unless a specific exemption is available for the security or transaction. (The contents of this registration statement are discussed in greater detail in chapter 10. The types of transactions that are exempt from the process and the expense of registering securities with the SEC are discussed in greater detail in chapter 7.)

In addition to compliance with the Securities Act of 1933, issuers of securities must comply with applicable state "blue-sky" laws. Virtually every state has adopted some form of securities regulation, and many state securities laws follow the Uniform Securities Act developed by the Commissioners on Uniform State Laws. The Uniform Securities Act has four central components: (1) provisions regulating fraud and misrepresentations in connection with the offer and sale of securities; (2) procedures for the registration of new securities offerings; (3) registration of brokers and dealers of securities; and (4) remedies for violations of these state securities laws. The state securities laws also provide a number of transactional exemptions from registration, which parallel some of the federal exemptions.

The Search for Capital

Once the company's optimal capital structure has been matched with its stage of development, and its management understands the types of securities it may issue and the legal procedures for issuing them, the management team is ready to embark on the search (and battle) for capital. There are a wide variety of sources to consider in this quest for financing, and each source has its own investment criteria and preferences in structuring the transaction.

An emerging-growth company will require different types of financing at different stages in its development. At the early stages, seed money for the company is usually gathered from the founder's personal savings, family, and friends. But even at this stage, the entrepreneur must plan the capital structure of the company and consider applicable securities laws. A founder who issues an excessive percentage of the company's common stock to a distant relative in New Jersey as appreciation for a $10,000 investment could face a legal and financial valuation nightmare when he or she seeks more sophisticated growth financing in a few years.

A company whose founders fail to document certain understandings among them will have difficulty when sophisticated lenders and investors, who typically engage in an investigation of the company commonly referred to as *due diligence* prior to extending growth financing, require that these problems be remedied before making the investment or loan.

Seed financing from family and friends is often supplemented with debt financing from a commercial lender, which will look toward the founder's personal assets or personal guaranty to serve as collateral for the financing. If the founder lacks assets available to pledge, a Small Business Administration (SBA) guaranty may be available by applying for a loan through an SBA certified or preferred lender.

Once the company has raised seed capital and managed to establish itself as an operating entity with a well-developed product or service and a well-rounded management team, it is ready to embark on the search for growth financing. Owners and managers of emerging-growth companies have a number of sources of capital.

Institutional Venture Capital

The term *venture capital* has been defined in many ways, but it refers generally to the early-stage financing of young emerging-growth companies at a relatively high risk attributable to the newness of the company or even the entire industry. Professional venture capitalists are usually a group of highly trained general partners who manage a pool of venture funds for investment in growing companies on behalf of a group of passive limited partners or a federally licensed small-business investment company (SBIC). Some private corporations and even state governments also manage venture funds for investment in rapidly growing small companies.

Most venture capitalists seek companies offering significant potential capital appreciation and return on investment, a strong management team, a company well positioned to exploit an opportunity within its industry, and a likelihood of an initial public offering within three to five years. Venture capitalists typically want to exercise some control and influence over the company's growth and development, both directly through a consulting arrangement or membership on the board of directors and indirectly through a plethora of restrictive covenants in the investment documentation.

Initial Public Offering (IPO)

The decision to offer the stock of a growing closely held company to the public carries with it a host of opportunities—and drawbacks. The net proceeds of the public offering will enable the company to carry on with its business plans, build up a reserve of working capital, consider acquisitions in order to enter into new markets, achieve horizontal or vertical integration and economies of scale, or acquire and protect valuable tangible assets and intellectual property rights. A public company also has increased visibility in the business and financial community, which may make additional rounds of debt and equity financing easier to obtain.

The drawbacks of going public are also numerous: time-consuming and expensive registration and periodic reporting requirements under federal and state securities laws, restrictions on transactions among the insiders of the corporation, greater exposure to the risk of legal action taken by a disappointed shareholder, and a certain loss of control (the extent will depend on the proportion of the shares sold to the public).

Private Placement

A *private placement* is an offering of the company's securities to a limited number of investors under an exemption from the registration requirements imposed by federal and state securities law. Many small companies that do not necessarily possess the characteristics required by an institutional venture capitalist or underwriter (in connection with a public offering) choose this method of equity financing. The private placement generally offers reduced transactional and ongoing costs because of its exemption from the registration and reporting requirements, as well as access to a wider variety of investors whose appetite for return on investment and operational control may be somewhat smaller than the institutional sources.

Commercial Banks

Smaller companies are much more likely to obtain an alternative audience with a commercial loan officer after the start-up phase has been completed. Beyond general credit ratings and the ability to repay the loan, bankers also look closely at the company's management team, competition, industry trends, anticipated use of proceeds, and the nature of the company's business in determining whether to extend debt financing. (This information should be contained in a formal loan proposal, discussed in chapter 9.) Growth financing from a commercial lender usually takes the form of a three- to five-year term loan and/or an operating line of credit.

Commercial Finance Companies

Many companies that seek debt financing but are rejected by banks turn to commercial finance companies for credit. These companies usually offer debt financing at considerably higher rates than an institutional lender but are often willing to provide lower rates if the company takes advantage of other services offered for fees, such as payroll and accounts receivable management. Commercial finance companies have more flexible lending policies than banks because of fewer state and federal regulations, but they are just as likely to mitigate their risk with higher interest rates for loans or credit to undeveloped companies.

Leasing Companies

Growing companies with a need to acquire specific assets to fuel their development should consider leasing as one alternative to debt financing. Leasing generally takes one of three forms:

1. *Sales and Leaseback Arrangements.* Under these, the company sells the asset to a third party and then immediately leases it back from that party for a specified period and under specific terms. The advantage for the seller/lessee is that the funds that would otherwise be used to pay the sale price of the asset remain available for other purposes, the use of the asset is retained, and the lease payments generally qualify as deductible business expenses.

2. *Operating Leases.* These usually provide the lessee with both the asset and a service contract over a period of time that is usually significantly less than the actual useful life of the asset. The aggregate payments under the lease contract are not sufficient to recover the full value of the equipment, which usually means lower monthly payments for the lessee. A well-negotiated operating lease contains a clause giving the lessee the right to cancel the lease (with little to no penalty). The cancellation clause provides management with more flexibility in the event that sales decline or the equipment leased becomes obsolete.

3. *Capital Leases.* These differ from an operating lease in that they usually do not include any maintenance services and involve the use of the equipment by the lessee over the full useful life of the asset.

Private Individual Investors

Growing companies may seek the support of wealthy individuals who share
the company's vision to serve as a source of debt or equity capital. This type of
investor can extend financing alone or in connection with others pursuant to a
private placement memorandum. Companies seeking private funds should explore state and local networks that are being established to facilitate the process
of matching interested investors with emerging-growth companies in search of
capital. Venture capital clubs, chambers of commerce, and small-business group
meetings in most metropolitan cities are good places to start building this network.

State and Local Government Programs

Many state and local governments provide direct or indirect financing to small
and growing companies in an effort to foster economic development. The
amount and terms of the financing are usually regulated by the statutes authorizing the creation of the state or local development agency.

Joint Ventures

Growing companies seeking capital to engage in specific projects or markets
may explore the possibility of a joint venture or cross-licensing arrangement
with a complementary company already operating in these markets or producing
these products or services. The mechanics of a joint venture agreement are discussed in greater detail in chapter 14. Joint ventures can serve as a viable alternative to capital formation for specific projects. These arrangements should be
analyzed under federal and state antitrust laws, discussed in greater detail in
chapter 15.

Research and Development Limited Partnerships

This financing vehicle has changed as the federal income tax laws have
changed but nevertheless remains a viable alternative for both new and established companies to finance research and development costs related to specific
projects or products. Typically, limited partners invest in a fund managed by one
or more general partners. The partnership then contracts with the owner of the
untested technology to conduct research and development in exchange for certain ownership rights in the end result of the project. The original developer of
the technology usually retains an option to repurchase the licensing and marketing rights to the actual products or services created, often in exchange for a
royalty payment based on a percentage of gross sales. This alternative enables a

growing company to shift the costs, as well as the risks, of developing a new technology into the hands of a third party in exchange for the opportunity to share in the rewards if the project is successful.

Trade Credit or Consortiums

Many growing companies overlook an obvious source of capital or credit when exploring their financing alternatives: suppliers and customers. Suppliers have a vested interest in the long-term growth and development of their customer base and may be willing to extend favorable trade credit terms or even direct financing to help fuel a good customer's growth. The same principles apply to the customers of a growing company who rely on the company as a key supplier of needed resources.

A trend emerging in customer-related financing is the consortium. Under such an arrangement, a select number of key customers finance the development of a particular product or project in exchange for the right of first refusal or territorial exclusivity for the distribution of the finished product. The consortium alternative should be carefully examined under applicable federal and state antitrust laws before negotiations are formalized.

Intermediaries

Many growing companies begin their search for capital with the assistance of an intermediary, such as an investment banker, broker, merchant banker, or financial consultant. These companies and individuals do not supply the capital but can assist in arranging the financing through commercial lenders, insurance companies, personal funds, or other institutional sources. Investment bankers also arrange for equity investment by private investors, usually in anticipation of a subsequent public offering of the company's securities. (More information on selecting an investment banking firm can be found in chapter 7.)

Small Business Innovation Research (SBIR) Program

The SBIR program was established by Congress through the enactment of the Small Business Innovation Development Act of 1982. Under the program, certain federal agencies must allocate a percentage of their budgets to fund research and development proposals submitted by small businesses.

Landlords

Commercial real estate developers have become more willing to take an equity position in a tenant company in exchange for a larger construction allowance or reduced monthly rental. This is especially prevalent in certain high-technology office parks or private business incubators where the developer is constructing the facility especially for this purpose.

Conclusion

There are countless numbers of other sources for capital and alternatives to direct financing. Although no stone should remain unturned in the search for capital, overly creative methods of financing often become short-term solutions to long-term problems, creating complexities in the capital structure that are difficult to remedy.

The team responsible for growth planning within the company must always take a long-term view in establishing and refining the firm's capital structure and in identifying capital formation alternatives. The cost of various forms of capital, the availability of and access to the capital, the attendant risks to the investors, the level of control over the company imposed by the lenders or investors, and the degree of operational flexibility required by management are important considerations.

7

Private Placements as a Strategy for Raising Capital

One of the most common methods growing companies use to raise additional equity capital is through a private placement of its securities. A private placement may be used as a vehicle for capital formation when a particular security or transaction is exempt from federal registration requirements under the Securities Act of 1933. It generally offers reduced costs, both transactional and ongoing, because it is exempt from many of the extensive registration and reporting requirements imposed by federal and state securities laws. Therefore the legal, accounting, and financial printing costs of the proposed offering tend to be lower. Private placement usually offers the ability to structure a more complex and confidential transaction since the offerees typically are a small number of sophisticated investors, and it provides for more rapid penetration into the capital markets than would a public offering of securities, which requires registration with the Securities and Exchange Commission (SEC).

Disclosure Requirements in a Private Placement

The degree of disclosure that must be made to investors in a private placement continues to be a source of controversy in the legal and business communities. Exhibit 7-1 notes the five basic factors that affect the type of information that must be provided and the format in which the data are presented.

Each transaction or proposed offering of securities must be carefully reviewed by legal counsel to determine, first, the minimum level of disclosure that must be provided to prospective investors under applicable federal and state law. Then the costs of preparing a more detailed document should be weighed against the benefits of the additional protection provided to the issuer by a more compre-

Exhibit 7-1. Factors affecting disclosure.

---

1. The minimum level of disclosure that must be made under federal securities laws, which depends, in part, on which exemption from registration is being relied upon
2. The minimum level of disclosure that must be made under applicable state securities laws, which depends on in which state or states an offer of the securities is to be made
3. The sophistication and expectations of the targeted investors (e.g., some investors will expect a certain amount of information presented in a specified form regardless of what the law may require)
4. The complexity of the nature of the offerer's business and the terms of the offering (e.g., many offerers should prepare detailed disclosure documents in order to avoid liability for misstatements, fraud, or confusion, especially if the nature of the offerer's business and/or the terms of its offering are complex)
5. Any special circumstances or history affecting the offerer, such as pending litigation, conflicts of interest, licensing arrangements, unique risk factors, or the presence of extraordinary debt or related obligations

---

hensive prospectus. The key question will always be, "What is the most cost-effective vehicle for providing the targeted investors with the information they require and that applicable law dictates that they must have?"

An Introduction to Federal Securities Laws

Section 5 of the Securities Act of 1933 requires the offerer to file a registration statement with the SEC prior to the offer to sell any security in interstate commerce unless an exemption is available under § 3 or 4.

Registration under § 5 is expensive and time-consuming, and a network of underwriters and brokers or dealers must be assembled to make a market for the security. An issuer registered under § 5 is also subject to strict periodic reporting requirements. The penalties for failing to register or for disclosing inaccurate or misleading information under §§ 11 and 12 of the 1933 Act are also quite stringent. Therefore growing companies that are not ready to register their securities for offering to the public must work with legal counsel to structure the transaction within the various categories of exemptions available, such as: (1) the broad private offering exemption, designed for "transactions by an issuer not involving a public offering" under § 4(2); (2) the intrastate exemption under § 3(a)(11); and (3) Regulation D, which sets forth three specific transactional exemptions from the registration provisions of the 1933 Act.

If the private placement is not structured under one of the three transactional exemptions offered by Regulation D, counsel will usually rely on either § 4(2) or § 3(a)(11).

Section 4(2)

The statutory language of § 4(2), which allows for an exemption from registration for "transactions by an issuer not involving a public offering," has been a source of controversy and confusion in the legal and financial communities. Over the years, court cases have established that targeted investors in a § 4(2) offering must have access to the same kind of information that would be available if the issuer were required to register its securities under § 5 of the Securities Act of 1933. However, terms like *access to* and *same kind* generally leave open to the discretion of the company and its counsel the exact method of presenting the necessary information to the prospective investors. In relying on an exemption under § 4(2), owners and managers of growing companies should structure the manner of the offering in accordance with the following additional, albeit vague, guidelines:

- The offering should be made directly to the prospective investors without the use of any general advertising or solicitation.
- The number of offerees should be kept small.
- The offering should be limited to insiders (such as officers of the company or family members) or sophisticated investors.
- The prospective investors should be provided, at a minimum, with a set of recent financial statements, a list of critical risk factors that influence the investment, and an invitation to inspect the facilities and records of the company.

If in doubt as to whether § 4(2) applies to the particular offering, *don't rely on it*; rather, attempt to structure the transaction within one of the Regulation D exemptions.

Section 3(a)(11)

The statutory language of § 3(a)(11), which allows for an exemption from registration for "any security which is part of an issue offered and sold only to persons resident within a single state . . . by an issuer which is a resident and doing business within such state," is not quite as controversial as § 4(2). The key issue in relying upon this exemption is ensuring that the offering is truly an intrastate one. This test is deceptive, however, and the SEC has adopted Rule 147 to assist the issuer and its counsel in determining whether the requirements of § 3(a)(11) have been met. Precautionary steps must be taken by the company to ensure that all offerees are residents of the particular state because even one nonresidential offeree will jeopardize the availability of the exemption.

Regulation D Transactional Exemptions

Rule 504

Rule 504 permits offers and sales of not more than $1 million (provided that no more than $500,000 is offered and sold without registration under state securities laws) during any 12-month period by any issuer that is not subject to the reporting requirements of the Securities Exchange Act of 1934 and that is not an investment company. It places virtually no limit on the number or the nature of the investors that participate in the offering.

Although no formal disclosure document needs to be registered and delivered to offerees, three procedures must be understood and followed:

1. The document provided to prospective investors must be accurate and not misleading in any material respect.
2. Form D must be filed for all offerings within 15 days of the first sale.
3. Applicable state laws must be examined carefully because although many states have adopted securities laws similar to Regulation D overall, most of these laws do not include an exemption similar to 504. As a result, a formal memorandum will need to be prepared.

Rule 505

This second exemption allows for the sale of the issuer's securities to an unlimited number of "accredited investors" and up to 35 unaccredited investors regardless of their net worth, income, or sophistication up to $5 million in a 12-month period. Many growing companies select Rule 505 over Rule 504 because its requirements are consistent with many state securities laws.

An accredited investor is any person who qualifies for one or more of the eight categories set out in Rule 501(a) of Regulation D. Included in these categories are officers and directors of the entity who have policy-making functions, as well as outside investors who earned $200,000 per year for the last two years (or $300,000 for each of the last two years as a family unit) or whose net worth exceeds $1 million. If one or more of the purchasers is not an accredited investor, a full private placement memorandum must be prepared and delivered to all purchasers, which substantially increases the overall costs of the offering.

Many of the same filing requirements and restrictions imposed by Rule 504 also apply to Rule 505, such as the need to file a Form D. There is an absolute prohibition on advertising and general solicitation for offerings, and certain restrictions on which companies may be an issuer under Rule 505. For example, any company subject to the "bad boy" provisions of Regulation A is disqualified from being a 505 offerer. These provisions apply to persons who have been subject to certain disciplinary, administrative, civil, or criminal proceedings or sanctions that involve the issuer or its predecessors.

Rule 506

For growing companies requiring large amounts of capital, this exemption is the most attractive because it has no maximum dollar limitation. Rule 506 is similar to Rule 505 in that the issuer may sell its securities to an unlimited number of accredited investors and up to 35 nonaccredited investors. The key difference under Rule 506 is that any nonaccredited investor must be "sophisticated." In this context, a sophisticated investor is one who does not fall within any of the eight categories specified by Rule 501(a) but is believed by the issuer to "have knowledge and experience in financial and business matters that render him capable of evaluating the merits and understanding the risks posed by the transaction, either acting alone or in conjunction with his purchaser representative." The best way to remove any uncertainty over the sophistication or accreditation of a prospective investor is to request that a comprehensive Confidential Offeree Questionnaire (discussed later in this chapter) be completed before the securities are sold.

Rule 506 does eliminate the need to prepare and deliver disclosure documents in any specified format if accredited investors exclusively participate in the transaction. The same absolute prohibition on advertising and general solicitation imposed by Rule 505 applies to Rule 506 offerings.

State Securities Laws

Full compliance with the federal securities laws is only one level of regulation that must be taken into account when developing plans and strategies to raise capital through an offering of securities. Even if an offering is exempt under federal laws, registration may still be required under applicable blue-sky laws in the states where the securities are to be sold. This often creates expensive and timely compliance burdens for growing companies and their counsel, who must contend with this bifurcated scheme of regulation. Regulation D was designed to provide a foundation for uniformity between federal and state securities laws.

Overall, there are a wide variety of levels of review among the states, ranging from very tough "merit" reviews (designed to ensure that all offerings of securities are fair and equitable) to very lenient "notice-only" filings (designed primarily to promote full disclosure). The securities laws of *each* state where an offer or sale will be made should be checked carefully prior to the distribution of the offering documents.

Owners and managers of growing companies considering a private placement must also be keenly aware of the specific requirements of the securities laws in the states in which the securities will be offered. Although a comprehensive discussion of the state securities laws is beyond the scope of this book, suffice to say that every state in the nation, plus the District of Columbia, has some type of statute governing securities transactions and securities dealers. These laws should be carefully reviewed in order to determine

- Whether the particular limited offering exemption selected under federal law will also apply in the state
- Whether presale or postsale registration or notices are required
- Whether special legends or disclosures must be made in the offering documents provided to investors
- What remedies are available to an investor who has purchased securities from a company that has failed to comply with applicable state laws

Preparing the Private Placement Memorandum

As you may recall, CleanWorld Consulting Company (CCC) has determined to offer up to $2 million of its convertible preferred stock pursuant to a private placement as a bridge prior to its public offering. Pureair and Cleansoil, who began the business, and the company's management team will prepare a private placement memorandum (PPM), which will serve as a combined business plan, offering document, and marketing tool. The PPM serves not only to protect the investor by providing full disclosure of the material information needed to make an informed investment decision but also to protect CCC by providing a written record of the information given to investors in the event of a future dispute.

Elements of the PPM

The contents of a PPM vary depending on the nature of the business of the offerer, the history of the company, the terms of the offering, and the exact exemption from registration upon which the company has relied. Its presentation varies too. It can be typeset and full of fancy color pictures and diagrams, or it can be prepared with an old typewriter and use simple diagrams. The text should be *descriptive, not persuasive,* and allow readers to reach their own conclusions as to the merits of the securities being offered. Regardless of aesthetic considerations (which should not necessarily be taken lightly depending on the nature of the company and targeted prospective investor), typically a PPM will have a number of core elements.

Introductory Materials

There are usually three main parts to the introductory materials:

1. The cover page, which should include a brief statement about CCC and its business, the terms of the offering (often in table form), and all "legends" (boldfaced disclosure paragraphs at the beginning of the document) as required by federal and state laws
2. A summary of the offering, which serves as an integral part of the introductory materials and a cross-reference point for readers
3. A statement of the investor suitability standards, which discusses the federal and state securities laws applicable to the offering and the definitions of an accredited investor as applied to the offering

Profile of the Company

The first substantive discussion in the PPM is a detailed profile of the issuer or its affiliates and predecessors. It should contain a discussion of CCC's principal officers and directors, products and services, management and operating policies, performance history and goals, competition, trends in the industry, advertising and marketing strategy, suppliers and distributors, intellectual property rights, key real and personal property, customer demographics, and any other material information relevant to the investor, such as dependence on a single customer or the availability of a vital raw material. This section, however, is not and should not be described in lieu of a business plan, since the PPM is *not* the place for an extensive discussion of the company's objectives, operations, and problems.

Risk Factors

This section, usually the most difficult to write yet of utmost importance to the prospective investor, outlines all of the factors that make CCC's offering or projected business plans risky or speculative. The exact risks to the investors posed by the offering will depend on the nature of the issuer's business and the trends within that industry. The more generic risk factors for emerging-growth companies such as CCC are

- Stage of development of the company
- Dependence on key personnel
- Limited management experience
- Lack of a public market for the issuer's securities
- Threats posed by competitors

The problems raised by this section can be attributed to three factors. First, the entrepreneur will usually believe that the offering is virtually risk free in that the company will not fail if it raises the needed capital and that investors will rapidly recover their investment and an attractive return. A second problem is the scope of the disclosure. The threat of nuclear war, for instance, is a risk for businesses of all sizes and capital structures, but that does not mean that it must be disclosed in this section. But what about closer calls, such as the threat by a recently terminated employee that he will "sue the firm for everything it's got," when in reality he was legitimately terminated for good cause? Or the risk that the product that will be marketed with the capital raised will be obsolete within three years? The third problem is to balance the fear of the company that an overly detailed risk-factor section will scare away investors against the fear that a skimpy section is a litigation breeder if an unanticipated surprise turns out to foil the plans of the company.

Capitalization of the Issuer

This section examines the capital structure of CleanWorld before and after the offering; the rights, restrictions, and special features of the securities being offered; and any applicable provision of the articles of incorporation or bylaws that affect CCC's capitalization, such as preemptive rights, total authorized stock, different classes of shares, or restrictions on declaration and distribution of dividends. It also addresses the issue of any dilution of CCC's securities, including a full explanation if the prospective investor is purchasing the security at a substantially different price from that paid by the company's founders or others in the recent past.

Management of the Company

The section on the company's management team provides a list of the names, ages, special skills or characteristics, and biographical information on each officer, director, or key consultant; compensation and stock option arrangements; bonus plans; special contracts or arrangements; and any transactions between CleanWorld and individual officers and directors, including loans, self-dealing, and related types of transactions. It identifies the issuer's legal and accounting firms and their roles and any other expert retained in connection with the offering.

Terms of the Offering

The terms and conditions of the offering must be stated: the number of shares offered and the price and whether the offering is "all or nothing" or "part or nothing" or neither; the right of the issuer to terminate, withdraw, or extend the offering; the right of the issuer to reject any prospective purchaser; and any arrangements with brokers or dealers or other persons or finders in connection with the sale of the securities offered, including commissions to be paid and indemnification arrangements.

Allocation of Proceeds

The PPM states the principal purposes for which the net proceeds will be used and the approximate amount allocated to each purpose. Careful thought should be given to this section because failure to use funds as described in the PPM could be found to be materially misleading and trigger liability of CleanWorld as well as Pureair, Cleansoil, and the rest of the management team. If no exact breakdown has been prepared, the issuer explains why the capital is being raised and the business objectives it expects to pursue with the proceeds of the offering.

Plan of Distribution

If the securities are to be offered through underwriters, brokers, or dealers (to the extent permitted by federal and state laws), the names of each "distributor" must be disclosed, as well as the terms and nature of the relationship between the issuer and each party. The commissions to be paid, the obligations of the distributor (e.g., guaranteed or best-efforts offering), and any special rights, such as the right of a particular underwriter to serve on the board of directors, should be fully disclosed.

Dilution

Because promoters and finders often have acquired their securities at prices substantially below those in the prospective offering, the book value of shares purchased by prospective purchasers pursuant to the offering will be substantially diluted. The PPM therefore discusses the number of shares outstanding prior to the offering, the price paid, the net book value, and the effect on existing shareholders of the proposed offering, as well as dilutive effects on new purchasers at the completion of the offering.

Financial Statements

The exact financial statements CleanWorld provides will vary depending on applicable federal and state regulations, the nature and stage of growth of its business, and any special permission obtained from the SEC to omit one or more of the required financial statements, so long as investor protection is not compromised. At a minimum, CCC must provide a consolidated balance sheet as of the end of the most recent fiscal year or within 135 days if the company existed for a period of less than one fiscal year and a consolidated statement of income, cash flows, and shareholders' equity for each of the last two fiscal years preceding the date of the balance sheet provided in the PPM. CCC's management should discuss and explain these financial statements, analyze the financial condition of the company, and disclose any disagreement with the company's accountants on financial and accounting matters.

To the extent that an issuer chooses to include financial projections in the PPM, the pro forma must be presented in good faith and have reasonable underlying assumptions for the forecasts provided. These assumptions must be fully disclosed and include the required caveats and warnings that the figures provided are projections provided by management and that no representations or warranties have been given as to their accuracy.

Exhibits

Any growth company raising capital through a private placement must always keep in mind its obligation to provide "all information material to an understanding of the issuer, its business and securities being offered." This means that many of the documents examined by the attorneys and accountants in the due diligence process, such as the articles of incorporation and bylaws, key contracts or leases, and resumes of the principals, may be appended as exhibits to the PPM. Other items typically included are

- Tax and securities opinions of counsel (to the extent that they are required)
- Partnership or shareholders' agreements
- Subscription and investment agreements
- Recent newspaper or magazine articles about the company
- Photographs, maps, sketches, and organizational structure wiring diagrams
- Any other nonproprietary information important to prospective investors

Legal Opinion

This section identifies the counsel for CleanWorld who will be rendering securities or tax opinions, if any, in connection with the offering.

Access to Further Information

Prospective purchasers should be given the opportunity to obtain additional information concerning the terms and conditions of the offering and such other information that CleanWorld possesses or can acquire without unreasonable effort or expense that may be necessary to verify the accuracy of the information furnished in the PPM.

Subscription Materials

The two key documents that make up the subscription materials that must be provided to a prospective investor are the Offeree Questionnaire and the Subscription Agreement.

Offeree and Purchaser Questionnaires

Offeree Questionnaires serve as evidence of the required sophistication level and the ability of prospective offerees to fend for themselves in a § 4(2) offering. The questionnaire also presents an opportunity for CCC to obtain information that may be required for credit evaluation by lenders or sureties or, in certain types of investments, regulatory matters such as citizenship or ownership of other assets.

Questionnaires generally contain personal information relating to the prospective investor's name, home and business addresses, telephone numbers, age, social security number, education, present employment and employment history, and investment and business experience. The requested financial information includes the prospective investor's tax bracket, income, and net worth.

Before CCC accepts the subscription of any particular investor, an attorney should carefully review the questionnaires. If any information seems unusual, inconsistent, or incomplete, counsel may decide to resolve these matters directly with the prospective investor.

Subscription Agreement

The Subscription Agreement is the contract between the investor and the issuer for the actual purchase of the securities. It contains acknowledgments of

- The receipt and review by the purchaser of the information given to him or her about the offering and the issuer
- The restricted nature of the securities to be acquired and the fact that the securities were acquired under an exemption from registration
- Any particularly significant suitability requirements, such as amount of investment or passive income, tax bracket, and so forth, that CCC feels may be crucial to the purchaser's ability to obtain the benefits of the proposed investment
- An awareness of specific risks disclosed in the information furnished
- The status of the purchaser representative, if one is used

The Subscription Agreement contains a reconfirmation by the purchaser of the accuracy and completeness of the information contained in the offeree or purchaser questionnaire; the number and price of the securities to be purchased and the manner of payment; and agreement to any special elections that may be contemplated, such as S corporation elections, accounting methods, and any relevant tax elections. Often it contains an agreement on the part of the purchaser to indemnify the issuer against losses or liabilities resulting from any misrepresentations on the part of the prospective purchaser that would void or destroy the exemption from registration that the issuer is attempting to invoke and representations on the part of the purchaser with respect to its authority to execute the agreement. The representations normally included are the following:

- The securities are being bought for investment, not distribution or resale.
- The investor has the ability to bear the risk of investment.
- The investor has received access to all material information about the issuer.
- The investor understands that there is no public market for the securities (or that the securities are not salable in any public market) and understands and agrees that the securities may be resold only through registration or under an exemption from the 1933 act's registration requirements.

The Subscription Agreement states the date when the closing will take place. The offering materials should describe the conditions under which the investor's offer to purchase the securities will be accepted and the nature of any escrow or segregated accounts. Issuers and their agents should always reserve the right to accept or reject any subscription received through the closing date.

Negotiating With the Investment Banker or Broker

If the issuer is permitted by applicable federal and state laws to employ the services of a brokerage or investment banking firm to assist in the marketing of its securities, it should make the necessary arrangements as early as possible because the intermediary will have the best understanding of the private capital market and what the investors in that market will expect from the standpoint of structure of the company and the transaction, as well as anticipated return on investment. The issuer should have some plans and preferences for the channels of distribution and manner of offering that the intermediary may pursue. For example, if the intermediary deals primarily with large institutional investors, then control of the issuer's stock will be concentrated in the hands of very few parties. In our example, CCC may prefer the stock to be distributed as widely as possible (within the limits of Regulation D, of course) to decentralize control. Or the intermediary may envision a series of expensive dinners to entertain its most sophisticated clients, whereas CCC may not have budgeted for such a lavish expense. These structural and promotional issues should be discussed and resolved early.

In searching for the appropriate intermediary, CCC should take into account the following factors:

- Size and local or national reputation of the firm
- Areas of specialization
- Distribution channels usually pursued by the firm
- Structure of prior transactions handled by the firm
- The terms of the selling agreement presented, such as the form and rate of commission or whether the offering will be limited to a best-efforts rather

than a firm commitment basis (for example, the underwriter has no obligation to itself purchase any securities that are not sold) or whether the firm is willing to hold the issuer harmless in the event that one of its account executives violates any securities regulations

- The ability of the firm to assist in future capital formation efforts
- The range of additional services the firm offers

Private placements of securities are clearly an attractive and widely used method to resolve the capital formation problems of the emerging-growth company, but this route is not without detours and difficulties. The management team assembled to put together the private placement and market the issuer's securities must be keenly aware of all applicable federal and state registration, disclosure, and advertising regulations; if they are not, the entire transaction will be put in jeopardy.

CHAPTER

8

Institutional Venture Capital

Today's institutional venture capital industry has its roots in the turn of the twentieth century, when wealthy families like the Rockefellers and du Ponts provided risk capital to small, growing companies. Following World War II, a few institutional venture capital companies were formed, the most notable being American Research and Development Corporation in Boston in 1946. In 1958 the enactment of the Small Business Investment Act established a national program for licensing privately owned small-business investment companies (SBIC). And since the mid-1970s a wide variety of privately owned, non-SBIC venture capital funds have been formed by investor groups, fund managers, investment banks, and industry-specific business executives. The SBICs, venture capital subsidiaries of large financial institutions, and industrial corporations and independent venture capital firms now collectively manage a capital base in excess of $20 billion.

Owners and managers of growing companies often have mixed views toward the institutional venture capital industry. Although they welcome the money and management support that they desperately need for growth, they abhor the loss of control and the restrictions typically placed on the company in the investment documents.

In order to achieve the delicate balance between the needs of the venture capitalist and the needs of the company, it is imperative that owners and managers understand the process of obtaining venture capital financing.

Narrowing the Field

Preparation is the key to obtaining an initial meeting with the institutional venture capitalist. The first component of the preparation process is a well-written business plan and financing proposal. It is a necessary prerequisite to serious consideration by any sophisticated source of capital.

Many institutional sources of capital, however, are flooded with unsolicited, nonintroduced plans, which are more likely to end up in a wastebasket than before an investment committee. Thus, the second component is effective networking: the use of professional advisers, commercial lenders, investment bankers, and consultants who may be able to assist the company in getting the business plan into the hands of the appropriate venture capitalists.

Third, the field must be narrowed. Most venture capitalists have certain investment preferences as to which companies to include in their investment portfolio. These preferences and biases may be based on the nature of the company's products and services, geographic location, projected rates of return, stage of development, or amount of capital required. Rather than waste precious resources by blindly sending business plans to any and all venture capitalists in the company's region, companies must take the time to research the venture capital industry to match the characteristics of the proposed investment with the investment criteria of the targeted fund.

Companies searching for venture capital should first identify the stage of business development financing they require before embarking on the search for capital. At the earliest stage is *seed financing*, in which small amounts of capital are provided for initial product feasibility and development, market research, refinement of strategies, and other preliminary analyses.

The next level of financing is *start-up* or *early-stage financing*, which is generally for completion of product development, recruitment of a management team, refinement of the long-term business plan, and the commencement of marketing efforts. Financing for companies at the starting point in their growth and development has become more difficult to obtain as a result of the elimination of the preferential treatment for capital gains, as opposed to ordinary income, by the Tax Reform Act of 1986. Venture capitalists are now investing in later-stage companies, with a greater emphasis on the company's ability to generate current income and return to the investors.

First-stage financing usually funds the first phase of the full-scale manufacturing, marketing, and sales and pays for any missing elements of the management team. *Second-stage financing* is typically for the company that has begun production and distribution and has established inventories, contracts, and accounts receivable but now needs working capital to fuel expansion. *Third-stage financing* is usually provided to a company that is already operating at a profit but needs capital for research and development of new products, expansion of its physical facilities, or a significant increase in sales and marketing efforts.

Finally, in *bridge financing*, venture capitalists provide capital to a company that expects to go public within the next 12 months and requires additional working capital to bridge the gap.

Venture capital firms also consider providing capital to finance mergers and acquisitions, joint ventures, leveraged management, buy-outs or recapitalization, efforts to go private, or other kinds of transactions if the return on investment meets their criteria.

Assume that Impasse, Inc., the West Coast consumer electronics products company that we met in chapter 1, decides to raise capital to fuel its internal growth in lieu of positioning itself for sale to a foreign competitor. This decision is based in part on a technological development that will significantly improve the audio quality of a new portable compact disc player. As an established company repositioning itself for growth, Impasse is looking for a combination of traditional commercial bank loans, secured by tangible assets, and second-stage equity financing from a regional venture capitalist experienced in the consumer electronics industry.

Central Components of the Venture Capitalist's Investment Decision

Regardless of the company's stage of development or geographic location, there are several key variables that all venture capital firms consider in analyzing the business plan presented for investment: (1) management team, (2) products and services, (3) markets, and (4) return on investment. In determining whether Impasse qualifies for venture capital, the management team must be prepared to answer the following questions:

Management Team

1. What are the background, knowledge, skills, and abilities of each member of the management team?
2. How is this experience relevant to the proposed business plan or project?
3. How are risks and problems identified, managed, and eliminated by the management team?
4. To what extent does each member of the team exhibit certain key entrepreneurial personality traits, such as self-confidence, leadership skills, tenacity, drive, and unbounded energy?

Products and Services

1. At what stage of development are the company's products and services? What specific opportunity has the company identified? How long will this window of opportunity remain open? What steps are necessary for the company to exploit this opportunity?
2. To what extent are the company's products and services unique, innovative, and proprietary? What steps have been taken to protect the proprietary features of the company's products and services?
3. To what extent does the company control the means of production of the products and services, or is it dependent on a key supplier or licensor?

4. To what extent does the company's products or services represent a technological breakthrough, or are the products and services more "low tech" with less risk of obsolescence? What rights are inherent in this technology or lack thereof?

Markets

1. What is the stage in the life cycle of the industry in which the company plans to operate?
2. What is the size and projected growth rate of the company's targeted market?
3. What methods of marketing, sales, and distribution will the company use in bringing its products and services to the marketplace?
4. What are the strengths and weaknesses of each of the company's direct, indirect, and anticipated competitors in the targeted market?
5. Will the development of the company's products and services create new markets? If yes, what are the barriers to entry in these markets?
6. What are the characteristics of the typical consumer of the company's products and services? What has consumer reaction been thus far?

Return on Investment

1. What is the company's current and projected valuation and performance in terms of sales, earnings, and dividends? To what extent have these budgets and projections been substantiated? Has the company overestimated or underestimated the amount of capital required?
2. How much money and time have the owners and managers of the company already invested? How much more time and money are they willing to commit before realizing a return on their own personal investments? How well are current assets and resources of the company being managed and allocated?
3. How much capital will be required, both currently and as projected, in order to bring the company's business plans to fruition? Could this capital be invested in stages or tied to the performance of the company, or is all of the capital required at once? What types of securities are being offered? To what extent will additional dilution be necessary to meet these growth objectives?
4. What is the projected return on investment to the venture capitalist? How will this projected return be affected if the company fails to meet its business plans or financial projections? To what extent is there a glass ceiling on the potential return to the investors? What rights, remedies, and exit strategies will be available to the venture capitalist if such failure occurs?
5. What are the ancillary financial rewards to the venture capitalist in terms of consulting and management fees, rights of first refusal on subsequent

rounds of financing, and registration rights in the event of a public offering?

All of the answers to these questions should be contained in the business plan Impasse and its advisers prepare; they will be explored further in any initial and subsequent meetings Impasse may have with the venture capitalist.

Impasse should be careful to avoid certain *negative factors* because they tend to disqualify what might be an otherwise workable deal—for example:

- An unqualified brother-in-law filling a key management position
- Projections that provide for excessive management salaries, company cars, and other unnecessary executive benefits
- An unwillingness to provide a personal guaranty for debt financing
- Incomplete or overly slick business plans
- Business plans that project overly optimistic or unrealistic goals and objectives

At the same time that the venture capitalist is evaluating Impasse's business plan, the company's leader, Eightrack, should be assessing the strengths and weaknesses of the prospective venture capitalist(s). Exhibit 8-1 sets forth some questions Impasse should ask in determining whether the venture capital firm fits within its current and projected requirements. In gathering the information

Exhibit 8-1. Assessing a prospective venture capitalist.

- How well does the venture capital firm know the consumer electronics industry? How often does this venture capitalist work with companies at a stage of development similar to Impasse? To what extent has it worked with owners and managers of more seasoned companies in a turnaround situation?
- What assistance beyond money—such as management expertise, industry contacts, and support services—can the venture capitalist bring to the company?
- What is the reputation of this venture capital firm within the financial community? If the venture capitalist is to serve as the lead investor, how effective will it be in helping to attract additional coinvestors? Has the firm asked for any special terms or reward for serving as lead investor? What effect will this have on the willingness of other coinvestors to participate?
- Will this venture capitalist be able to participate in later rounds of financing if the new product line is successful and the company continues to grow?

to answer these questions, Impasse's owners and managers should speak with investment bankers, attorneys, accountants, and other venture capitalists familiar with this particular firm. Most important, they should speak with owners and managers of other companies in the portfolio of this particular venture capitalist to determine the level of support, conflict, and communication typically provided by this firm. The review should include both successful and unsuccessful portfolio companies; it should find out how the venture capitalist has reacted to companies that get into trouble, not just those that annually outstrip projections.

Negotiating and Structuring the Venture Capital Investment

The negotiation and structuring of most venture capital transactions depend less on industry standards, black-letter law, or structural rules of thumb and more on the need to strike a balance between the needs and concerns of the founders of the company and the investment criteria of the venture capital firm.

The company often has concerns that relate to

- Loss of management control
- Dilution of founder's stock
- Repurchase of founder's stock in the event of employment termination, retirement, or resignation
- Amount of financing adequate to meet goals and objectives
- Security interests being taken in key assets of the company
- Future capital requirements and founder's dilution
- Intangible and indirect benefits of venture capitalist participation

The following issues are the principal concerns of the venture capitalist:

- Current and projected valuation of the company
- Level of risk associated with this investment
- Investment objectives and criteria of the fund
- Projected levels of return on investment
- Liquidity of investment, security interests, and exit strategies in the event of business distress or failure ("downside protection")
- Protection of investment or return if company meets or exceeds projections ("upside protection")
- Influence on and control of management strategy and decision making
- Registration rights in the event of a public offering
- Rights of first refusal to provide future financing

Both parties typically have the following concerns:

- Retention of key members of the management team (and recruitment of any key missing links)
- Resolution of any conflicts among the syndicate of investors (especially where there is a lead investor representing several venture capital firms)
- Flexibility of organizational structure to allow for additional financing
- Financial strength of the company postinvestment
- Tax ramifications of the proposed investment

Once the venture capitalist and the key members of Impasse's management team have analyzed all of these factors from a risk, reward, and control perspective, they typically prepare a *term sheet*, which sets forth the key financial and legal terms of the transaction and then serves as a basis for preparation of the definitive legal documentation. The term sheet may also identify certain rights and obligations of Impasse and the venture capitalist, such as an obligation to maintain an agreed valuation, an obligation to be responsible for certain costs and expenses in the event the proposed transaction does not take place, or an obligation to secure commitments for financing from additional sources, such as the supplemental debt financing Impasse plans to obtain, prior to closing.

Structure of the Transaction

Negotiation regarding the structure of the transaction between Impasse and the venture capitalist will usually revolve around the types of securities to be used and the principal terms of the securities. The type of securities ultimately selected and the structure of the transaction usually fall within one of the following categories:

1. *Preferred stock.* This is the most common form of security issued in connection with a venture capital financing of an emerging-growth company at various stages in its development. Preferred stock can be structured to offer a number of advantages to an investor, such as convertibility into common stock, dividend and liquidation preference over the common stock, antidilution protection, mandatory or optional redemption schedules, and special voting rights and preferences.

2. *Convertible debentures.* This is basically a debt instrument (secured or unsecured) that may be converted into equity upon specified terms and conditions. Until converted, it offers the venture capitalist a fixed rate of return and offers tax advantages (e.g., deductibility of interest payments) to the company. Venture capital companies often prefer this type of security for higher-risk transactions, where the venture capitalist prefers to enjoy the elevated position of a creditor until the risk is mitigated, or in connection with bridge financing, whereby the venture capitalist expects to convert the debt to equity when additional capital is raised. Finally, if the debentures are subordinated, commercial

lenders often treat them as equity on the balance sheet, which enables the company to obtain institutional debt financing.

3. *Debt securities with warrants.* Venture capitalists generally prefer debentures or notes in connection with warrants, often for the same reasons that convertible debt is used: the ability to protect downside by enjoying the elevated position of a creditor and the ability to protect upside by including warrants to purchase common stock at favorable prices and terms. The use of a warrant enables the investor to buy common stock without sacrificing the preferred position of a creditor, as would be the case if only convertible debt was used in the financing.

4. *Common stock.* Venture capitalists rarely prefer to purchase common stock initially from a company, especially at early stages of its development, because it offers the investor no special rights or preferences, no fixed return on investment, no special ability to exercise control over management, and no liquidity to protect against downside risks. If the company wishes to preserve its Subchapter S status under the Internal Revenue Code, which would be jeopardized if a class of preferred stock were to be authorized, it might select common stock. Companies should be aware that common stock investments by venture capitalists could create "phantom income": adverse tax consequences to employees if stock is subsequently issued to them at a cost lower than the price per share paid by the venture capital company.

After Impasse and the venture capitalist determine the type of security to offer, they must ensure that its authorization and issuance are properly effectuated under applicable state corporate laws. For example, assume that Impasse's corporate charter does not currently provide for a class of preferred stock. Therefore, articles of amendment must be prepared, approved by Impasse's board of directors and shareholders, and filed with the appropriate state corporation authorities.

Terms and Conditions of the Preferred Stock

The nature and scope of the various rights, preferences, and privileges granted to the holders of the newly authorized preferred stock will be the focus of negotiation between Impasse and the venture capitalist. Specifically, the terms and conditions of the voting rights, dividend rates and preferences, mandatory redemption provisions, conversion features, liquidation preferences, and the antidilution provisions (sometimes referred to as *ratchet clauses*) are likely to be hotly contested. If any portion of the financing provided includes convertible debentures, negotiations will also determine term, interest rate and payment schedule, conversion rights and rates, extent of subordination, remedies for default, acceleration and prepayment rights, and underlying security for the instrument.

The nature and scope of the protection that the venture capitalist demands will depend in part on Impasse's history and its corporate and capital structure. Assume that several of Impasse's majority shareholders are family members and that, in the past, certain shares of common stock have been authorized for issuance at low prices to relatives. In order to protect against dilution upon conversion of the preferred stock (or the convertible debentures), the venture capitalist may require that certain ratchet provisions be built into the conversion terms of the preferred stock when Impasse's corporate charter is amended. These provisions will adjust the conversion price to allow the venture capitalist to receive a greater number of shares upon conversion than originally anticipated. A *full ratchet* adjusts the conversion price to the lowest price at which the stock issuable upon conversion has been sold. An example of such a provision is as follows:

> *Adjustment of Conversion Price From the Issuance or Deemed Issuance of Additional Shares of Common Stock.* If and whenever the Corporation shall issue or sell, or is, in accordance with the provisions of this subparagraph, deemed to have issued or sold any shares of Common Stock for a consideration per share less than the Conversion Price in effect immediately prior to the time of such issue or sale, then forthwith upon such issue or sale the Conversion Price shall be reduced to the price at which such shares of Common Stock are issued or sold or are deemed to have been issued or sold. Shares issued without consideration shall be deemed issued or sold at a price of $0.01 per share or the then par value of a share of Common Stock of the Corporation, whichever is less.

There are several other types of ratchet clauses, generally known as *partial ratchets*, which adjust the conversion price based on some weighted average formula where shares issuable upon conversion have been issued at a variety of different prices. This type of partial ratchet is generally fairer to Impasse and its current stockholders. Finally, Impasse may wish to negotiate certain types of stock sales, such as those pursuant to an incentive-based employee stock option plan, which will be exempt from the ratchet provisions.

Understanding the Legal Documents

The legal documents prepared in Impasse's venture capital financing contain all of the legal rights and obligations of the parties, striking a balance between the needs and concerns of Impasse and the investment objectives and necessary controls of the venture capitalist. The documents typically prepared are, where applicable: Preferred Stock or Debenture Purchase Agreement ("Investment Agreement"), Stockholders' Agreement, Employment and Confidentiality

Agreement, Warrant, Debenture or Notes, Preferred Stock Resolution (to amend the corporate charter), Contingent Proxy, Legal Opinion of Company Counsel, and a Registration Rights Agreement.

Investment Agreement

This document describes all of the material terms of the financing and serves as a form of disclosure document in which relevant historical and financial information is disclosed in the Representations and Warranties by Impasse to the investors. The Representations and Warranties (along with any exhibits) are designed to provide full disclosure to the investors, which will provide a basis for evaluating the risk of the investment and structure of the transaction.

The Investment Agreement also provides for certain conditions precedent that Impasse must meet prior to the closing. These provisions require the company to perform certain acts at or prior to closing as a condition to the investor's providing the venture capital financing. The conditions to closing are often used in negotiations to mitigate or eliminate certain risks the investor identifies, but usually they are more of an administrative checklist of actions that must occur at closing, such as execution of the ancillary documents discussed below.

Perhaps the most burdensome aspect of the Investment Agreement, and thus the most hotly negotiated, are the covenants that will govern and restrict Impasse's business affairs and operations in the future. Affirmative covenants might include an obligation to

- Maintain certain insurance policies.
- Protect its intellectual property.
- Comply with key agreements.
- Prepare forecasts and budgets for review and approval by the investors.
- Ensure that certain investors are represented on the board of directors of Impasse.

Impasse must undertake all acts described in the affirmative covenants, unless express prior approval is obtained from the investors.

Negative covenants might include obligations *not* to

- Change the nature of the business or capital structure of the company.
- Declare any cash or asset dividends.
- Issue any additional stock or convertible securities.
- Compensate any employee or consultant in excess of agreed amounts.
- Pledge any company assets to secure debt or related obligations.

In most cases, Impasse cannot undertake the acts that the negative covenants cover without the express prior approval of the investors. These restrictions on activity will last for as long as the venture capitalist owns the securities purchased in the financing.

Finally, the Investment Agreement will provide for certain remedies for any breach of the covenants or misrepresentation by Impasse. These remedies may require a civil action, such as a demand for specific performance, a claim for damages, or a request for injunctive relief. In other cases, the remedies will be self-executing, such as an adjustment in the equity position of the investor, a right of redemption of the investment securities, rights of indemnification, super-majority voting rights, or a right to foreclose on assets securing debt securities.

Stockholders' Agreement

Venture capitalists often require the principal stockholders of the company to become parties to a Stockholders' Agreement as a condition to closing on the investment. Any existing stockholders' or buy/sell agreements will also be carefully scrutinized and may need to be amended or terminated as a condition to the investment.

The Stockholders' Agreement typically contains certain restrictions on the transfer of the company's securities, voting provisions, rights of first refusal and cosale rights in the event of a sale of the founder's securities, antidilution rights, and optional redemption rights for the venture capital investors. For example, the investors may want to reserve a right to purchase additional shares of Impasse's preferred stock in order to preserve their respective equity ownership in the company if another round of the preferred stock is issued subsequently. This is often accomplished with a contractual preemptive right (as opposed to such a right being contained in the corporate charter, which would make these rights available to *all* holders of the preferred stock), which might read as follows:

> Each of the investors shall have a preemptive right to purchase any share of Common Stock or any securities that Impasse shall issue that are convertible into or exercisable for shares of Common Stock. In determining such right, each investor holding shares of Preferred Stock shall be deemed to be holding the shares of Common Stock into which such shares of Preferred Stock are convertible. Such preemptive right must be exercised by each investor within fifteen (15) days from the date that each investor receives notice from Impasse stating the price, terms, and conditions of the proposed issuance of the shares of Common Stock and offering each investor an opportunity to exercise its preemptive rights.

Employment and Confidentiality Agreements

Venture capitalists often require key members of the company's management team to execute certain Employment and Confidentiality Agreements as a condition to the investment. These agreements define the obligations of each employee, the compensation package, the grounds for termination, the obligation to preserve and protect the company's intellectual property, and posttermination covenants, such as covenants not to compete or to disclose confidential information. (For more information on employment agreements, see chapter 2, and for more information on protecting intellectual property, see chapter 13.)

Contingent Proxy

This document provides for a transfer of the voting rights attached to any securities held by a key principal of Impasse to the venture capitalist upon death or disability. The proxy may also be used as a penalty for breach of a covenant or warranty in the Investment Agreement.

Registration Rights Agreement

Many venture capitalists will view the eventual public offering of Impasse's securities pursuant to a registration statement filed with the SEC under the Securities Act of 1933 as the optimal method of achieving investment liquidity and maximum return on investment. As a result, the venture capitalists will protect their right to participate in the eventual offering with a Registration Rights Agreement. Generally these registration rights are limited to Impasse's common stock, which would require the venture capital investors to convert their preferred stock or debentures prior to the time that the registration statement is approved by the SEC.

The registration rights may be in the form of demand rights, which are the investors' right to require the company to prepare, file, and maintain a registration statement, or "piggyback rights," which allow the investors to have their investment securities included in a company-initiated registration. The number of each type of demand or piggyback rights, the percentage of investors necessary to exercise these rights, the allocation of expenses of registration, the minimum size of the offering, the scope of indemnification, and the selection of underwriters, brokers, and dealers will be areas of negotiation in the Registration Rights Agreement.

9

Debt Financing
for Growing Companies

The optimal capital structure of an emerging-growth company will most
likely include debt financing. The use of debt in the capital structure, commonly known as leverage, affects the valuation of the company and its overall
cost of capital. The determination of the proper debt-to-equity ratio depends on
a wide variety of factors, which include but are not limited to

- The risk of business distress or failure created by the contractual obligation
  to meet debt-service payments
- The direct and indirect costs to the company of obtaining the capital
- The need for flexibility in the capital structure in order to respond to changing economic or market conditions
- The ability of the company to get access to various sources of financing
  (access to capital issues)
- The nature and extent of the tangible or even intangible assets of the company available to serve as collateral to secure the loan
- The level of dilution of ownership and control that the shareholders and
  managers of the company are willing to tolerate
- Certain tax considerations (interest payments are a deductible expense,
  whereas dividends are not)

To determine its maximum debt capacity, an emerging-growth company usually balances the costs and risks of a default of a debt obligation against the
desire of the owners and managers to maintain control of the enterprise by protecting against the dilution that an equity offering causes. Many entrepreneurs
prefer to retain their control over the affairs of the company in exchange for the
higher level of risk inherent in taking on additional debt obligations.

A company whose pro forma analysis reveals that its ability to meet debt-service obligations will strain its cash flow or that it has insufficient collateral available should explore equity alternatives. It is not worth driving the company into voluntary or involuntary bankruptcy solely to maintain a maximum level of control.

A company that is trying to determine the optimal level of debt financing should examine key business ratios for the particular industry, such as those published by Robert Morris Associates and Dun & Bradstreet. Once they arrive at the optimum debt-to-equity ratio, owners and managers of growing companies must be aware of the various sources of debt financing, as well as the business and legal issues involved in borrowing funds from a commercial lender.

Sources of Debt Financing

Although most small companies turn to traditional forms of financing from commercial banks, such as term loans and operating lines of credit, there exists a wide variety of alternative sources of debt financing.

Trade Credit

The use of credit with key suppliers is often a means of survival for rapidly growing companies. When a company has established a good credit rating with its suppliers but as a result of rapid growth tends to require resources faster than it is able to pay for them, trade credit becomes the only way that its growth can be sustained. A key supplier has an economic incentive to help a loyal customer grow and prosper and therefore may be willing to negotiate credit terms acceptable to both parties.

Equipment Leasing

Most rapidly growing companies are desperately in need of the use but not necessarily the ownership of certain key resources to fuel and maintain growth. Equipment leasing, in which monthly lease payments are made in lieu of debt-service payments, offers an alternative to ownership of the asset. There are many forms of equipment leasing. *Operating leases* are generally shorter in term and include repair and maintenance services; *capital leases* are generally longer in term, do not include ancillary services, and virtually transfer ownership to the lessee, due in part to the attractive terms of the option to purchase the asset at the end of the lease term.

Factoring

Under the traditional factoring arrangement, a company sells its accounts receivable to a third party in exchange for immediate cash. The third party, or "factor," assumes the risk of collection in exchange for the ability to purchase the accounts receivable at a discount. The amount of the discount is usually determined by the level of risk that debtors will default and prevailing interest rates. Once notice has been provided to debtors of their obligation to pay the factor directly, the seller of the accounts receivable is no longer liable to the factor in the event of a default.

As factoring has become more commonplace in a variety of industries, less traditional forms of factoring have emerged that are more akin to pure accounts receivable financing: The lender does not assume the credit risk, the accounts are assigned to the lender without notice to the debtors, and the accounts receivable merely become the principal source of collateral to secure the loan agreement.

Miscellaneous Sources of Nonbank Debt Financing

Debt securities, such as bonds, notes, and debentures, may be offered to venture capitalists, private investors, friends, family, employees, insurance companies, and related financial institutions. Many smaller companies turn to traditional sources of consumer credit, such as home equity loans, credit cards, and commercial finance companies, to finance the growth of their business. In addition to the Small Business Administration (SBA) loan programs, many state and local governments have created direct loan programs for small businesses.

Commercial Loans

Although all available alternative sources of debt financing should be strongly considered, traditional bank loans from commercial lenders are the most common source of capital for small, growing companies. Before an attempt is made to understand the types of loans available from commercial banks, it is important to understand the perspective of the average commercial bank when it analyzes the loan proposal prepared by an emerging-growth company.

Understanding the Lender's Perspective

Despite the fact that almost every small business at some point borrows from a commercial lender, there remains a lot of confusion and resentment in the relationship between bankers and entrepreneurs. Owners and managers of small companies are likely to relate countless stories about heartless bankers who do not understand and appreciate their business requirements. Loan officers either describe the "idea-rich and asset-poor" entrepreneur who expects to borrow $1 million collateralized only by a dream or relate the horrible experience they had foreclosing on yet another default by a small business.

Given these problems, it is crucial to understand the lender's perspective. Banks are in the business of selling money. Capital is the principal product in their inventory. Bankers, however, are both statutorily and personally adverse to risk. The bank's shareholders and board of directors expect that loan officers will take all necessary steps to minimize the risk to the institution in each transaction and obtain the maximum protection in the event of default. Therefore the types of loans available to growing companies, the terms and conditions of loan agreements, and the steps the bank takes to protect its interest have a direct relationship to the level of risk that the lending officer and the loan committee perceive.

The management team of the growing company that has been assigned to obtain the debt financing from a commercial bank must embark on an immediate risk mitigation and management program in preparation for negotiation of the loan documentation.

Preparing for Debt Financing: The Loan Proposal

Most lenders require candidates for debt financing to prepare and present a loan proposal package. Although the exact elements of such a package vary depending on the size of the company, its industry, and its stage of development, most lenders have some fundamental questions requiring answers (see Exhibit 9-1).

The answers to these questions are designed to assist the banker in assessing the risk factors in the proposed transaction *and* by providing him or her with the information necessary to persuade the loan committee to approve the transaction. Therefore, a small and growing company should put together a loan proposal package that points to the presence of a strong management team and an aggressive internal control and accounts receivable management program, con-

Exhibit 9-1. Questions bankers need to know.

- Who is the borrower?
- How much capital is needed and when?
- How will the capital be allocated? For what specific purposes?
- How will the borrower service its debt obligations (e.g., application and processing fees, interest, principal, or balloon payments)?
- What protection (e.g., tangible and intangible assets to serve as collateral) can the borrower provide the bank if the company is unable to meet its obligations?

tains financial statements and projections that demonstrate the ability to service the debt, shows well-developed relationships with suppliers, distributors, and employees, and demonstrates an understanding of the trends in the marketplace. In addition, many commercial loan officers apply the traditional test of the four Cs of creditworthiness: *character* (reputation and honesty), *capacity* (business acumen and experience), *capital* (ability to meet debt-service payments), and *collateral* (access to assets that can be liquidated in the event of a default).

A loan officer who is convinced of the company's creditworthiness then serves as an advocate on behalf of the business in presenting the loan proposal to the bank's loan committee. The loan documentation, terms, rates, and covenants that the loan committee will specify as a condition to making the loan will be directly related to the ways in which the applicant is able to demonstrate its ability to mitigate and manage risk as described in its business plan and formal loan proposal.

Recall from chapter 1 that Far East Imports Company (FEIC) determined that it needed commercial debt financing to finance its launch into wholesale operations. It required capital to build a larger warehouse and distribution facility and extended credit to finance the significantly larger purchases of inventory.

FEIC's management team's first task was to assemble a formal loan proposal to present to local and regional commercial lenders. The director of purchasing, Sarah Thinkbig, was confident that given the company's proven track record of profitable operations at the retail level, its reputation with manufacturers in the Far East, and its strong management team, it could obtain favorable terms and rates from the lender of its choice. Its loan proposal featured the following categories of information:

1. *Summary of the Request.* An overview of FEIC's history, the amount of capital needed, proposed repayment terms, the intended use of the capital, and the collateral available to secure the loan.

2. *History of the Borrower.* A brief background of the business, its capital structure, its key founders, its stage of development, and its plans for growth; a list of key customers, suppliers, and service providers; its management structure and philosophy; its plant and facility; its key products and services; and an overview of the intellectual property it owns or has developed.

3. *Market Data.* An overview of trends in the industry, the size of the market, the company's market share, the competition (direct and indirect), proprietary advantages, marketing strategies, public relations and advertising strategies, market research studies, and future industry prospects.

4. *Financial Information.* Pro forma financial statements, federal and state tax returns, appraisals of key assets or company valuations, current balance sheet, credit references, and a two-year income statement. This section explains the role of the capital requested with respect to the company's plans for growth, an allocation of the loan proceeds, and the company's

ability to repay. The discussion of the company's ability to service the debt must be supported by a three-year projected cash flow statement on a monthly basis.

5. *Schedules and Exhibits.* A schedule of supporting documents (such as agreements with manufacturers, Letters of Intent for its planned operations, insurance policies, key contracts, employment agreements, and leases) must be made available to the lender for inspection upon request. Resumes of the company's principals, recent articles about the company, a picture of the company's products or site, and an organizational chart of the management structure should be appended.

Types of Commercial Bank Loans

The various types of loans available from commercial banks are usually categorized by the term of the loan, the expected use of proceeds, and the amount of money to be borrowed. The availability of these various loans to FEIC will depend on the nature of the industry, as well as the bank's assessment of the company's creditworthiness.

Short-Term Loans. Ordinarily, small companies use short-term loans for a specified purpose, and lenders expect that the loan will be repaid at the end of the project. For example, a seasonal business may borrow capital in order to build up its inventory in preparation for the peak season; at the end of the season, the lender expects to be repaid immediately. A short-term loan could be used to cover a period when the company's customers or clients are in arrears; when the accounts receivable are collected, the bank must be repaid.

Short-term loans are usually made in the form of a promissory note payable on demand. The note may be secured by the inventory or accounts receivable that the loan is designed to cover, or it may be unsecured (no collateral is required). Unless the company is a start-up or operates in a highly volatile industry (thereby increasing the risk in the eyes of the lender), most short-term loans are unsecured, which keeps the loan documentation and the bank's processing time and costs to a minimum. Lenders view short-term loans as self-liquidating in that they can be repaid by foreclosing on the current assets the loan has financed. The fact that the bank's transactional costs are low, along with its perception of the lower risk during this short period of time, makes short-term borrowing somewhat easier for a growing business to obtain. It also serves as an excellent means for establishing a relationship with a bank and demonstrating creditworthiness.

Operating Lines of Credit. A line of credit consists of a specific amount of capital made available to the borrower on an as-needed basis over a specified period of time. It may be for a short term (60–120 days) or a longer term (one to three years), renewable or nonrenewable, and at a fixed or fluctuating rate of interest.

FEIC will seek an operating line of credit for the purchase of its inventory. Decor and Thinkbig should be careful to negotiate ceilings on interest rates; to avoid excessive commitment, processing, application, and related up-front fees; and to ensure that repayment schedules will not be an undue strain for it. FEIC should also ensure that its obligations to make payments against the line of credit are consistent with its own anticipated cash flow projections.

Intermediate-Term Loans. An intermediate-term loan is usually provided over a three- to five-year period for the purposes of acquiring equipment, fixtures, furniture, and supplies or for expanding existing facilities, for acquiring another business, or for working capital. It is likely that FEIC will be able to secure this type of financing to expand existing warehousing facilities or acquire a new site.

The intermediate-term loan is almost always secured by the assets being purchased with the loan proceeds and by other assets of the company, such as inventory, accounts receivable, equipment, and real estate, that may be available to serve as security. It usually calls for a loan agreement, which typically includes restrictive covenants that govern the operation and management of the company during the term of the loan. These restrictive covenants are designed to protect the interests of the lender and ensure that all payments are made on a timely basis, before any dividends, employee bonuses, or noncritical expenses are paid.

Long-Term Loans. Generally, commercial banks do not provide long-term financing to small businesses; the risk of market fluctuations and business failure over a 10- or 20-year term is too high for the commercial lender to feel comfortable. But there are exceptions to this rule for specific, highly secured transactions, such as the purchase of real estate or a multiuse business facility. In this case the lender will consider extending a long-term loan to a small company for 65–80 percent of the appraised value of the land or building.

Letters of Credit. Until recently, letters of credit were issued primarily by commercial banks solely in connection with international sales transactions, such as transactions between FEIC and foreign manufacturers, as a method of expediting the shipping and payment process. Typically the seller of goods demands that payment be made in the form of a letter of credit. The buyer of the goods must then make arrangements with its bank to issue the letter of credit. The buyer's bank, often in conjunction with a corresponding bank, then communicates with the seller of the goods, explaining the documents that it requires, such as a negotiable bill of lading, as a condition to releasing the funds. It is important to understand that banks issuing the letter of credit may be liable to the seller of the goods for payment if the bill of lading and related documents are properly presented, even if there are problems in the performance of the underlying contract between the buyer and the seller. Any defenses available to the buyer relating to the underlying contract are generally not available to the bank issuing the letter of credit.

In more recent years, the standby letter of credit has emerged as an indirect debt financing that serves as a guaranty of performance. Standby letters of credit are often issued by a bank on behalf of a customer in order to secure payments to a builder, landlord, or key supplier. The operative term of such an instrument is *standby*, because if the transaction goes as planned, the instrument will never be drawn upon.

Negotiating the Loan Documents

Negotiating the financing documents that will be executed by the growing company in a typical commercial bank financing requires a delicate balancing between the requirements of the lender and the needs of the borrower. The lender wants to have all rights, remedies, and protection available to mitigate the risk of loan default. The borrower wants to minimize the level of control exercised by the lender (generally through the affirmative and negative covenants of the loan agreement) and achieve a return on its assets that greatly exceeds its debt-service payments.

Before each document involved in a typical debt financing is examined, it is important to understand some general rules of loan negotiation.

Interest Rates

A banker generally calculates the rate of interest in accordance with prevailing market rates, the degree of risk inherent in the proposed transaction, the extent of any preexisting relationship with the lender, and the cost of administering the loan.

Collateral

The commercial lender may request that certain collateral be pledged that has a value equal to or greater than the proceeds of the loan. Under such circumstances, owners and managers of growing companies should attempt to keep certain assets of the business outside the pledge agreement so that they are available to serve as security in case they need additional capital later.

Beyond the traditional forms of tangible assets that may be offered to the lender as collateral, borrowers should also consider intangibles—such as assignment of lease rights, key-man insurance, intellectual property, and goodwill—as candidates for serving as collateral. These assets could be very costly to a firm in the event of default and should be pledged only when the ability to repay is in no doubt.

Restrictive Covenants

The typical loan agreement includes a variety of restrictive covenants designed to protect the interests of the lender. *Affirmative covenants* encompass the obligations of the borrower (and its subsidiaries, except as otherwise provided) during the period that the loan is outstanding. These may include the following affirmative acts by the borrower:

- Furnishing audited statements of income and expenses and balance sheets at regular intervals (usually quarterly and annually), the annual statement to be prepared and certified by an independent certified public accountant who renders an opinion either unqualified or with qualifications satisfactory to the lender
- Furnishing other information regarding the business affairs and financial condition of the borrower as the lender may reasonably request
- Furnishing the lender with copies of all financial statements, reports, and returns sent to shareholders of the borrower or to governmental agencies. The latter may be limited to filings with the Securities and Exchange Commission.
- Giving the lender access to properties and to books of account and records of the borrower, on reasonable conditions, including maintenance of confidentiality
- Keeping and maintaining proper books of account in accordance with sound accounting practices
- Complying with all applicable laws, rules, and regulations
- Maintaining the corporate existence and all rights, privileges, and franchises of borrower and any subsidiaries
- Maintaining all property in good order and repair
- Maintaining any agreed dollar amount of net worth or any agreed ratio of current assets to current liabilities
- Keeping and maintaining proper and adequate insurance on all assets
- Paying and discharging all indebtedness and all taxes as due except such as are contested in good faith
- Purchasing and paying premiums as due on life insurance on named key personnel, naming the borrower as the beneficiary
- Retaining existing management

Loan agreements generally contain covenants on the part of the borrower (and its subsidiaries, except as otherwise provided) *not* to take certain action or to permit specified happenings to occur except with the consent of the lender or the owners and holders of a designated percentage of the principal amount of the outstanding notes or indebtedness. The scope of these *negative covenants* is generally negotiable, depending in large part on the borrower's financial strength and economic and operational requirements. The following negative covenants are usually included in the loan requirement whereby the borrower agrees not to do the following without the written consent of the lender:

- Engage in any business not related to present business.
- Create any mortgage, lien, or other security other than pending security on the property securing the instant loan.
- Create any mortgage, lien, or other encumbrance, including conditional sales agreements, other title-retention agreements, or lease-purchase agreements, on any property of borrower or, unless excepted, of its subsidiaries.
- Incur any new indebtedness except for trade credit or renewals, extensions, or refunding of any current indebtedness. The borrower's right to incur indebtedness may be conditioned on compliance with a specified ratio (actual or pro forma) of pretax income to interest expense for a designated period.
- Enter into leases of real or personal property, as lessee, in excess of a specified aggregate amount. The borrower's right to make leases may be conditioned on compliance with a specified ratio (actual or pro forma) of pretax income to fixed charges for a designated period.
- Purchase, redeem, or otherwise acquire or retire for cash any of the borrower's capital stock, with stated exceptions, such as from posttax earnings in excess of a specified amount or for regular sinking-fund requirements on preferred stock.
- Pay any cash dividends, with stated exceptions, such as from posttax earnings earned subsequent to a specified date or in excess of a specified amount.
- Become a guarantor (except as to negotiable instruments endorsed for collection in ordinary course).
- Make loans or advances to or investments in any person or entity other than borrower's subsidiaries.
- Merge or consolidate with any other corporation or sell or lease substantially all or the entirety of the borrower's assets. There may be exceptions where the borrower is the surviving corporation.
- Permit net worth or current assets to fall below a specified level.
- Permit capital expenditure to exceed a specified amount (which may be on an annual basis, with or without a right to cumulate).
- Permit officers' and directors' remuneration to exceed a specified level.
- Sell or dispose all of the stock of a subsidiary (subject to permitted exceptions) or permit subsidiaries to incur debt (other than trade debt).

Covenants may be serious impediments to the ability of the company to grow and prosper over the long run. They should be carefully reviewed for consistency in relation to other corporate documents, such as by-laws and shareholders' agreements.

Owners and managers of growing companies should note, however, that under the rapidly changing area of lender liability law, some commercial bankers are backing away from the level of control that has traditionally been imposed on the borrower.

Prepayment Rights

The borrower should always negotiate a right to prepay the principal of the loan without penalty or repayment charges. Many commercial lenders, however, will seek to attach prepayment charges to term loans with a fixed rate of interest in order to ensure that a minimum rate of return is earned over the projected life of the loan.

Hidden Costs and Fees

Many commercial banks attempt to charge the borrower a variety of direct and indirect costs and fees in connection with the debt financing, among them closing costs, processing fees, filing fees, late charges, attorney's fees, out-of-pocket-expense reimbursement (courier, travel, photocopying, etc.), court costs, and auditing or inspection fees. Another way that commercial lenders earn ancillary revenue on a loan is by imposing certain depository restrictions on the borrower, such as a restrictive covenant to maintain a certain deposit balance in the company's operating account or the use of the bank as a depository as a condition to closing on the loan.

Understanding the Legal Documents

A typical intermediate-term loan transaction usually has five primary documents.

Loan Agreement

This agreement sets forth all of the terms and conditions of the transaction between the lender and the borrower. It specifies the amount, term, repayment schedules and procedures, special fees, insurance requirements, conditions precedent, restrictive covenants, the borrower's representations and warranties (with respect to status, capacity, ability to repay, title to properties, litigation, etc.), events of default, and remedies of the lender in the event of default.

The provisions of this agreement and the implications of these covenants should be reviewed carefully by an experienced attorney and a knowledgeable accountant, who should also analyze the long-term legal and financial impact of the restrictive covenants. The company should negotiate to establish a timetable under which certain covenants will be removed or modified as the company's ability to repay is clearly demonstrated. The company should never rely on any verbal assurances the loan officer makes that a waiver of a default on a payment or a covenant will subsequently be available.

Security Agreement

This agreement identifies the collateral to be pledged in order to secure the loan. The agreement will usually reference terms of the Loan Agreement, as well as the Promissory Note, especially with respect to the restrictions on the use of the collateral and the procedures upon default of the debt obligation. The remedies available to the lender under the Security Agreement in the event of default range from selling the collateral at a public auction to taking possession of the collateral and using it for an income-producing activity. The proceeds of any alternative chosen by the lender will be principally for repaying the outstanding balance of the loan.

Financing Statement

This is the document filed with the state and local corporate and land records management authorities in order to record the interests of the lender in the collateral. It is designed to give notice to other potential creditors of the borrower that a senior security interest has been granted in the collateral specified in the financing statement. Specific rules regarding this document and the priority of competing creditors can be found in the applicable state's version of the Uniform Commercial Code.

Promissory Note

This instrument serves as evidence of the obligation of the borrower to the lender. Many of its terms—the interest rate, the length of the term, the repayment schedule, the ability of the borrower to prepay without penalty, the conditions under which the lender may declare an event of default, and the rights and remedies available to the lender upon such default—also appear in the more comprehensive Loan Agreement.

Guaranty

Many small-business owners will be asked to execute a Guaranty as further security in order to mitigate the risk of the transaction to the lender. The owner should review and negotiate the terms of this Guaranty carefully, especially with respect to the term of it, the scope, the rights of the lender in the event of default, and the type of guaranty provided. For example, under certain circumstances, the lender can be forced to exhaust all possible remedies against the borrower before being able to proceed against the guarantor or may be limited to proceed against certain assets of the guarantor. Similarly, the extent of the Guaranty could be negotiated such that it is reduced on an annual basis as the company grows stronger and its ability to service the debt independently becomes more evident.

Periodic Assessment of Banking Relationships

Many commercial lenders, recognizing the value and importance of growing businesses in the economy, have begun to compete fiercely for the business of smaller borrowers and customers. They have broadened their services and provide growth companies greater access to debt capital. From time to time owners and managers of growing companies must reassess their banking relationships to ensure that they are receiving the best rates and services available to businesses of their size and within their industry. This does not mean that a company should discard a long-standing and harmonious banking relationship over a one percentage point difference in an interest rate, but it also does not mean that it should remain loyal to a bank not offering a full range of services.

The following questions are useful in a reassessment of the banking relationship:

1. When did you last hear from your designated loan officer?
2. What was the bank's reaction to your most recent request for another term loan or increase in the company's operating line of credit?
3. How well does the bank know and understand your industry?
4. How strict has the bank been in enforcing loan covenants, restrictions, or late charges?
5. What support services has the bank offered your company?
6. How do your bank's interest rates and loan terms compare to those of other local commercial lenders?
7. What is the bank's general reputation in the business community? What has it done lately to strengthen (or damage) its reputation?
8. Is the bank basically operating on a solid financial foundation (e.g., given the recent wave of bank failures)?

9. Is the bank large enough to grow with the financial needs of your company as the business expands and additional amounts of capital are required? (This should be considered early in the company's development so that the relationship is not outgrown just at the time when you need it the most.)

10. Does this bank really want your company as a customer? What has it done for you lately?

CHAPTER

10

Preparing for an
Initial Public Offering

An *initial public offering* (IPO) is a process whereby an emerging-growth company registers its securities with the Securities and Exchange Commission (SEC) for sale to the general investing public for the first time. Many owners and managers of growing companies view this process of "going public" as the epitome of financial success and reward.

The decision to go public requires considerable strategic planning and analysis from both a legal and business perspective. The planning and analysis process encompasses (1) a weighing of the costs and benefits of being a public company; (2) an understanding of the process and costs of becoming a public company; and (3) an understanding of the obligations of the company, its advisers, and its shareholders once the company has successfully completed its public offering.

Costs and Benefits of the IPO

For the rapidly expanding privately held company, the process of going public represents a number of benefits, including:

- Significantly greater access to capital
- Increased liquidity for the company's shares
- Market prestige
- Enhancement of the company's public image
- Flexibility for employee ownership and participation
- Improved opportunities for mergers, acquisitions, and further rounds of financing
- An immediate increase in the wealth of the company's founders

The many benefits of going public are not without their corresponding costs, however, and the downside of being a public company must be strongly considered in the strategic planning process. Among these costs are

- A dilution in the founders' control of the entity
- The pressure to meet market and shareholder expectations regarding growth and dividends
- Changes in management styles and employee expectations
- Compliance with complex regulations imposed by federal and state securities laws
- Stock resale restrictions for company insiders
- Vulnerability to shifts in the stock market
- The sharing of the company's financial success with hundreds, even thousands, of other shareholders

Hidden Legal Costs of Being a Public Company

Often the most expensive aspect of registering securities for public offering is the hidden costs of the transaction imposed by federal and state securities laws. SEC rules and regulations make going public a time-consuming and expensive process that begins several years before the actual offering and continues, through the SEC periodic reporting process, for as long as the company remains public. From a legal perspective, the following costs and factors involved in being a public company should be strongly considered:

1. *Planning and preparing the business for the IPO.* From the day that it is formed, the company must avoid a host of legal and structural pitfalls if an IPO is in its future. Some pitfalls will serve as a significant impediment to a successful IPO and will be expensive to remedy. Because a public company requires a more formal management style from a legal perspective—for example, more regular meetings of the board of directors—small companies are well advised to operate as if they were public right from the start.

2. *Due diligence and housecleaning.* Federal and state securities laws dictate that prospective investors have access to all material information about a company offering its securities to the public. Well before a growing company is ready to file its registration statement with the SEC, the due diligence process occurs. Usually it identifies a variety of housecleaning chores that the company must accomplish *before* it files any documents. It may need to formalize, amend, or even terminate corporate charters, bylaws, shareholders' agreements, employment agreements, leases, licenses, accounting methods, and related docu-

ments and procedures before the company is ready to operate in a public fishbowl.

3. *Registration process.* The time, effort, and expense required to prepare the registration statement for SEC approval should not be underestimated. In fact, the 6- to 12-month time frame and the out-of-pocket expenses alone make the cost of going public a prohibitive capital formation alternative for many growing businesses. Costs vary depending on a number of factors, but a company planning to offer its securities to the public should be prepared to spend anywhere from $200,000 to $500,000 in legal and accounting fees, appraisal costs, printing expenses, and consulting and filing fees. This amount does not include the underwriters' and brokers' commissions, which may run as high as 10 percent or more of the total offering. These are sunk costs and must be paid regardless of how few shares are actually sold.

In addition to the registration statement, exhibits and attachments documenting major business transactions, customer and vendor arrangements, and financial statements must be filed with the SEC prior to the offering. These required disclosures result in a loss of confidentiality, which may be costly for the issuer, especially since competitors, creditors, labor unions, suppliers, and others have access to these documents once they become available to the public.

4. *Periodic reporting and ongoing compliance.* Most public companies are subject to the ongoing periodic reporting requirements imposed by the SEC, such as quarterly financial reporting (Form 10-Q), annual financial reporting (Form 10-K), reporting of current material events (Form 8-K), and related reporting requirements such as those for sale of control stock and tender offers. Other ongoing costs of being a public company include an increased use of attorneys, accountants, and other advisers; a dedication of staff time to meet with securities analysts and financial press; the implementation of a shareholder and media relations program; and the significantly greater cost of annual reports, shareholders' meetings, and solicitations of proxies when shareholder approval is needed for major corporate transactions.

Preparing for the Due Diligence Process

Regardless of whether going public or some other financing strategy is ultimately adopted, the due diligence process means that the company's corporate records, personnel, products, agreements, and financial data will be viewed by underwriters and their counsel under a microscope. Growth companies can prepare for this process well in advance and avoid the significant expenses incurred by being unprepared by observing all formalities imposed by applicable corporate laws, maintaining accurate and detailed minutes of corporate decisions, and ensuring that the documents listed in Exhibit 10-1 are at their disposal when the due diligence team arrives.

Planning for the IPO

As you may recall, CleanWorld Consulting Company (CCC) planned to sell privately up to $2 million of convertible preferred stock as bridge financing in anticipation of a public offering within 18 months following the closing of the private placement. The time for CCC to begin planning for the IPO is well before the private placement memorandum (PPM) is even drafted. In fact, if it fails to take certain key steps in preparation for an IPO, it will face a significant, if not prohibitive, cost barrier to the offering.

Of greatest interest to any prospective underwriter or investor analyzing CCC will be the three Ps of due diligence: people, products, and profits. From a legal perspective, these key assets should have been adequately protected from the inception of CCC. For example, key employees, such as environmental engineers and field consultants, should be carefully selected since their background and role in the company will have to be subsequently disclosed in the prospectus. These employees should be subject to reasonable employment agreements, nondisclosure agreements, and incentive programs that ensure a long-term commitment to CCC. Professional advisers such as attorneys and accountants should have a strong corporate and securities law background and should possess the capability to grow with the company as its requirements for professional services become more comprehensive and complex.

Second, CCC's products and services should be protected to the fullest extent possible under patent, trademark, and copyright laws. Any key vendor, licensee, customer, or distributor agreement that materially affects the production or distribution of these products and services should be negotiated and reduced to writing as formally as possible, with the eventual disclosure of these documents kept in mind.

Finally, CCC's capital structure and financial performance will be scrutinized by any potential underwriter looking at the company.

An inefficient management structure, overly restrictive shareholder agreements that affect control of the company, self-dealing among the board of directors and key stockholders, inadequate corporate records, a capital structure with excessive debt, a series of unaudited and uncertain financial statements, and a poor earnings history will have a negative effect on the valuation of CCC and the willingness of an underwriter to take the company public.

In preparing for an eventual public offering, CCC should also implement a more formalized management structure with monthly or quarterly formal board meetings, maintenance of complete and accurate corporate minutes and resolu-

Exhibit 10-1. Documents required for the underwriter's due diligence.

1. The company's articles of incorporation and any amendments, by-laws, organizational resolutions, minutes of corporate board and shareholder meetings, and any shareholder agreements or voting trusts
2. Executed copies of all material supplier, distributor, and customer contracts or other written evidence of such arrangements
3. Any business, marketing, or management plans prepared by the company, along with any pro forma financial projections and allocation of proceeds
4. Completed copies of officers' and directors' questionnaires that contain information regarding possible conflicts of interest or insider transactions, as well as information on each person's qualifications and experience
5. All files pertaining to previous, current, or threatened litigation with creditors, customers, vendors, or employees
6. All leases, title reports or title insurance policies, deeds of trust, mortgages, invoices, and bills of sale for real estate and equipment held by the company
7. All investment agreements, loan agreements, warrants, stock options, or any other documentation relating to the issuer's capital structure, debt obligations, or duties to issue additional stock
8. All insurance policies, government permits and licenses, and other documents or certificates of authority to operate the issuer's business that may be subject to governmental regulation
9. Copies of any patents, copyrights, trademarks, or franchise or license agreements which the issuer may own or be a party to

tions, and the recruitment of an experienced and independent board of directors who would be acceptable to the investing public.

Selecting an Underwriter

The managing underwriter is at the heart of the network established for taking CCC's securities public. The underwriter will organize a group of co-underwriters to share in the risk of the offering and to establish the network of registered broker-dealer firms to participate in the distribution process by selling the issuer's securities to their clientele. Therefore, the appropriate selection of and negotiation with the managing underwriter is a key ingredient for the success of the IPO.

Underwriters offer a wide range of support services: management consulting services, business valuations, development of media and shareholders' relations programs, assistance in developing an optimum capital structure or location, and analysis of merger or acquisition candidates. CCC (or any other growth company considering a public offering) may not need all of these services and must consider which are most important. It must also examine the reputation, experience, distribution capability, market-making ability, research capabilities, and specific industry expertise of the potential underwriter. In turn, the size and reputation of the underwriter CCC is able to attract will depend on the strength of the issuer, the amount of stock being offered, and the issuer's future business plans.

Once CCC selects a managing underwriter that it hopes will meet its present and future requirements, the two parties execute a Letter of Intent, which sets forth the terms and conditions of the proposed distribution of the issuer's securities. The Letter of Intent governs the relationship throughout the preparation and registration process because the final underwriting agreement is usually not signed until the morning of the day that the registration statement becomes effective following SEC approval. An understanding of the key terms of the Letter of Intent is crucial to any company considering a public offering.

1. *Type of underwriting.* There are two basic forms of commitment by the managing underwriter. The more attractive to CCC is the *firm commitment*, in which the underwriter pledges to purchase all of the securities offered by the company. It then bears the responsibility for resale to the public.

Not nearly so attractive is the *best-efforts commitment*, under which the managing underwriter merely promises to use its best efforts to offer and sell the securities of the issuer. The underwriter makes no assurance that the amount of capital that CCC requires to meet its business objectives will be received. The company nevertheless still incurs the extensive costs of the offering and the legal burden of being a publicly held company.

One type of protection is the *all-or-nothing* or *go–no go amount*; if a certain minimum number of shares are not sold, the entire offering is withdrawn. An underwriter may also want to negotiate an *overallotment option* under which it is granted an option to purchase a specific number of additional shares if the maximum number of shares of CCC to be sold is exceeded.

2. *Compensation of the underwriter.* The commission schedules, ongoing consulting fees, and any warrants to purchase shares of CCC (during a certain period of time and at a fixed price) usually are the elements of the compensation package to the underwriter. The rate of commission, the amount of advance payment, the number of warrants to be issued, and other issues will depend on CCC's negotiating leverage, the risk of the offering, and the underwriter's projected internal time and effort to manage the distribution network.

3. *Offering, size, price, and special characteristics.* The number of shares to be sold, the type of security to be issued, the price of the security per share, and any special characteristics or restrictions regarding these securities are identified in the Letter of Intent. CCC's principals must remember that the final decisions regarding these factors may not be made until just prior to the actual offering, depending on market conditions and completion of the due diligence process. Under such circumstances, CCC and the underwriter should at least agree on price ranges in the Letter of Intent, which will be subject to the terms of the final pricing amendment filed with the SEC just prior to the public offering.

4. *Responsibility for fees and expenses.* The issuer is usually responsible for all of its own costs in connection with the preparation and registration of the offering statement, as well as some portion of the underwriter's expenses. CCC should expect that the managing underwriter will want to hold a series of parties and "dog and pony shows" on behalf of the issuer, but it should establish a ceiling on these expenses.

5. *Miscellaneous provisions.* The other key terms to be negotiated in the Letter of Intent are: rights of first refusal on future financing; responsibility for state blue-sky law registration; selection of professional advisers; representations and warranties of the issuer; restrictions on the issuer's activities before and after the sale of the securities; and accessibility of the issuer's employee records for further due diligence.

Preparing the Registration Statement

The first step in preparing the CCC registration statement required by the SEC is an initial meeting of all key members of the registration team (attorneys, accountants, the underwriter, the chief executive officer, the chief financial officer, etc.) at which delegation of responsibility for preparation of each aspect of the registration statement is assigned, along with a timetable for completion of each task.

In connection with the commencement of the preparation of the registration statement, several preliminary tasks must be completed:

- Extensive due diligence by legal counsel to both CCC and the underwriter
- Meetings of the company's board of directors to authorize the offering
- Preparation and completion of the confidential questionnaire for CCC's officers and directors
- Research by legal counsel as to compliance with applicable state blue-sky law and National Association of Securities Dealers (NASD) regulations
- Meetings with underwriters to establish marketing and distribution strategies

The registration statement consists of two distinct parts: the *offering prospectus*, a document widely distributed to underwriters and prospective investors to assist them in analyzing CCC and the securities being offered, and the *exhibits* and *additional information*, which are provided directly to the SEC as part of the disclosure and registration regulations. The registration statement becomes part of the public record and is available for public inspection.

The SEC provides several different forms of registration statement alternatives. CCC's choice will depend on the company history and the size and nature of the specific offering. The form most commonly used is the S-1, which is required for all issuers unless an alternative form is available. Two other forms, the S-2 and the S-3, are available to companies already subject to the reporting requirements of the Securities Exchange Act of 1934. The S-4 form is limited to corporate combinations. The S-1 through S-4 are filed and processed at the principal office of the SEC in Washington, D.C., by the Division of Corporate Finance.

The SEC has also established special provisions for small offerings by companies not already subject to the reporting requirements of the 1934 Act. This is the Form S-18, which is available for offerings that will not exceed $7.5 million over a 12-month period. The S-18 is the best alternative for CCC because it is somewhat less detailed from a disclosure perspective and requires less detailed financial statements. It can be filed with the regional office of the SEC closest to the principal place of business of the issuer. The ability to file in the regional office usually means a quicker turnaround; however, in the event of a backlog, the S-18 can also be filed in SEC headquarters.

All forms of registration statement contain a series of core procedural rules and disclosure items that must be addressed in the registration statement. These rules are enumerated in the SEC's Regulation C, which is a counterpart to the SEC's Regulation 12b, Regulation S-K, and Regulation S-X. Regulation C also contains rules on the distribution process, the use of the preliminary prospectus (the "red herring"), and shelf registration (the filing of a registration statement well in advance of the time the securities will actually be offered to the public). The core contents of any registration statement filed under Regulation C are found in Regulation S-K, which outlines the requirements for all nonfinancial information, and in Regulation S-X, which specifies the form and content of the financial statements filed as part of the registration statement.

The following key disclosure items must be addressed in the registration statement:

1. *Cover Page/Forepart.* Must fulfill the SEC's very specific requirements regarding information that must be set forth on the cover page and forepart of the prospectus, including summary information pertaining to the nature of CCC's business, the terms of the offering, the determination of the offering price, dilution, plan of distribution, risk factors, and selected financial information.

2. *Introduction to the Company.* An overview of CCC: its business, employees, financial performance, and principal offices.

3. *Risk Factors.* A description of the operating and financial risk factors affecting CCC's business with particular regard to the offering of the securities, such as any dependence on a single customer, supplier, or key personnel, an absence of operating history in the new areas of business CCC wants to pursue, an unproved market for the products and services offered by the company, or a lack of earnings history.

4. *Use of Proceeds.* A discussion of CCC's anticipated use of the proceeds that will be raised by the offering.

5. *Capitalization.* A description of the capital structure of CCC's debt obligations and its anticipated dividend policy and dilution of purchaser's equity.

6. *Description of Business and Property.* A description of the key assets, principal lines of business, human resources, properties, marketing strategies, and competitive advantages of CCC and any of its subsidiaries for the last five years.

7. *Management and Principal Shareholders.* A discussion of CCC's key management team and description of each member's background, education, compensation, and role in the company, as well as a table of all shareholders who hold a beneficial interest of 5 percent or more.

8. *Litigation.* A statement of any material litigation (past, pending, or anticipated) affecting CCC, or any other adverse legal proceedings that would affect an investor's analysis of the securities being offered.

9. *Financial Information.* A summary of financial information regarding CCC, such as sales history, net income or losses from operations, long-term debt obligations, dividend patterns, capital structure and founder's equity, and shareholder loans.

10. *Securities Offered and Underwriting Arrangements.* A description of the underwriting arrangements, distribution plan, and the key characteristics of the securities being offered.

11. *Experts and Other Matters.* A brief statement regarding the identity of the attorneys, accountants, and other experts retained in connection with the offering, as well as the availability of additional information (such as indemnification policies for the company's directors and officers, recent sales of unregistered securities, a breakdown of the expenses of the offering, and a wide variety of corporate documents and key agreements) from Part II of the registration statement filed with the SEC.

The Registration Process

When the initial draft of the registration statement is ready for filing with the SEC, CCC has two choices: to file the document with the transmittal letter and required fees *or* to schedule a prefiling conference with an SEC staff member to discuss any anticipated questions or problems regarding the disclosure document or the accompanying financial statements.

Once the registration statement is officially received by the SEC, it is assigned to an examining group, composed usually of attorneys, accountants, and financial analysts, within a specific industry department of the Division of Corporate Finance. Traditionally at this time the first press releases are distributed to the financial press, and the marketing strategies by the underwriters are further defined and developed. The length of time the examining group devotes to the statement, and the depth of its review, depend on the company's history and the nature of the securities offered. For example, a company operating in a troubled or turbulent industry that is publicly offering its securities for the first time should expect a detailed review by all members of the examining group.

Following its initial review, the group sends a deficiency or comment letter to the issuer and its counsel, suggesting changes to the registration statement. The modifications of the statement that it suggests focus on the quality of the disclosure (such as an adequate discussion of risk factors or the verbiage in management's discussion of the financial performance of the company), *not* on the quality of the company or the securities being offered. In most cases, the issuer will be required to file a material amendment in order to address the staff's concerns, which may require a reprinting and redistribution of the preliminary prospectus distributed to the underwriters.

This process continues until the issuer and its counsel have addressed all concerns raised by the examining group. Then the final pricing amendment is filed following the pricing meeting of the underwriters and the execution of the final underwriting agreement. The registration statement then is declared effective, and the securities can be offered to the public when the final prospectus is sent to the financial printers and distributed. The registration statement is declared effective 20 days after the final amendment has been filed, unless the effective date is accelerated by the SEC. Most issuers and their underwriters seek an accelerated effective date, which is usually made available if the issuer has complied with the examining group's suggested modifications.

A company offering its securities to the public must also meet NASD requirements and state securities laws. The NASD is a self-regulatory body that reviews underwriting and distribution agreements prepared in connection with the public offering in order to ensure that the terms and conditions are consistent with industry practices. It analyzes all elements of the proposed corporation package for the underwriter in order to determine reasonableness. The SEC will not deem a registration statement effective for public offering unless and until the NASD has approved the underwriting arrangements.

All states have some type of law regulating the offer and sale of securities within its borders. Section 18 of the Securities Act of 1933 states that federal securities laws do not supersede compliance with any state securities laws. Although various exemptions from formal registration are often available, a company and its counsel must check state securities laws carefully in connection with an IPO as to filing fees, registered agent requirements, disclosure obligations, and underwriter or broker-dealer regulations for each state in which the securities will be offered.

The Closing and Beyond

Once the final underwriting agreement is signed and the final pricing amendment is filed with the SEC, the registration statement will be declared effective, and the selling process begins. Throughout the selling period, CCC must wait patiently and hope that any minimum sales quotas (such as for all-or-nothing offerings) are met and that the offering is well received by the investing public.

To facilitate the mechanics of the offering process, most issuers retain the services of a registrar and transfer agent, who will be responsible for issuing stock certificates upon closing, maintaining stockholder ownership records, and processing the transfer of shares from one investor to another. These services are usually offered by commercial banks and by trust companies, which also offer ongoing support services such as annual report and proxy mailing, disbursement of dividends, and custody of the authorized but unissued stock certificates. Once the offer and sale of the shares to the public has been completed, a closing must be scheduled to exchange documents, issue stock certificates, and disburse net proceeds to the company.

The issuer is required by the SEC to file a Form SR, a report on the company's use of the proceeds raised from the sale of the securities. The information the company provides should be substantially similar to the discussion contained in the prospectus provided to prospective investors. An initial Form SR must be filed within 90 days after the registration statement becomes effective and then once every six months thereafter until the completion of the offering and the application of the proceeds toward their intended use.

Ongoing Reporting and Disclosure Requirements

The Securities Exchange Act of 1934 generally governs the ongoing disclosure and periodic reporting requirements of the publicly traded company. Section 13 of the Act grants broad powers to the SEC to develop documents and reports that companies that register their securities for sale to the general public must file. The three primary reports required by § 15(d) of the Exchange Act are Form 10-K, Form 10-Q, and Form 8-K.

1. *Form 10-K.* The annual report that CCC must file within 90 days after the close of the fiscal year covered by the report. The form must include a report of all significant activities of the company during its fourth quarter, an analysis and discussion of CCC's financial condition, a description of CCC's current officers and directors, and a schedule of certain exhibits.

2. *Form 10-Q.* The quarterly report that must be filed no later than 45 days after the end of each of the first three fiscal quarters of each fiscal year. This filing includes copies of CCC's quarterly financial statements (accompanied by a discussion and analysis of the company's financial condition by its management), a report on any litigation affecting CCC, and steps the company has taken that affect shareholder rights or may require shareholder approval.

3. *Form 8-K.* A periodic report designed to ensure that all material information pertaining to significant events (such as a sale of key assets of the company or the involvement of the company in critical litigation) that affect CCC is disclosed to the investing public as soon as it is available but not later than 15 days after the occurrence of the particular event that triggers the need to file the Form 8-K.

The duty to disclose material information, whether as part of a Form 8-K filing or otherwise, to the general public is an ongoing obligation that continues for as long as the company's securities are publicly traded. CCC must establish an ongoing compliance program to ensure that all material corporate information is disclosed as fully and as promptly as possible. A fact is generally considered to be material if there is a substantial likelihood that a reasonable shareholder would consider it important in his or her investment decisions (whether to buy, sell, or hold or how to vote on a particular proposed corporate action). The following kinds of information are examples of what is typically considered to be a significant event that is material for disclosure purposes:

- Acquisitions and dispositions of other companies or properties
- Public or private sales of debt or equity securities
- Bankruptcy or receivership proceedings affecting the issuer
- Major contract awards or terminations
- Changes in the key management team

Pursuant to § 12(g) of the Exchange Act, certain issuers of publicly traded securities are subject to additional reporting and disclosure requirements. If the issuer elects to register its securities under § 12(g) (in order to become more attractive to underwriters and shareholders because of the additional reporting requirements) *or* it has greater than 500 shareholders and at least $5 million worth of total assets, it will also be subject to the rules developed by the SEC for proxy solicitation, reporting of beneficial ownership, liability for short-swing transactions, and tender offer rules and regulations.

1. *Proxy solicitation.* Due to the difficulty of assembling every shareholder of a corporation, which may have thousands of owners, for matters that require a shareholder vote, voting by proxy is a fact of life for most publicly held corporations. When management solicits the proxies of its shareholders for voting at annual or special meetings, it must follow special statutory rules. The request for the proxy must be accompanied by a detailed proxy statement specifying the matters to be acted upon and any information the shareholder requires in reaching a decision.

2. *Reporting of beneficial ownership.* Section 16(a) of the Exchange Act requires that all officers, directors, and any shareholders owning more than 10 percent of the outstanding shares file a statement of ownership (either direct or indirect) of CCC's securities with the SEC. This initial statement is filed on Form 3 and must reflect all holdings, direct and indirect, in CCC's securities. Section 16(a) also requires that whenever the officers and directors increase or decrease their holdings of CCC's securities by purchase, sale, gift, or otherwise, the transaction must be reported to the SEC no later than the tenth day of the month following the month in which the transaction occurred. These statements of change are filed on Form 4.

3. *Liability for short-swing transactions.* Section 16(b) requires that CCC's officers, directors, employees, or other insiders return to it any profit they may have realized from any combination of sales and purchases, or purchases and sales, of CCC's securities made by them within any six-month period. Any acquisition of CCC's securities, regardless of what form of consideration is paid, is considered to be a purchase. The purpose of § 16(b) is to discourage even the possibility of directors and officers taking advantage of inside information by speculating in a company's stock. Liability occurs automatically if there is a sale and purchase within six months, even if the individual involved in the transaction did not actually take advantage of inside information.

4. *Tender offer rules and regulations.* Sections 13 and 14 of the Exchange Act generally govern the rules for parties who wish to make a tender offer to purchase the securities of a publicly traded corporation. Any person acquiring, directly or indirectly, beneficial ownership of more than 5 percent of an equity security registered under § 12 of the Exchange Act must report the transaction by filing a Schedule 13D within ten days from the date of acquisition. Schedule 13D requires disclosure of certain material information, such as the identity and background of the purchaser, the purpose of the acquisition, the source and amount of funds used to purchase the securities, and disclosure of the issuer. If the purchase is in connection with a tender offer, then the provisions of § 14(d) also apply; the terms of the tender offer must be disclosed, as well as the plans of the offerer if it is successful and the terms of any special agreements between the offerer and the target company. Section 14(e) of the Exchange Act imposes a broad prohibition against the use of false, misleading, or incomplete statements in connection with a tender offer.

Defenses to Tender Offers and Hostile Takeovers

Growing companies considering going public must risk being acquired by an unwanted suitor and in defense must consider adopting plans and strategies to avoid takeover threats. One of the most challenging responsibilities of being a publicly held company is determining which tender offer defenses can be adopted without a legal challenge by the company's shareholders, creditors, or competitors against the management team that developed the strategy. Some of the most commonly used defensive tactics are listed in Exhibit 10-2.

Growing companies considering restructuring or related steps as a defensive tactic against a hostile takeover should carefully consult with counsel. Not all of the tactics listed in Exhibit 10-2 have been met with direct approval by federal and state courts and regulators.

Rule 10b-5 and Insider Trading

The business and financial press has devoted a great deal of attention to the SEC's Rule 10b-5 and its application in the prosecution of insider trading cases. The text of 10b-5 is as follows:

It shall be unlawful for any person, directly or indirectly, by the use of any means or instrumentality of interstate commerce, or of the mails or of any facility of any national securities exchange to:

Exhibit 10-2.   Defensive tactics against hostile takeovers.

- **The Porcupine**. Acquisition of another business that will increase the chances that the hostile takeover will trigger antitrust law problems.

- **Pac-Man**. The company subject to the tender offer itself makes a counter-tender offer for the bidder. Also known as the counter-tender.

- **Poison Pill**. Steps taken that relate to issuance of shares, removal of directors, supermajority voting provisions, or redemption by shareholders, for example, that prevent or deter the threat of a hostile takeover.

- **Lockup**. The issuance or threat of issuance of options to acquire additional shares of the target company to a nonadversarial party in order to make the acquisition more expensive or more difficult.

- **Shark Repellent**. Amendments to the corporate charter specifically designed to make takeover attempts more difficult.

- **White Knight**. Soliciting bids to sell the company (or the actual issuance of stock or warrants) to a more congenial suitor.

- **Golden Parachute**. Steps taken by management that trigger special bonuses and related forms of compensation if the management team is removed or replaced in connection with a tender offer.

- **Fair Price Amendments**. Plans and provisions added to the corporate charter requiring that shareholders receive equivalent prices for their shares at both ends of a multitiered hostile bid for the company. These provisions, also known as lollipops, are designed to protect all shareholders equally but do not necessarily deter a hostile takeover.

(a) employ any device, scheme, or artifice to defraud;

(b) make any untrue statement of a material fact or to omit to state a material fact necessary in order to make the statements made, in light of the circumstances under which they were made, not misleading; or

(c) engage in any act, practice, or course of business which operates or would operate as a fraud or deceit upon any person, in connection with the purchase or sale of any security.

Rule 10b-5 has been applied most frequently in insider trading cases, typically those in which an officer, director, or other person with a fiduciary relationship with a corporation buys or sells the company's securities while in the possession of material, nonpublic information. The rule is also used in at least five other situations:

1. When a corporation issues misleading information to the public, or keeps silent when it has a duty to disclose
2. When an insider selectively discloses material, nonpublic information to another party, who then trades securities based on the information (generally called tipping)
3. When a person mismanages a corporation in ways connected with the purchase or sale of securities
4. When a securities firm or another person manipulates the market for a security traded in the over-the-counter market
5. When a securities firm or securities professional engages in certain other forms of conduct connected with the purchase or sale of securities

Officers, directors, employees, and shareholders of publicly traded companies (or companies considering being publicly traded) must be keenly aware of the broad scope of this antifraud rule in their transactions that involve the company.

Disposing of Restricted Securities

All shares of a public company held by its controlling persons—which typically include its officers, directors, and 10 percent shareholders (if any)—are deemed "restricted securities" under the 1933 Act. The sale of restricted securities is generally governed by Rule 144 under the 1933 Act, which requires as a condition of sale that

1. The company be current in its periodic reports to the SEC;
2. The restricted securities have been beneficially owned for at least two years preceding the sale;
3. The amount of securities that may be sold in any three-month period be limited to the greater of 1 percent of the outstanding class of securities or the average weekly reported volume of trading in the securities on a registered national security exchange, if the securities are listed;
4. The securities be sold only in broker's transactions and notice of the sale be filed with the SEC concurrently with the placing of the sale order; and
5. A sale involving 500 shares or $10,000 be reported to the SEC on Form 144.

CHAPTER

11

Growth Through Acquisitions

U nder certain circumstances, corporate growth objectives can best be achieved by the purchase or sale of privately held companies. This chapter will examine growth through acquisition from the perspective of an emerging-growth company, such as Impasse, Inc. (discussed in chapter 1), considering the purchase of another business of a smaller size. The planning and implementation of the acquisition program that Impasse's consulting firm, Compactdisc & Associates, develops will typically involve the steps outlined in Exhibit 11-1.

Very few other business transactions are as complex or raise as many legal issues as the acquisition or disposition of a business, even if the deal does not involve a hostile takeover attempt. In fact, the planning and structuring of a merger or acquisition typically involves all of the corporate, securities, employment, intellectual property, and antitrust law principles already discussed in this book, as well as certain special industry regulatory approvals and tax accounting, environmental and hazardous waste, real property, product liability, bulk transfer, and labor law issues.

Impasse must begin the acquisition process with a plan that identifies the specific objectives of the transaction and the criteria to be applied in analyzing a potential target company. Although the reasons for considering growth through acquisition vary from industry to industry and from company to company, the following strategic advantages provided by acquisitions should be considered:

- The growth company may be able to achieve certain operating and financial synergies and economies of scale with respect to production and manufacturing, research and development, management, or marketing and distribution.

- The target company may own proprietary rights to products or services that it cannot fully develop unless it is acquired by a firm with capital to allocate to these projects.

- The target company may be in danger of losing a talented management team due to the lack of career growth potential unless it is acquired by a growing

Exhibit 11-1. Planning an acquisition program.

- Developing acquisition objectives
- Analyzing projected economic and financial gains to be achieved by the acquisition
- Assembling an acquisition team (managers, attorneys, accountants, and investment bankers) and beginning the search for acquisition candidates
- Due diligence analysis of prime candidates
- Initial negotiations and valuation of the selected target
- Selection of the structure of the transaction
- Identification of sources of financing for the transaction
- Detailed bidding and negotiations
- Obtaining all shareholder and third-party consents and approvals
- Structuring the legal documents
- Preparing for the closing
- The closing
- Postclosing tasks and responsibilities
- Implementation of the strategic integration of the two companies

business that can offer higher salaries, increased employee benefits, and greater opportunity for advancement. (Conversely, the acquiring company may have a surplus of strong managers who are likely to leave unless the company acquires other businesses for these managers to operate and develop.)

- The growth company may wish to stabilize its earnings stream and mitigate its risk of business failure by diversifying its products and services through acquisition rather than internal development.
- The growing company may need to deploy excess cash into a tax-efficient project, such as an acquisition, since the distribution of dividends and stock redemptions are generally taxable events to its shareholders.
- The growing company may want to achieve certain production and distribution economies of scale through vertical integration, which would involve the acquisition of a key supplier or customer.
- The target company's management team may be ready for retirement, or a key manager may have recently died, leaving the business with residual assets that an acquiring company can exploit.

- The emerging-growth company may wish to increase its market power by acquiring its competitors, which may be a less costly alternative for growth than internal expansion.

- The acquiring company may be weak in certain key business areas, such as research and development or marketing, and it may be more efficient to fill these gaps through an acquisition rather than attempting to build these departments internally.

- An emerging-growth company may have superior products and services but lack the consumer loyalty or protected trademarks needed to gain recognition in the marketplace. The acquisition of an older, more established firm becomes a more efficient method of establishing goodwill.

- A growing company may wish to penetrate new geographic markets and finds that it is cheaper to acquire firms already doing business in those areas rather than attempt to establish market diversification from scratch.

- The target company may lack the technical expertise or capital needed to grow to the next likely stage in its development unless it is acquired by a firm with such resources already in place.

- The target company may have excess plant or production capacities that the buyer can use to achieve greater economies of scale.

- The target company may be available at a distressed price (which tends to pique the interest of a growing company even if it is not necessarily looking for an acquisition candidate) due to mismanagement or undercapitalization resulting in a turnaround situation.

- The target company may own certain patents, copyrights, trade secrets, or other intangible assets that the buyer can acquire only by acquisition.

A company considering an acquisition should not rely too heavily on a target's last year's earnings or a "multiple of sales" formula to determine its valuation. Rather, it should look closely at the target business's underlying foundation—economic and technological trends affecting its outlook, the quality of its assets and management team, its dependency on a particular key supplier or customer, and the extent to which it has protected its intellectual property. It should examine financial data about the company beyond its sales figures—cash flows, accounts receivable management, credit ratings, and cost of goods sold.

In our example, Impasse should probe beyond the data contained in the target's financial statements. Statements provided by the prospective seller tend to be incomplete or misleading, especially because most target companies have spent years trying to understate their performance in order to avoid excessive tax liability or percentage to lessors and licensors and now, for the first time, are seeking to overstate their financial performance. In addition, the seller's management can take certain steps to make the financial statements more attractive in anticipation of a sale, such as capitalizing items that are normally taken as a direct expense, overstating the value of assets, or understating the extent of liabilities.

A common acquisition misperception is that diversification significantly reduces the risk of business failure. Although a diversified line of products and services does tend to stabilize a growing company's earnings stream, it can also be a dangerous and expensive acquisition strategy. For example, the negotiation and structure of the transaction is often driven by an awareness of the special issues affecting the industry in which the target operates. A buyer who misunderstands or lacks enough knowledge of the particular industry will be at an extreme disadvantage during the negotiations and beyond the closing. Members of the acquisition team must be able to conduct meaningful due diligence as a result of their background and prior experience with a business similar or related to the target company. The team can also structure part of the purchase price in the form of a postclosing long-term consulting contract with the prior owner.

An emerging-growth company considering an acquisition should not necessarily assume that the best opportunities are found in turnaround situations. A financially distressed target company may be available at a lower price than a healthy firm, but the lower price may not be worth the drain on the acquirer's resources that will be necessary in order to rehabilitate the entity. Some businesses available for acquisition should have never been started in the first place, or they may be spin-offs of divisions of larger companies that have been a resource drain for the parent since inception. In such cases, it will be especially difficult, if not impossible, for the acquiring company to bring enough talent, expertise, and capital to bear to achieve a successful turnaround. The most effective way to distinguish between a target that has truly kinetic energy and salvageable assets, as opposed to one that has too many skeletons in the closet or will always be the walking dead, is through effective due diligence and analysis.

Analysis of Target Companies

Once Impasse has identified its acquisition objectives and developed criteria for analyzing a target company, it must narrow the field of candidates. The acquisition should achieve one or more of the objectives that Compactdisc and Associates has developed, and the target company should meet many, if not all, of the criteria listed in Exhibit 11-2.

Once the field of candidate companies has been narrowed, the acquirer will select the finalist. Its rating and analysis of the finalists will encompass two phases: the preacquisition review and the detailed legal and business due diligence.

Exhibit 11-2.   Criteria for target company in an acquisition.

- The target operates in an industry that demonstrates growth potential.
- The target has taken steps to protect any proprietary aspects of its products and services.
- The target company has developed a well-defined and established market position.
- The target company should be involved in a minimal amount of litigation (especially if the litigation is with a key customer or supplier).
- The target company should be in a position to readily obtain key third-party consents from lessors, bankers, creditors, suppliers, customers, and franchises (failure to obtain necessary consents to the assignment of key contracts will serve as a substantial impediment to the completion of the transaction).
- The target company should be positioned for a sale (except in hostile takeover situations) so that negotiations focus on the terms of the sale, not whether to sell in the first place (dissension among the ranks could substantially delay the closing of the transaction, especially if the company lacks the necessary majority for shareholder approval of the transaction).
- The target's principal place of business should be within one hour's plane trip of the acquiring company's headquarters or satellite offices (unless the primary acquisition objective is to enter new geographic markets).

Preacquisition Review

The preacquisition review is the preliminary analysis conducted on the two or three finalists that most closely meet the acquiring company's objectives. Typically the prospective targets have different strengths and weaknesses, which must be weighed.

The central goal of the preacquisition review is to collect data that will be useful in determining the value of the finalists for negotiation and bidding purposes. The key areas of inquiry at this stage in the transaction are the target's management team; financial performance to date and projected; areas of potential liability to a successor company; identification of any legal or business impediments to the transaction; confirmation of any facts underlying the terms of the proposed valuation and bid; and the extent to which the intellectual property of the company has been protected. The acquirer can gather this information from meetings, from the target's management team, or from external sources—trade associations, customers and suppliers of the target, industry publications, chambers of commerce, securities law filings, or private data sources such as Dun & Bradstreet, Standard & Poor's, and Moody's.

Once the data have been assembled on the finalists, a preacquisition team is assembled to analyze the information and begin to structure the terms of the offering. The result of their analysis should be a Letter of Intent or preliminary agreement with the target selected.

The Letter of Intent is often executed between buyer and seller as an agreement in principle to consummate the transaction in accordance with the broad terms and conditions contained in it. The parties should be clear as to whether the Letter of Intent is a binding preliminary contract or merely a memorandum from which the formal legal documents can be drafted once the due diligence is completed. The Letter of Intent has many advantages to both parties, including a psychological commitment to the transaction, a way to expedite the formal negotiations process, and an overview of the matters requiring further discussion.

One difficult issue is whether the Letter of Intent should set out a price. From the buyer's perspective, the purchase price should not be set until after due diligence. The seller, however, may be hesitant to proceed without a price commitment. Both parties should agree on a range, with a clause specifying the factors that will influence the final price. The buyer should always reserve the right to change the price and terms if information is discovered during the due diligence that will offset the value of the target.

It is not unusual for a seller to request that a buyer execute a confidentiality agreement prior to conducting extensive due diligence. Acquiring companies should negotiate the narrowest possible scope in connection with such agreements, especially if the buyer is in the same or a similar industry to the seller.

Conducting the Due Diligence

Once a preliminary agreement has been reached, Impasse and its acquisition team should embark on the extensive legal and business due diligence that must occur prior to the closing of the transaction. The legal due diligence will focus on the potential legal issues and problems that may serve as impediments to the transaction, as well as shed light on how the documents should be structured. The business due diligence will examine the strategic issues surrounding the transaction, such as the integration of the human and financial resources of the two companies; confirmation of the operating, production, and distribution synergies and economies of scale to be achieved by the acquisition; and gathering of information necessary for financing the transaction.

The due diligence process can be tedious, frustrating, time-consuming, and expensive. But it is necessary to a well-planned acquisition. It can be informative and revealing in analyzing the target company and in measuring the costs and risks associated with the transaction. Buyers should expect sellers to become defensive, evasive, and impatient during the due diligence phase of the transaction because the latter do not like having their business policies and decisions under the microscope, especially for an extended period of time and by a party searching for skeletons in the closet. Eventually the seller may issue an ultimatum to the prospective buyer: "Finish the due diligence soon or the deal is off." If negotiations reach this point, the best response is to end the examination process promptly. Buyers should avoid "due diligence overkill," keeping in mind that due diligence is not a perfect process; information can and often will slip through the cracks. Thus, broad representations, warranties, and indemnification provisions should be structured into the final purchase agreement in order to protect the buyer.

Due diligence preparation and planning can expedite the process and ensure that virtually no stone remains unturned. The following two checklists should be helpful to growing companies considering an acquisition to prepare for the due diligence process. The first is written from a legal perspective, and the second is designed to provide the acquisition team with a starting point for analysis of the target from a management, marketing, and financial perspective.

Legal Due Diligence

In analyzing the target company, the acquisition team and its counsel should review the following legal documents and records.

Corporate Matters

1. The target's corporate records
   Certificate of incorporation and all amendments
   By-laws (as amended)
   Minute books, including resolutions and minutes of all director and shareholder meetings
   Current shareholders' list (certified by the corporate secretary) and stock transfer books
   List of all states, countries, and other jurisdictions in which the target transacts business or is qualified to do business
   Applications or other filings in each state just listed for qualification as foreign corporation and evidence of qualification

2. Agreements among the target's shareholders

3. All contracts restricting the sale or transfer of shares of the company, such as buy-sell agreements, subscription agreements, offeree questionnaires, or contractual rights of first refusal, as well as all agreements for the right to purchase shares, such as stock options or warrants

Financial Matters

1. List of and copies of management and similar reports or memoranda relating to the material aspects of the business operations or products

2. Letters of counsel in response to auditors' requests for the preceding five years

3. Reports of independent accountants to the board of directors for the preceding five years

4. Revolving credit and term loan agreements, indentures, and other debt instruments, including, without limitation, all documents relating to shareholder loans

5. Correspondence with principal lenders to the target

6. Personal guarantees of target's indebtedness by its shareholders or other parties

7. Agreements by the target where it has served as a guarantor for the obligations of third parties

8. Federal, state, and local tax returns and correspondence with federal, state, and local tax officials

9. Federal filings regarding the Subchapter S status (where applicable) of the target

10. Any private placement memorandum prepared and used by the target (as well as any document used in lieu of a private placement memorandum, such as an investment profile or a business plan)

11. Financial statements for the past five years of the target, including:
    Annual (audited) balance sheets
    Monthly (or other available) balance sheets
    Annual (audited) and monthly (or other available) earnings statements
    Annual (audited) and monthly (or other available) statements of shareholders' equity and changes in financial position
    Any recently prepared projections for the target
    Notes and material assumptions for all statements described above

12. Any information or documentation relating to tax assessments, deficiency notices, investigations, audits, or settlement proposals

13. Informal schedule of key management compensation (listing information for at least the ten most highly compensated management employees or consultants)

14. Projected budgets, accounts receivable reports, and related information

Management and Employment Matters

1. All employment agreements

2. Agreements relating to consulting, management, financial advisory services, and other professional engagements

3. Copies of all union contracts and collective bargaining agreements

4. Equal Employment Opportunity Commission (and any state equivalent) compliance files

5. Occupational Safety and Health Administration files and records

6. Employee benefit plans (and copies of literature issued to employees describing such plans), including the following:
   Pension and retirement plans, including union pension or retirement plans
   Annual reports for pension plans, if any
   Profit-sharing plans
   Stock option plans, including information concerning all options, stock appreciation rights, and other stock-related benefits granted by the company
   Medical and dental plans
   Insurance plans and policies, including the following:
      Errors and omissions policies
      Directors' and officers' liability insurance policies
   Any employee stock ownership plan and trust agreement
   Severance pay plans or programs
   All other benefit or incentive plans or arrangements not covered by the foregoing, including welfare benefit plans

7. All current contracts and agreements with or pertaining to the target and to which directors, officers, or shareholders of the target are parties, and any documents relating to any other transactions between the target and any directors, officers, or shareholders, including receivables from or payables to directors, officers, or shareholders

8. All policy and procedures manuals of the target concerning personnel, business operations, sales, etc.

9. The name, address, and telephone number of any officer who has left the target within the past two years

Tangible and Intangible Assets of the Target

1. List of all commitments for rented or leased real and personal property, including location and address, description, terms, options, and annual costs

2. List of all real property owned, including location and address, description of general character, and encumbrances

3. List of all material, tangible assets

4. List of all liens on all real properties and material tangible assets

5. Mortgages, deeds, title insurance policies, leases, and other agreements relating to the properties of the target

6. Real estate tax bills for the real estate of the target

7. List of patents, patents pending, trademarks, trade names, copyrights, franchises, licenses, and all other intangible assets, including registration numbers, expiration dates, and copies of all correspondence relating to this intellectual property

8. Copies of any survey, appraisal, engineering, or other reports as to the properties of the target

Material Contracts and Obligations of the Target

1. Material purchase, supply, and sale agreements currently outstanding or projected to come to fruition within 12 months, including the following:
   List of all contracts relating to the purchase of products, equipment, fixtures, tools, dies, supplies, industrial supplies, or other materials having a price under any such contract in excess of $5,000
   List of all unperformed sales contracts

2. Documents incidental to any planned expansion of the target's facilities

3. Consignment agreements

4. Research agreements

5. Franchise, licensing, distribution, and agency agreements

6. Joint venture agreements

7. Agreements for the payment of license fees or royalties

8. Documentation relating to all property, liability, and casualty insurance policies owned by the target, including for each policy a summary description of:
   Coverage
   Policy type and number
   Insurer
   Premium
   Expiration date
   Deductible
   Any material changes in any of the foregoing since the inception of the target
   Claims made under such policies

9. Agreements restricting the target's right to compete in any business

10. Agreements for the target's current purchase of services, including, without limitation, consulting and management

11. Contracts for the purchase, sale, or removal of electricity, gas, water, telephone, sewage, power, or any other utility service

12. List of waste dumps, disposal, treatment, and storage sites

13. Agreements with any railroad, trucking, or any other transportation company or courier service

14. Letters of credit

15. Copies of licenses, permits, and governmental approvals applied for or issued to the target that are required in order to operate the businesses of the target, such as zoning permits, operating permits, or health and safety certificates

Litigation and Claims

1. Opinion letter from each lawyer or law firm prosecuting or defending significant litigation to which the target is a party (letter should describe such litigation)

2. List of material litigation or claims for more than $5,000 against the target asserted or threatened with respect to the quality of the products or services sold to customers, including pending or threatened claims

3. List of settlement agreements, releases, decrees, orders, or arbitration awards affecting the target

4. Description of labor relations history

5. Documentation regarding correspondence or proceedings with federal, state, or local regulatory agencies

In reviewing the applicable legal documents and business records, the acquisition team and its legal counsel should be gathering data necessary to answer the following types of preliminary legal questions relevant to the transaction:

1. What legal steps will need to be taken to effectuate the transaction (e.g., director and stockholder approval, share transfer restrictions, restrictive covenants in loan documentation)?

2. What antitrust problems, if any, are raised by the transaction? Will filing be necessary under the Hart-Scott-Rodino Act, which requires that proposed mergers matching certain terms and conditions be approved by the Federal Trade Commission prior to consummation of the transaction?

3. Will the transaction be exempt from registration under applicable federal and state securities laws under the sale-of-business doctrine, which provides that certain stock purchase transactions are exempt from securities laws filings if all the shares are sold to a single purchaser?

4. What potential adverse tax consequences to the buyer, seller, and their respective stockholders may be triggered by the transaction?

5. What are the potential postclosing risks and obligations of the buyer? To what extent should the seller be held liable for such potential liability? What steps, if any, can be taken to reduce these potential risks or liabilities? What will it cost to implement these steps?

6. What are the impediments to the assignability of key tangible and intangible assets of the target company desired by the buyer, such as real estate, intellectual property, favorable contracts or leases, human resource, or plant and equipment?

7. What are the obligations and responsibilities of the buyer and seller under applicable environmental and hazardous waste laws, such as the Comprehensive Environmental Response Compensation and Liability Act?

8. What are the obligations and responsibilities of buyer and seller to the creditors of the target (e.g., bulk transfer laws under Article 6 of the applicable state's commercial code)?

9. What are the obligations and responsibilities of buyer and seller under applicable federal and state labor and employment laws (e.g., will the buyer be subject to successor liability under federal labor laws and as a result be obligated to recognize the presence of organized labor and therefore be obligated to negotiate existing collective bargaining agreements)?

10. To what extent will employment, consulting, confidentiality, or noncompetition agreements need to be created or modified in connection with the proposed transaction?

Finally, the acquisition team and legal counsel should carefully review the documents and records received from the seller in order to determine how the information gathered will affect the structure or the proposed financing of the transaction.

Business and Strategic Due Diligence

At the same time that legal counsel is performing its share of the investigation of the target company, Impasse should assemble a management team to conduct business and strategic due diligence by addressing the following topics.

The Target's Management Team

1. Has the target's organizational chart been carefully reviewed? How are management functions and responsibilities delegated and implemented? Are job descriptions and employment manuals current and available?

2. What is the general assessment of employee morale at the lower echelons of the corporate ladder? To what extent are these rank-and-file employees critical to the long-term health of the target?

3. What are the future growth prospects of the principal labor markets from which the target depends on attracting key employees? Are employees with the skills necessary to operate and manage the target generally available? How are the target's employees recruited, evaluated, trained, and rewarded?

4. What is the background and experience of the target's key management team? What is the reputation of this management team within the industry?

Has there been a high turnover rate among the target's top management? Why (or why not)? Who are the target's key professional advisers and outside consultants?

5. What are the basic management styles, practices, and strategies of the target's current team? What are the strengths and weaknesses of the management team? To what extent has the target's current management engaged in long-term strategic planning, developed internal controls, or structured management and marketing information systems?

Operations of the Target

1. What are the target's production and distribution methods? To what extent are these methods and systems protected by contract or proprietary rights?

2. To what extent is the target operating at its maximum capacity? Why? What are the significant risk factors (e.g., dependence on raw materials or key suppliers or customers) affecting the target's production capacity and ability to expand? What are the significant costs of producing the target's goods and services? To what extent is the production and output of the target dependent on economic cycles or seasonal factors?

3. Are the target's plant, equipment, supplies, and machinery in good working order? When will these assets need to be replaced? What are the annual maintenance and service costs for these key assets? At what levels are the target's inventories? What are the break-even production efficiency and inventory turnover rates for the target company, and how do these compare with industry norms?

4. Does the target maintain production plans, schedules, and reports? Have copies been obtained and analyzed by the buyer? What are the target's manufacturing and production obligations pursuant to long-term contracts or other arrangements?

Sales and Marketing Strategies of the Target

1. What are the target's primary and secondary markets? What is the size of these markets, and what is the target's market share within each? What strategies are in place to expand this market share? What are the current trends affecting either the growth or the shrinkage of these particular markets? How are these markets segmented and reached by the target?

2. Who are the target's direct and indirect competitors, and what are their strengths and weaknesses? In what principal ways do companies within the target's industry compete (e.g., price, quality, or service)? (For each material competitor, the buyer should seek to obtain data on the competitor's products and services, geographic location, channel of distribution, market share, financial health, pricing, policies, and reputation within the industry.)

3. Who are the target's typical customers? What are their purchasing capabil-

ities and patterns? Where are these customers principally located? What political, economic, social, or technological trends or changes are likely to affect the demographic makeup of the target's customer base over the next three to five years? What key factors influence the demand for the target's goods and services?

4. What sales, advertising, public relations, and promotional campaigns and programs are in place at the target company? To what extent have these programs been effectively monitored and evaluated?

Financial Management of the Target

1. Based on the financial statements and reports collected in connection with the legal due diligence, what key sales, income, and earnings trends have been identified? What effect will the proposed transaction have on these aspects of the target's financial performance? What are the various costs incurred in connection with bringing the target's products and services to the marketplace? In what ways can these costs be reduced or eliminated?

2. What are the target's billing and collection procedures? How current are the target's accounts receivable? What steps have been (or can be) taken to expedite the collection procedures and systems? How credible is the target's existing accounting and financial control system?

3. What is the target's capital structure? What are the key financial liabilities and debt obligations of the target? How do the target's leverage ratios compare to industry norms? What are the target's monthly debt-service payments? How strong is the target's relationship with creditors, lenders, and investors?

In conducting the due diligence from a business perspective, owners and managers of growing companies are likely to encounter a wide variety of financial problems and risk areas when analyzing the target: undervaluation of inventories, overdue tax liabilities, inadequate management information systems, incomplete financial documentation or customer information, related-party transactions (especially in small, closely held companies), an unhealthy reliance on a few key customers or suppliers, aging accounts receivable, unrecorded liabilities (e.g., warranty claims, vacation pay, sales returns, and allowances), or an immediate need for significant expenditures as a result of obsolete equipment, inventory, or computer systems. Each of these problems poses different risks and costs that Impasse must weigh against the potential benefits to be gained from the transaction.

Valuation, Pricing, and Sources of Financing

Following the completion of well-planned and -executed due diligence but prior to the structuring and drafting of the actual formal legal documentation, the acquisition team needs to reach certain conclusions regarding the valuation, pricing, and source of financing for the proposal transaction.

Valuation of the Closely Held Company

The acquisition team should always include a qualified business appraiser or financial analyst who understands the special issues raised in assessing the value of a closely held company. By determining the valuation parameters of the target, he or she plays an important role in determining the proposed structure, pricing, and source of financing for the acquisition. Most of the information that an appraiser requires to analyze the value of the target can be gathered as part of the ordinary due diligence process. He or she also must attempt to gather the information necessary to answer the following types of questions:

1. How will the value of the target be affected by the loss of its current management (if applicable)?
2. How should the goodwill of the target be valued? What are the various components that make up the company's goodwill?
3. How and to what extent should the target's intangible assets, such as customer list, intellectual property, license and distributorship agreements, regulatory approvals, leasehold interests, and employment contracts, be assigned some relative tangible value?
4. If less than complete ownership of the target is being acquired, what effect do the remaining minority shareholders have on the company's overall value?
5. If the transaction is structured as a stock rather than an asset acquisition, what effects do the unknown contingent liabilities have on overall value (absent a comprehensive indemnification provision)?
6. What effect should the target company's accounting methods, credit ratings, business plans, projections, or income tax returns have on the overall value of the business?

Although a comprehensive discussion of the various methods of valuation is beyond the scope of this book, the acquisition team must understand how the appraiser will arrive at the range of values for the target company. Most methods of valuation fall into one of three general categories: comparable worth, asset valuation, or financial performance. The determination of which method or methods should be used by the appraiser will depend on the individual facts and circumstances surrounding each target company.

Comparable Worth

A comparative analysis is a commonly used valuation method. The appraiser identifies other companies engaged in the sale of similar products and services and then comparatively measures them against the target with respect to total revenues, market position, earnings, inventory turnover, cost of goods sold, and overall financial history. Because this type of information may be available only for publicly held companies, the appraiser must also try to gather information regarding recent sales of privately held companies similar to the target.

Asset Valuation

An asset-based valuation attempts to determine the overall worth of the target's tangible and intangible assets from both a book value and fair market value perspective. The starting point for this method is the book value of the target's tangible assets, such as real estate, equipment, machinery, inventory, and supplies. The presence of either undervalued assets or intangibles desired by the buyer will likely drive the price well over the initial book value.

In conducting an asset-based valuation, the appraiser will be concerned with such issues as the following:

- Is real estate leased or owned by the target company? If leased, what are the key terms and conditions of the lease? What restrictions (zoning, easements, or covenants), if any, are there on the current or future use of the property?
- What is the age, condition, and remaining useful life of the target's plant, equipment, and machinery? What are the anticipated replacement costs of any equipment or machinery that may be obsolete? What is the salvage value and secondary market for old or excess equipment? What depreciation methods did the target employ for its fixed assets?
- To what extent are the accounts receivable of the target collectible? To what extent do aging reports reflect a cash flow problem? What steps (and costs) will be necessary to collect from the company's debtors? Will the target guarantee all or part of the collections in the purchase agreement?

Financial Performance

The broadest category of business valuation methods is based on the financial performance of the target company, which can be determined by sophisticated financial formulas and ratio analysis focusing on the target company's past, current, and projected sales, earnings, cash flows, and dividends. Although these ratios and formulas play an important role in determining an objective value of the target, it is dangerous to place too much emphasis on any method of valuation based entirely on financial performance. Most of these methods depend on the appraiser's predictions of the target's projected financial performance, which will be only as reliable and credible as the expertise of the appraiser and the underlying data on which such financial projections are based. Of the methods of valuation based on financial performance, two are used most commonly:

1. *Discounted Cash Flow (DCF)*. The projected annual earnings of the target over a specific time period are calculated, added, and then discounted to deter-

mine the present worth of these aggregate projected earnings. The discount rate applied usually depends on the cost of the capital necessary to finance the acquisition. The acquiring company's cost of capital must be analyzed from both a debt and equity perspective, with an emphasis on other capital investments of similar risk that the buyer could make in lieu of the proposed transaction. The principal risk in using this method is that projected earnings are difficult to predict over long periods of time and therefore typically result in a very subjective valuation of the target. Nevertheless, this method attempts to provide the acquiring company with an estimate of whether the expected returns of the transaction exceed the costs and risks involved in acquiring the target company.

2. *Accounting Measures and Rates of Return.* Business appraisers often look to the financial performance of the target from an accounting perspective as a measure of the company's value. These methods usually involve some multiple of the company's prior gross revenues, earnings, or dividends as a means of determining its present value. Historical data rather than anticipated performance are at the heart of the analysis. The obvious weaknesses with business valuations based on accounting information are: (1) the possibility of "cooked books" where the financial records of the target have been either negligently maintained over the years or altered in anticipation of a sale; (2) the target company's projected value (or lack thereof) is not adequately taken into account; and (3) varying accounting methods and conventions may have been followed by the target company that affect the numbers used in the valuation.

Role of the Valuation Report and Pricing

Assuming that the appraiser is able to gain the full support and cooperation of the target company in gathering necessary data, he or she will issue a formal valuation report to the acquisition team, which then determines the effect of the report on the pricing of the transaction. There is often only an indirect relationship between reported value and actual purchase price. For example, if the range of values established by the appraiser is between $3.2 million and $3.6 million, the acquiring company's willingness to pay a price equal to or greater than the valuation ceiling will depend on the extent to which operating synergies and long-term economies of scale will be achieved as a result of the transaction.

On the other hand, if the acquiring company seeks only to buy certain key assets owned by the target (known as cherry picking the crown jewels), then it is likely to be far less concerned with long-term synergies and more concerned with paying the lowest possible price for the target. Similarly, if the acquiring company plans to structure the transaction as a leveraged buy-out, where the purchase price is financed primarily by borrowing against the assets and cash flow of the target, then the operating synergies will be less important than the need to acquire the assets necessary to serve as collateral for the transaction. Ultimately, pricing issues will be determined by the negotiations between buyer and seller, as well as the type of financing selected by the acquiring company.

Financing the Acquisition

Many smaller-scale acquisitions are financed primarily with the acquiring company's excess cash or retained earnings. Under such circumstances, it needs little to no external debt, and the only key issues become pricing the stock or assets to be purchased and the terms of payment between buyer and seller. But if the acquiring company lacks the excess cash required to finance the transaction, such as may be the case with Impasse, it has essentially two choices: offer the shareholders of the target some consideration other than cash, such as equity securities, promissory notes, or a share of the postclosing earnings, or identify an external source of capital.

When the acquiring company must identify external sources of financing for the transaction, it faces many of the issues discussed in Part II. Many growing companies have successfully used private placements, commercial lenders, venture capitalists, and even public offerings of their securities to finance the acquisition of a target. Depending on the size and complexity of the transaction, the acquisition team may want to retain the services of an investment banker to assist in arranging and negotiating the necessary financing for the transaction, usually in exchange for a consulting fee and a percentage of the capital raised. The investment banker may also assist in preparing the proposal necessary to present to the potential sources of capital, structuring the transaction, and valuing the target company. For smaller-scale transactions, these services may be available from accountants, lawyers, business brokers, and merchant bankers.

Once the decision has been made to acquire the target company, strategies must be developed regarding the structural alternatives for the transaction. The key legal and strategic issues in structuring an acquisition are discussed in the next chapter.

Structuring the Acquisition

A wide variety of corporate, tax, and securities law issues affect the decision as to the structure of an acquisition, and each must be carefully considered from a legal and accounting perspective. At the heart of each alternative are the following basic issues:

1. Will the buyer be acquiring stock or assets of the target?
2. In what form will the consideration from the buyer to the seller be made (e.g., cash, notes, securities)?
3. Will the purchase price be fixed, contingent, or payable on an installment basis?
4. What are the tax consequences of the proposed structure for the acquisition?

Stock Versus Asset Purchases

Perhaps the most fundamental issue in structuring an acquisition is whether the transaction will take the form of an asset or stock purchase. Each form has advantages and disadvantages:

Advantages of a Stock Purchase

- The business identity, licenses, and permits of the target can usually be preserved.
- The continuity of the target's corporate identity, contracts, and structure can be retained.

Disadvantages of a Stock Purchase

- There is less flexibility to cherry-pick key assets of seller.

- The buyer may be liable for unknown, undisclosed, or contingent liabilities (unless it is adequately protected in the purchase agreement).
- The buyer will be forced to contend with the seller's minority shareholders unless it purchases all shares of the company.
- The offer and sale of the securities may need to be registered under federal or state securities laws.

Advantages of an Asset Acquisition

- The buyer can be selective as to which assets of the target to purchase.
- The buyer is generally not liable for the seller's liabilities unless specifically assumed under contract.

Disadvantages of an Asset Acquisition

- The bill of sale must be comprehensive, with exhibits attached, to ensure that no key assets are overlooked and as a result are not transferred to the buyer.
- A variety of third-party consents, from such parties as a franchisor, lender, or lessor, will typically be required to transfer key tangible and intangible assets to the purchaser.
- The seller will be responsible for liquidating the remaining corporate shell and distributing the proceeds of the assets sale to its shareholders, which may result in a double taxation unless an alternative election is made under federal tax laws.
- The buyer must comply with applicable state bulk sales statutes, as well as pay state and local sales and transfer taxes.

Overview of the Tax Aspects of the Acquisition

The Tax Reform Act of 1986 (TRA), as well as the Revenue Act of 1987, have played a significant role in how corporate acquisitions are structured. An experienced tax accountant must serve as a key member of the acquisition team to ensure that the tax consequences of the transaction are carefully considered.

Most corporate acquisitions will be deemed to be taxable transactions under TRA if they are structured as a purchase of stock or assets in exchange for cash, promissory notes, or other forms of consideration. Nontaxable transactions usually fall more into the category of a merger in that they involve an exchange of the target company's stock or assets for the purchaser's or its subsidiary's equity securities, coupled with some direct or indirect continuing relationship between the buyer and the seller and their respective shareholders. These nontaxable transactions must fall within one of several reorganization categories contained in TRA § 368. Among the more important aspects of the TRA to consider in structuring acquisitions are the following:

1. The restructuring of individual and corporate tax rates
2. Repeal of the favorable treatment for capital gains
3. Special restrictions pertaining to the allocation of the purchase price by the buyer and the seller in an asset acquisition*
4. Repeal of the general utilities doctrine†

Taxable Versus Tax-Free Transactions

In most acquisitions, the tax benefits to a buyer result in a detriment to the seller, and vice versa, thereby creating conflicting objectives regarding the structure of the transaction. For example, a seller may want to defer its current tax liabilities by structuring the transaction as a tax-free reorganization; the gain it realizes upon the sale of the business is generally not recognized until the seller disposes of the securities issued to it by the buyer. In contrast, the buyer may prefer the tax benefits it enjoys from a taxable acquisition: that the tax basis in the stock or assets acquired is stepped up to the fair market value of the consideration paid, resulting in a wide variety of expenses that may be amortized. Similarly, the buyer may prefer a taxable transaction where the consideration is cash or promissory notes in order to prevent a dilution in the ownership of its common stock.

If the parties choose to structure the transaction as a tax-free reorganization, they have three principal forms set forth under the Internal Revenue Code to consider: Type A Statutory Merger, Type B Stock-for-Stock Merger, and Type C Stock-for-Assets Merger.

1. *Type A Statutory Merger.* A Type A reorganization is a statutory merger or consolidation under state law. No express limitations are imposed on the

---

*Prior to 1986, a seller and a purchaser could independently negotiate an allocation of the purchase price to the assets being acquired. Negotiations focused on how much of the purchase price would be attributed to capital assets such as goodwill—preferred by the seller—and how much to depreciable assets—preferred by the buyer. TRA provides a specific statutory formula under the residual method of allocation found in § 338.

†Prior to 1986, there was no double tax on gains in connection with liquidating distributions, except for recapture taxes and limited related items, so that in an asset acquisition, a seller could distribute the cash and other consideration received for its assets directly to its shareholders, who would then be responsible for taxes only at the personal level. Under TRA, the general utilities doctrine was repealed, and as a result there is recognition of gain or loss at both the corporate level and the shareholder level on liquidating distributions or sales.

type of consideration that can be used in the transaction or on the disposition of assets prior to the merger. This is a flexible acquisition device that permits shareholders to receive property, including cash, in addition to stock of the acquiring corporation.

2. *Type B Stock-for-Stock Merger.* Type B reorganizations are an acquisition by one corporation in exchange solely for all or part of the voting stock (or in exchange solely for all or part of the voting stock of a corporation in control of the acquiring corporation) of another corporation if, immediately after the acquisition, the acquiring corporation has control (at least 80 percent of the total combined with power of all classes of stock and at least 80 percent of the total number of shares of all other classes of stock) of such other corporation (whether or not the acquiring corporation had control immediately before the acquisition). A purchase of stock for cash within one year preceding the B exchange may destroy the tax-free nature of the exchange. Counsel to the acquiring company must be made aware of any cash payment such as a finder's fee or the payment of appraisal rights to dissenting shareholders.

3. *Type C Stock-for-Assets Merger.* Type C reorganizations are an acquisition by one corporation, in exchange solely for all or part of its voting stock (or in exchange solely for all or part of the voting stock of a corporation in control of the acquiring corporation), of substantially all of the properties of another corporation. The transferor corporation must distribute the stock, securities, and other properties its receives from the acquiring corporation, as well as any retained assets, as part of the plan of reorganization.

The tax aspects of the proposed transaction are among the most important issues the acquisition team must address. Because these laws are complex and constantly changing, knowledgeable advisers should be consulted.

Federal Securities Laws and Acquisitions

Mergers and acquisitions among small and growing privately held companies do not generally raise many issues or filing requirements under the federal securities laws. But if either or both of the parties to the transaction have registered their securities under the Securities Act of 1933, a host of reporting obligations is triggered. Growing companies should be aware of the following general requirements, which they should review carefully with legal counsel:

1. *10-Q and 10-K Reports.* A discussion of the acquisition may need to be included in either or both of the acquiring company's and the target's quar-

terly and annual filings with the Securities and Exchange Commission
(SEC). The acquiring company will usually be obligated to include the
information in its scheduled reports (or make an 8-K filing as the case may
be) if the acquisition is deemed to be "significant," typically defined as one
where the target's assets or pretax income exceeds 10 percent of the acquiring company's assets or pretax income.

2. *Registration Statements.* If the acquiring company plans to issue new securities as part of the consideration to be given to shareholders of the
target, it may need to file a registration statement with the SEC.

3. *Proxy Information.* If the proposed transaction must be approved by the
shareholders of either the acquiring company or the target, it is essential
that the SEC's special proxy rules and regulations be followed very carefully.

4. *Tender Offers.* When a growing company elects to make a tender offer
directly to the shareholders of the target rather than negotiating through
management, antifraud regulations set forth in the Williams Act, administered by the SEC, must be carefully followed. The Williams Act consists
of the federal securities laws that regulate tender offers. Its regulations
include the filing of the SEC's Schedule 13D whenever the purchaser becomes the beneficial owner of more than 5 percent of the target's equity
securities.

Corporate Authorization and Consent

The extent to which the directors and shareholders of both buyer and seller will
be required to authorize or consent to the proposed acquisition will depend on
applicable state corporate law and the specific provisions of each company's
charter and bylaws.

Generally an acquisition of all or substantially all of the target's assets requires
the approval of a specified percentage of the shareholders and the directors of
the target. The acquiring company usually needs only a resolution of its board
of directors to accomplish the asset purchase.

The rights of the minority shareholders of the target should be carefully considered; in most states, shareholders are granted a statutory right of dissent and
appraisal in connection with the disposition of substantially all of the assets of
the corporation not in the ordinary course of business. Similarly, in transactions
where the two parties are not dealing at arm's length or if the acquisition is
designed to freeze out a particular minority shareholder, the acquisition team
must consider legal challenges to the transaction under theories of self-dealing
or fraud.

Preparation of the Definitive Legal Documents

Once the due diligence has been completed, valuations and appraisals conducted, terms and price initially negotiated, and financing arranged, the acquisition team and legal counsel structure and begin preparing the definitive legal documentation for the transaction. The drafting and negotiation of these documents usually focuses on the nature and scope of the seller's representations and warranties, the terms of the seller's indemnification to the buyer, the conditions precedent to closing of the transaction, the responsibilities of the parties between the execution of the purchase agreement and the actual closing, the terms of payment of the purchase price, the scope of postclosing covenants of noncompetition, and any predetermined remedies for breach of the covenants, representations, or warranties.

Preliminary Legal Matters

Following the execution of a Letter of Intent or Memorandum of Understanding and well before the due diligence begins, one of the first responsibilities of purchaser's legal counsel is to prepare a comprehensive Schedule of Activities. The primary purpose of the Schedule is to outline all of the events that must occur and the documents that must be prepared prior to the closing and beyond. The purchaser's legal counsel assigns primary areas of responsibility to the various members of the acquisition team, as well as to the seller and its counsel. Once all tasks have been identified and assigned and a realistic timetable has been established for completion, a closing time and date can be preliminarily determined.

The list of legal documents that must be prepared and the specific tasks to be outlined in the Schedule vary from transaction to transaction, usually depending on the specific facts and circumstances of each deal, such as whether the transaction is a stock or asset purchase, the form and terms of the purchase price, the nature of the business being acquired, the nature and extent of the assets being purchased and/or liabilities being assumed, and the sophistication of the parties and their respective legal counsel.

Assume for the balance of this chapter that Growth Co. Corp. (GCC) has identified Target Co., Inc. (TCI), a closely held manufacturer, as an acquisition candidate but is concerned about unknown or contingent liabilities stemming from TCI's uncertain past. A Memorandum of Understanding is negotiated by the parties by which GCC will acquire substantially all of the assets of TCI for $3.5 million. The financing arranged by GCC will come from the following sources:*

*This financing structure may be more complex than the typical asset acquisition at this level; how-

1. $500,000 from retained earnings of GCC;
2. $1.5 million in debt financing provided by Business Bank Corp. (BBC), which will be secured by the assets being acquired; and
3. $1.5 million in seller's takeback financing by TCI, payable as follows:
   $750,000 secured five-year promissory note
   $250,000 warrants to purchase shares of common stock in Growth Co. Subsidiary, Inc. (GCS), (a new subsidiary established by GCC to manage and operate the assets being acquired)
   $250,000 earnout over five years based on GCS's financial performance
   $250,000 assumption of TCI liabilities by GCS

Based upon the structure discussed above, a number of legal documents must be prepared and negotiated (see Exhibit 12-1). Exhibit 12-1 lists 26 sample documents; however, different transactions will require different types of protection.

Had the transaction been structured as a stock purchase rather than an asset transaction, TCI shareholders would also have to produce duly endorsed stock certificates, current corporate financial statements, certified copies of the corporate financial statements, certified copies of the corporate articles and bylaws, certificates of good standing, officer and director release, termination and resignation agreements, termination of personnel and retirement plans (where applicable), and all other material corporate documentation at the closing.

Negotiating the Documents

The acquisition team must understand the key points to be negotiated in the primary documents in the transaction.

1. *Asset purchase agreement.* At the heart of any acquisition is the asset or stock purchase agreement. All other documents in the transaction flow from it. There are several key components and issues in the purchase agreement:

   a. *Indemnification.* Among the most contested areas are the indemnification provisions, usually because the purchaser wants to be reimbursed for any transaction or occurrence that took place before closing that subsequently gives rise to some claim or liability. The seller, on the other hand, wants to make a clean break from the company, including any responsibility for events that arose even before closing.

   b. *Representations and warranties.* The seller is expected to make a wide range of written and binding representations and warranties to the buyer

---

ever, it is designed to provide readers with examples of the alternative methods of structuring such an acquisition.

Exhibit 12-1. Acquisition documentation.

- Asset Purchase Agreement (among GCC, GCS, and TCI)
- Intercreditor Agreement (between BBC and TCI)
- Loan Agreement (among BBC, GCC, and GCS)
- Promissory Note, Security Agreement, and Financing Statements (for BBC loan)
- Promissory Note, Security Agreement, and Financing Statements (for TCI takeback financing)
- Board of Directors' and Shareholders' Resolutions of TCI approving the transaction
- Board of Directors' Resolutions of GCC and GCS approving the transaction
- Warrants to Purchase GCS Common Stock (for TCI shareholders)
- Assumption of Liabilities Agreement (also known as a "Liabilities Undertaking" by GCS to TCI; in addition, TCI may want to obtain estoppel certificates or novation agreements from creditors covered by this agreement)
- Bill of Sale (for TCI assets sold to GCC and GCS)
- Bulk Sales Affidavits (if applicable under Article 6 of the state commercial code) (from TCI to its creditors)
- Disclosure Documents to TCI shareholders for issuance of GCS Warrants (if required by federal or state securities laws)
- Noncompetition and Nondisclosure Agreements (for TCI management team to GCC and GCS)
- Employment or Consulting Agreements (to the extent that any of TCI's employees will be hired to manage GCS)
- Assignment of Key Contracts and Third-Party Consent Agreements (e.g., Leases or Loan Agreements) (from TCI to GCS)
- Opinion of TCI Counsel (to GCC and GCS)
- Lien Search Reports on TCI Assets
- Certificates of Compliance with representations, warranties, and conditions precedent by TCI president and secretary
- Earnout Agreement (may be included in main body of Asset Purchase Agreement or be separate)
- Indemnification Agreement (may be included in main body of Asset Purchase Agreement or be separate) (*continued*)

Exhibit 12-1. (continued).

- Escrow Agreement (if negotiated) (proceeds of sale price to be placed in escrow until certain postclosing conditions are met and postclosing adjustments are made by TCI or as a contingency reserve fund in the event that representations and warranties are subsequently found to be untrue)
- Resignation and Release Agreements (from TCI employees who will not be retained after the transaction)
- Personal Guarantees (by key shareholders of GCC if demanded by BBC or TCI to secure the Promissory Notes)
- License Agreements (if any, to the extent that intellectual property rights are being retained by TCI and exclusively licensed by GCS)
- Allocation Certificates for federal, state, and local tax filings (as well as Uniform Commercial Code filings where applicable)
- List of Schedules and Exhibits to the Asset Purchase Agreement (to be compiled and prepared by TCI and its counsel)

---

in connection with the acquisition: that the sale is not in breach of any other agreement or obligation of the seller, that the assets are free and clear of all liens and encumbrances, that the assets are in good operating condition, that all material facts have been disclosed, and so forth. The buyer wants the scope of these representations and warranties to be as broad and comprehensive as possible, primarily because these clauses serve as a form of an insurance policy for the buyer. It will be incumbent on the seller and its counsel to negotiate limitations on the scope of these provisions where necessary.

c. *Conditions precedent to closing.* This section is essentially a checklist of events that must occur as a condition to closing the transaction. Both buyer and seller will have items that must be accomplished and documents or consents that must be signed. The nature and scope of these conditions must be carefully considered. Failure to satisfy these conditions will give the opposing party the right to walk away from the transaction.

d. *Conduct of business prior to closing.* The seller must have a contractual obligation to preserve the goodwill of the business and condition of the assets during the time between execution of the purchase agreement and closing of the transaction. The parties should negotiate all affirmative and negative covenants that will be imposed on the conduct of the seller during this time, as well as the penalties for noncompliance (e.g., reduction of purchase price, ability to walk away from deal by purchaser).

2. *Intercreditor agreement*. An intercreditor agreement is a contract among multiple lenders (in this case, TCI and BBC) and a particular borrower (GCC and GCS). The document governs the priority rights of the various lenders in the collateral (the assets acquired by GCC and GCS), otherwise known as *subordination*. Subordination and standby provisions govern "who gets what proceeds when" in the event of a default by the borrower. In the GCC-TCI transaction, it is likely that BBC and its counsel will prepare this agreement and demand that BBC receive the senior priority rights.

3. *Noncompetition agreements*. Covenants against competition and disclosure of confidential information are commonly a key part of any business acquisition. This is especially true in situations like the GCC-TCI transaction where the management team of the target may be left out of the transaction and its members are therefore likely candidates to be future competitors. Counsel to the purchaser will want to include covenants that are broad in terms of the scope of subject matter, duration, and geographic territory. Although these agreements will be carefully scrutinized by the courts as potential restraints of trade, agreements prohibiting sellers from competing against buyers in a business purchase transaction are given considerably more latitude than in other agreements, such as employment or consulting agreements.

4. *Earnout agreements*. When earnout agreements are negotiated as part of the purchase price in an acquisition agreement, part of the consideration payable to the seller essentially becomes contingent on the ability of the buyer to meet its financial and growth projections. In the example, TCI shareholders are betting on the ability of the GCS management team to manage and operate the assets being acquired efficiently and profitably. If any of the TCI shareholders will become members of the GCS management team, the earnout provides an incentive for performance from which both GCC and TCI can gain. The key terms of the earnout agreement negotiated are the type of earnout and the formula to be used (e.g., tied to gross sales, earnings), the duration of the earnout, the floor and ceiling on the payout to be provided to TCI shareholders, the controls that TCI shareholders will have, if any, over the budgets and expenditures made by GCS or GCC, the effect of business distress or bankruptcy of GCS on the earnout, and the tax implications of the transaction.

Many of the other documents involved in a typical acquisition have been discussed in earlier chapters of this book. For example, chapter 7 provides the appropriate information if a private placement memorandum needs to be prepared as a result of the warrants issued to TCI shareholders, and chapter 9, "Debt Financing for Growing Companies," discusses the loan documents that GCC and GCS will be expected to sign in connection with the financing provided by BBC.

Postclosing Matters

A wide variety of legal and administrative tasks must be accomplished by the acquisition team and its counsel following the closing in order to complete the transaction. The nature and extent of these tasks vary depending on the size and type of financing selected by the purchaser. (The parties to any acquisition must be careful to ensure that the pure jubilation of closing does not cause any postclosing matters to be overlooked.)

In an asset acquisition, these postclosing tasks might include a final verification that all assets acquired are free of liens and encumbrances; the recording of financing statements and transfer tax returns; the recording of any assignments of intellectual property with the Library of Congress or U.S. Patent and Trademark Office; notification of the sale to employees, customers, distributors, and suppliers; and adjustments to bank accounts and insurance policies. In a stock acquisition or merger, postclosing matters may encompass, in addition, filing articles of amendment to the corporate charter or articles of merger, completion of the transfer of all stock certificates, amendments to the corporate bylaws, and the preparation of all appropriate postclosing minutes and resolutions.

PART

III

Marketing

Academics and consultants whose professional lives are devoted to sales and marketing agree that inventing the best mousetrap in the world is of minimal economic value if you do not know who to sell it to and how to reach them once identified. Only recently have growing companies placed market research, market segmentation, nichemanship, and distribution strategy at the heart of their strategic planning priorities.

The development, marketing, and distribution of goods and services raises a host of legal issues that must be understood by the management teams of growing companies. At the core of product development is the initial and ongoing legal protection of the company's intellectual property (e.g., trademarks, patents, copyrights, and trade secrets). The forms of intellectual property are outlined in chapter 13. Various methods of distribution and growth of market share are discussed in chapter 14. Finally, chapter 15 examines the various legal aspects of the regulation of the marketing process.

PART

III

Marketing

Protecting Intellectual Property

The development and continued success of a growing company is dependent in part on its ability to invent and exploit new products and services, open up new distribution channels, foster new production and training techniques, implement new promotional and marketing campaigns, establish new pricing methods, and adapt to changes in competition, consumer preferences, or demographic trends. The culmination of this research and development will often result in a continuing flow of intellectual property—patents, trade names, and so on—which owners and managers of fast-growing companies must adequately protect. The ability to identify, develop, and protect intellectual property rights generally helps the emerging-growth company achieve the following growth objectives:

1. Improves the ability to raise capital and the overall value and rate of growth of the company by increasing its intangible assets, as well as protecting the time, effort, and cost of developing these assets.

2. Creates competitive advantages and barriers to entry for current and potential competitors as the result of having exclusive ownership of key assets needed in the marketplace.

3. Assists management in understanding the intellectual property rights of other firms in the marketplace, necessary in order to avoid being the defendant in a civil action for infringement, misappropriation, or unfair competition.

4. Creates licensing opportunities and additional revenue sources for the company (e.g., under which the rights to exploit the intellectual property developed by the company will be licensed to third parties in exchange for an initial fee and ongoing royalties).

5. Builds consumer goodwill and brand loyalty to the company's protected trade identity and proprietary names for its products and services, which also prevents competitors from misrepresenting the source of production to consumers.

6. Provides growing companies with the maximum ability to control the de-velopment and ownership of the ideas and inventions of their employees.

The development and protection of intellectual property plays a key role in building a foundation for fostering growth. If the emerging-growth company does not protect its new products, services, systems, methods, distribution chan-nels, or operational techniques, it will have difficulty maintaining and expanding its market share because competitors will be free to copy these ideas and inven-tions.

Types of Intellectual Property

Patents

A *patent* is a grant by the federal government to the inventor of the right to exclude third parties from making, using, or selling the subject matter of the invention throughout the United States for a limited period of time. Most patents granted by the U.S. Patent and Trademark Office (USPTO) are for utility patents (issued for the protection of new, useful, and nonobvious processes, machines, compositions of matter, and articles of manufacture for a period of 17 years from the date the patent is actually issued). Also issued are design patents (issued for new, original, ornamental, and nonobvious designs for articles of manufacture) for a period of 14 years from the date of issuance and, less frequently, plant patents (issued for certain new varieties of plants that have been asexually repro-duced), which have a term of 17 years.

Trademarks, Service Marks, and Trade Names

A *trademark* is defined by the Lanham Act of 1946 as any word, name, sym-bol, or device adopted and used by a manufacturer or merchant to identify and distinguish its goods from those manufactured or sold by others and to indicate the source of the goods.

A *service mark* serves similar purposes but is generally used in connection with the advertising and marketing of services rather than products. A *trade name* is the name that a business or other organization has selected to identify itself as a distinct entity. Although certain companies use their trade name as a trademark or service mark, these two types of intellectual property must be viewed in a separate fashion. Most important, it is not necessarily the case that just because the company has been offering its goods or services pursuant to a particular company name that such name has acquired any trademark or service mark rights under federal or state law.

Copyrights

A *copyright* is a form of protection available to the author of original "literary, dramatic, musical, artistic and certain other intellectual works which are fixed in any tangible medium of expression." The owner of a copyright generally has the exclusive right to do or authorize others to do the following: reproduce the copyrighted work, prepare derivative works, distribute copies of the work, and perform or display the copyrighted work.

Trade Secrets

A *trade secret* may consist of any type of information a company uses to provide it with an advantage over competitors and that it treats as confidential and proprietary. The scope of protection available for trade secrets may be defined by a particular contract or fiduciary relationship, as well as by state statutes and court decisions.

Show-How and Know-How

Certain types of intellectual property are treated as such primarily because some third party is willing to buy or license them from a company or individual possessing a particular expertise. *Show-how* consists of technical support and related educational services, such as the nonwritten portions of a specific training program. *Know-how* usually takes the form of information that has been reduced to writing rather than spoken form, such as instructions for the use of a particular tool or machine.

Know-how and show-how usually arise in the context of a licensing agreement where the licensee is requesting support services in addition to the rights to the tangible technology or patent. To the extent that the know-how or show-how is confidential and proprietary, it will generally be governed by the law of trade secrets unless otherwise covered by a patent. To the extent that the know-how or show-how is nonproprietary and constitutes common knowledge, it will be governed by the term and conditions of the agreement between the parties.

Ideas and Concepts

Generally a mere idea or concept does not qualify for patent, copyright, trade secret, or trademark protection. The right to the exclusive use of an idea is generally lost by voluntary disclosure unless three elements are present: the idea is in a concrete form, the idea is original and useful, and the idea is disclosed in a situation where compensation is contemplated. If this test is satisfied, the idea may qualify as a "property right" and may be protected under theories of implied contract, unjust enrichment, misappropriation, breach of a fiduciary relationship, or passing off. Recovery under these circumstances usually will depend on the relationship between the idea submitter and the idea receiver, as well as the facts surrounding the disclosure.

Registration, Ownership, and Protection of Intellectual Property

Owners and managers of growing companies must establish a formal intellectual property protection and compliance program. Each type of intellectual property raises its own set of legal and management issues and tasks.

Patents

The first step in determining whether to protect a new product or invention with a patent is to understand the costs and benefits of patent protection. The patent application and registration process generally takes four to six years and is costly. An emerging-growth company with a new invention must first determine whether the benefits of excluding others from the manufacturing, distribution, or exploitation of the invention far outweigh the high costs of prosecution and protection of the patent (for example, attorney's fees alone in an average patent infringement civil suit could cost hundreds of thousands of dollars)—see Exhibit 13-1.

Timing is a key issue in determining whether to pursue a patent. Changes in the marketplace, economy, or state-of-the-art technology may occur while the patent is pending, after issuance, or after expiration. The timing issue is complicated by the statutory requirement that the application for a patent must be filed with the USPTO within one year of the public use or publication of the invention. Thus, there are significant limitations on the level of market research or testing that a company may conduct in connection with its evaluation of whether to apply for patent protection.

One of the examples from chapter 1 will be used to examine the steps that should be taken to file a patent application. Assume that the manufacturing of the BagDough product required a proprietary piece of bakery equipment that Eatalot had developed for Sweet-Tooth. Any franchisee or licensee of Sweet-Tooth that produced BagDough at its retail site would need this equipment. As a result, the management team determined that patent protection would be a worthwhile allocation of resources. Before Sweet-Tooth instructs its patent counsel to prepare the documents for filing with the USPTO, certain preliminary matters must be addressed.

First, Sweet-Tooth must compile and maintain records relating to the research

Exhibit 13-1. Strategic issues to consider prior to applying for a patent.

1. What is the projected commercial value of the invention?
2. What are the projected out-of-pocket expenses incurred to register the patent with the USPTO? In addition to legal fees, what advertising, marketing, or even retooling expenses will be incurred?
3. How close (from both an infringement and commercial exploitation perspective) is the subject matter of the invention to existing patented and nonpatented technology (current knowledge relating to an invention or discovery is generally known as the prior art)?
4. What are the costs and risks of choosing not to file for the patent? Is adequate protection available under state trade secret laws? To what extent do the business plans of the company call for exploiting the technology before the patent is issued?
5. What existing domestic and international patents directly or indirectly affect the subject matter of this invention? (A patent search is strongly recommended prior to filing any application.)
6. How will the subject matter of the invention be manufactured, distributed, and exploited in the marketplace? What is the anticipated market demand? If the technology will be licensed or sold, to what extent would the existence of a patent affect the price to be paid by the buyer or licensee? To what extent will the existence of the patent be an effective deterrent against competition and imitations? What other barriers to entry exist in lieu of a patent?
7. Can the subject matter of the invention be exploited within the time frame granted by the federal statute? Alternatively, will the market value of the technology or invention be lost during the three to six years that it takes to obtain a patent?
8. How difficult will the patent be to protect? How easily could a competitor create a similar invention or device without infringing on the claims made in the patent?
9. To what extent has the subject matter of the patent already been disclosed to the public? Has the statutory period expired for applying for a patent prior to such disclosure?

and testing of the special equipment. These records must contain certain key dates, such as the date that the invention was conceived and the date that it was actually or constructively reduced to practice. In this context, *reduction to practice* means that the invention is well beyond the conceptual phase; the equipment has been developed and tested or is described so clearly in the application that a third party skilled in the particular art could understand and develop the technology. The extent to which the invention must satisfy its exact intended purpose will vary, depending on the complexity of the technology involved. The records should also demonstrate that Sweet-Tooth was diligent in developing and testing the subject matter of the invention. Finally, the records should contain the corroboration of independent witnesses who are capable of understanding the nature and scope of the invention and can verify dates of conception, the actual or constructive reduction to practice, and the continued diligence of the inventor. These documents, records, and witness statements will be crucial during the initial prosecution of the patent, as well as in any subsequent proceeding regarding the scope of patent protection or the priority to be assigned to competing inventors who may be claiming patent rights in similar subject matter.

Sweet-Tooth next conducts a search at the USPTO Public Search Room in Arlington, Virginia. This step will reveal the nature and extent of the available prior art and will provide the basis for the scope of the claims that will be made in the patent application. Since the application must describe how the potential patentable subject matter differs from existing techniques, technologies, processes, or structures, the search will be especially useful in determining and describing the prior art.

Because a patent application is a complicated process, a qualified patent attorney should be retained. The application is made up of several distinct parts, among them a clear and concise description of the invention, a sworn statement by Sweet-Tooth declaring itself to be the original and sole inventor of the claimed subject matter, technical drawings (where necessary) of the invention, the prescribed filing fees, and one or more of the claims of exclusivity that Sweet-Tooth seeks to be granted.

The claims are the most important part of the application. They define the boundaries of the exclusive rights that will be granted to the inventor during the term of the patent. If the claims are drafted too narrowly, imitators and competitors will be able to develop similar technologies without worrying about infringement. If they are drafted too broadly, the USPTO may reject the patent or the courts may declare it invalid in a subsequent proceeding when and if the validity of the patent is challenged by a competitor.

When the USPTO receives the application, it examines the documents to ensure that all initial statutory filing requirements have been satisfied. If the application is in order, the USPTO assigns it a serial number and filing date, which will determine the priority to be accorded to the application as it is processed by the designated patent examiner. If the application is deficient, it will be returned to Sweet-Tooth's counsel without the serial number, unless the defect is minor.

The review and ultimate determination of the patentability of the invention depend on Sweet-Tooth's ability to demonstrate to the examiner that the following statutory requirements have been satisfied:

1. The invention constitutes patentable subject matter (e.g., process, machine, composition of matter, article of manufacture, or some new and useful improvement thereof).

2. Sweet-Tooth is the original inventor or discoverer of the subject matter of the technology described in the application.

3. The subject matter must be novel or new. It is not patentable if it is already known or used by others and already covered by another patent; is merely a new use of an existing product or technology; or if the subject matter has already been described in a printed publication. (Patents will not be awarded for inventions that are already part of the public knowledge or to applicants who prematurely exploit their technology.)

4. The subject matter of the invention is useful and not merely of scientific or philosophical interest.

5. The subject matter of the invention is nonobvious to one ordinarily skilled in the art. In other words, a patent may not be obtained for an invention if the difference between the subject matter sought to be patented and the current scope and content of the prior art is nominal or would be obvious to others in that particular trade or industry.

Once the patent has been issued, Sweet-Tooth's owners and managers must embark on an aggressive patent protection program. They must use proper notices and labeling of the registered patent for the product; monitor the developments in the industry; police the activities of licensees, employees, and others who came into contact with the patented machine or technology; exploit the marketplace created by the patented product; and aggressively pursue known or suspected infringers of the patent.

Although the costs of patent litigation may be high, the rewards of stopping an infringer are also very worthwhile. Damages and equitable remedies (such as injunctions or an accounting for profits) are available, and the federal patent law allows a court to triple the damages for extraordinary cases (also known as treble damages).

Trademarks and Trade Names

A trademark or service mark is a word, name, symbol, or device used to indicate the origin, quality, and ownership of products and services. To be afforded federal protection, a trademark or service mark must be used in interstate commerce, or the owner must have a bona fide intention to use the mark in connection with the product or service. Not all words and symbols are eligible for trademark protection. For example, a chain of stores that repair transmissions under the name Transmission Repair Shop could not get a service mark because its name is too generic, yet AAMCO is a nationally known mark for the same services. A properly selected, registered, and protected trademark can be of great utility to a growing company fighting to establish, maintain, and expand its market share (see Exhibit 13-2). There is perhaps no better way to maintain a strong position in the marketplace than to build goodwill and consumer recognition in the identity selected for products and services that can be protected under federal and state trademark laws.

Recall that Sweet-Tooth Bakery Products Company has decided to call its latest product "BagDough." This word by itself means nothing until it is introduced to the consumer as a bakery product combining the qualities and taste of a doughnut and a bagel. To protect and defend the name it has selected for its new proprietary line of products, Sweet-Tooth first should have a trademark search conducted to determine whether a competitor already has secured rights in this trade name or any similar name for the same or a related type of product. Perhaps one of the most important benefits to be gained from federal registration is that it serves as notice that the trademark belongs to the registrant. This becomes an important right if it is later discovered that a remote company in a different geographic market has subsequently decided to sell competing products under the registrant's marks, damaging goodwill and creating confusion when the registrant enters that local market. So long as a registration predates another's use of the mark, the registrant has the right to demand that others discontinue use of the mark, as well as the right to institute a civil action for damages and even lost profits. It is important to note, however, that because common-law trademark rights are still grounded in actual and prior use, even federal registration does not give a registrant a right to stop others who used the same mark in their local markets prior to the registrant's application.

From a marketing and distribution perspective, a trademark serves several distinct functions:

Exhibit 13-2.   Issues to consider when selecting a trademark.

- Nature of the product or service
- Purchasing habits of target consumers
- Difficulty of recognition and pronunciation (keep it short and easy to read if possible)
- Trademarks already used or registered by competitors and others
- Avoiding misdescriptive, egotistical, trendy, or laudatory claims
- Anticipated size of promotional budget
- Adaptability to various applications and media

1. It serves an identifying function by indicating the origin of the goods, distinguishing an individual manufacturer's goods from those of its competitors.

2. It provides a guarantee of quality and consistency. It assures the consumer that the products and services purchased today are of the same quality as any purchased previously.

3. It serves as an advertising device for the commercial exploitation of the goods and services.

The promotional function is perhaps the most easily understood yet most troublesome area of trademark usage. Manufacturers often invest great sums in the advertising and promotion of a particular mark in the hope of building goodwill and consumer recognition. Yet if the manufacturer is too successful, it can lose its trademark rights if the word falls into the vernacular due to misuse and overuse, such as the term *escalator*, which was once a registered trademark for mechanical steps.

The trademark is the consumer's first impression of the nature and quality of the product or service. Some companies select a mark that the public can understand easily. In this regard, the trademark serves as a compressed advertisement (such as "Great-Tasting Chicken"), which may please the advertising staff, but such a mark would be very difficult to register because it is often descriptive in nature. On the other end of the spectrum, coined words such as Kodak or arbitrary marks such as Camel for cigarettes independently mean nothing to a consumer until the manufacturer invests the promotional dollars to establish customer understanding and brand recognition. Growth companies ready to launch a new product or service should generally resist the temptation to select a trademark that is too descriptive. The costs of establishing that the mark has special or secondary meaning to the public (regardless of its descriptive nature) can be very high.

The selection of a trademark or a service mark generally falls into one of the following four categories, which will directly affect the ability of the growing company to register and protect the mark selected:

1. *Arbitrary or Fanciful.* The trademark is either a coined word, such as Xerox, or a word in common usage that has no meaning when applied to the goods and services in question, such as Dove for dish detergent or body soap. Such marks are the easiest to register and protect and are inherently distinctive for legal and registration purposes; however, because of the obscurity of the mark, the burden is on the manufacturer to establish goodwill.

2. *Suggestive.* A suggestive mark requires the consumer to use some imagination in determining what product or service is identified by the mark and as such is the next strongest category of mark that may be protected. Owners of suggestive trademarks are usually not required to establish second-

ary meaning (see below). Examples of suggestive marks are Seven-Up and Orange Crush, which merely suggest that they identify refreshing beverages.

3. *Descriptive*. Trademarks that describe the goods or services they identify cannot be protected unless the manufacturer can establish distinctiveness by demonstrating that the public associates this particular mark with the goods of the specific producer (known as secondary meaning). This category includes names like Holiday Inn, which is descriptive but nevertheless registered because it is distinctive and has established a secondary meaning.

4. *Generic*. Generic trademarks belong to everyone and may never be protected. A baker could never get a trademark for a product called Bread, or a handyman for his store called Hardware Store.

The rights of a growing company to a registered trademark arise from the *continued use of the mark to identify the origin of goods and services*. So long as the owner of the trademark continues such actual use, the rights may go on forever, provided that the proper documents are filed with the USPTO to renew the registration.

The Registration Process

Prior to the passage of the Trademark Law Revision Act of 1988, eligibility for the federal registration of a trademark arose only if the mark had been actually used in interstate commerce. This requirement was different from most other countries, which generally allow a company to register a mark even if no actual use had been established. To the growing business owner, this meant that a substantial amount of time and expense might be invested in a proposed trade identity for a new product or service, with virtually no assurance that the mark could ever be properly registered and protected.

Under the new law, a company may apply to file for registration of a trademark based on actual use or upon a bona fide intention to use the mark in interstate commerce. This allows the applicant to conduct some market research and further investigation without the need to put the mark into the stream of commerce as a prerequisite to obtaining federal protection.

The USPTO is developing guidelines for registration under the new intent-to-use provisions, with the following procedure contemplated:

1. The company files application for registration, which is subject to all of the current tests for registrability (e.g., likelihood of confusion, descriptiveness), except for proof of use in interstate commerce and the requirement for actual specimens of the mark.

2. If the application is approved by the examiner, a Notice of Allowance will be issued to the applicant.

3. The applicant then has six months to file a Statement of Use, with actual specimens attached. After the USPTO reviews the Statement of Use and specimens, the mark will be registered. An applicant may request time extensions for filing of the Statement of Use for up to four successive six-month periods. Failure to file by this deadline will result in an abandonment.

Regardless of whether the growing company files under the actual-use or intent-to-use provisions, an application must be prepared and filed, usually by an attorney, at the USPTO for the trademark in the appropriate classification. A trademark examiner will then review the application to determine if it meets the statutory requirements and whether similar trademarks have already been registered in the same or similar lines of business. The examiner usually enumerates his or her concerns in a formal Office Action. Then Sweet-Tooth's counsel must respond to all of the concerns.

This process continues until the examiner refuses the application or recommends it for publication in the *Official Gazette*, the publication that serves as notice to the general public. Any parties who believe that they would be injured by registration may file a Notice of Opposition within 30 days of the publication date. If the parties cannot resolve their differences, they will appear before the Trademark Trial and Appeal Board, which is also the appropriate body to appeal a final refusal of the examiner.

Registration is a complex and often lengthy process—anywhere from 12 to 18 months even if there are only minimal problems—but the commercial rewards may be substantial if the registered mark is properly used to provide the growing company with a competitive edge. A registration under the federal trademark laws, known as the Lanham Act, is effective for ten years but may be renewed for additional ten-year terms thereafter so long as it is still in actual use in interstate commerce. The registration may be cancelled after six years unless an affidavit of continued use is filed with the USPTO demonstrating that the registrant has not abandoned the trademark.

Enforcing Your Trademark Rights

When the battle with the USPTO is finally over, a new battle against the rest of the world begins.

Once the mark is registered, Sweet-Tooth's owners and managers must develop an active trademark protection program designed to educate company staff, consultants, distributors, suppliers, and all others who may come in contact with the company marks as to proper usage and protection of the marks. As with trade secret laws, the courts will usually help only those who have attempted to help themselves. A growing company that tolerates misuse of its marks by the public and/or fails to enforce quality control standards in any licensing of the mark may lose its trademark rights—and one of its most valuable weapons in the war for market share.

A well-managed trademark protection program begins with a formal Compliance Manual drafted with the assistance of trademark counsel and Sweet-Tooth's
advertising agency. This manual contains guidelines for proper trademark usage
and grammar—for example, "The trademark is correctly used only as a proper
adjective, and therefore it should always be capitalized and modify a noun" and
"The trademark should always be used in conjunction with the generic name of
the class of products to which it belongs."

In addition, strategies should be developed to monitor competitors and other
third parties for improper usage or potential infringement of the mark. A staff
member of Sweet-Tooth should be designated to read trade publications, business press, marketing materials of competitors, and in-house productions, labeling, and correspondence to ensure that the mark is properly used and not stolen
by competitors. If a clipping service, company field representative, franchisee,
trade association, or supplier discovers an infringing use, the owner must be
vigilant in protecting the mark by ensuring that all potential infringers receive
letters demanding that such practices be immediately discontinued and infringing materials destroyed. Sweet-Tooth must gather as much evidence as possible
on each potential infringer and keep accurate files in case trademark infringement litigation is necessary to settle the dispute.

A registrant considering litigation should carefully weigh the costs and likely
result of the suit against the potential loss of goodwill and market share. It may
be wiser to allocate those funds toward advertising rather than toward legal fees,
especially if the likelihood of infringement is remote.

Trademark Infringement and Dilution

The principal reason for a trademark monitoring program is to guard against
trademark infringement or dilution. Under the Lanham Act, infringement is a
demonstration by the owner of a registered mark that some third party is using
a reproduction or imitation of the registered mark in connection with the offer or
sale of goods and services in such a way as to be likely to cause confusion,
mistake, or deception from the perspective of the ordinary purchaser.

The exact definition of the "likelihood of confusion" standard has been the
source of much debate. The focus has always been on whether the ordinary
purchaser of the product in question is likely to be confused as to source of
origin or sponsorship. The courts have listed a wide variety of factors as criteria
for determining whether a likelihood of confusion exists. These include:

- The degree of similarity and resemblance of the infringer's marks to the
  registered marks (in terms of visual appearance, pronunciation, interpreta-
  tion, etc.)
- The strength of the registered mark in the relevant industry or territory
- The actual or constructive intent of the infringer
- The similarity of the goods or services offered by the infringer and the owner
  of the registered mark

- The overlap (if any) in the distribution and marketing channels of the infringer and the owner of the registered mark
- The extent to which the owner of the registered mark can demonstrate that consumers were actually confused (usually demonstrated with consumer surveys and affidavits)

In addition to a federal cause of action for trademark infringement, many state trademark statutes provide owners of registered marks with an antidilution remedy, which is available when a third party is using a mark in a manner that has the effect of diluting the distinctive quality of a mark registered under the state statute or used under common law. The owner of the registered mark and the diluting party need not be in competition, nor must a likelihood of confusion be demonstrated. In order for the owner to make a claim for dilution, the trademark must have a "distinctive quality," which means that it must enjoy strong consumer loyalty, recognition, and goodwill.

Trademark rights are often the most valuable asset of an emerging-growth company in today's competitive marketplace. The goodwill and consumer recognition that trademarks and service marks represent have tremendous economic value and are therefore usually worth the effort and expense to register and protect them.

Copyrights

Copyright law dates back to Elizabethan England when lawmakers had to grapple with the legal ramifications of a new invention, the printing press. The rights of authors of original works had to be protected, such that they could create, reproduce, and distribute the copyrighted work without others' infringing on their share of the literary market. The U.S. Constitution also recognized this important right and authorized Congress to create laws to "promote the Progress of Science and the Useful Arts, by securing for limited times to authors and inventors the exclusive right to their respective writings and discoveries."

Congress has struggled to keep up with the many modes of authorship that were not contemplated when the original copyright laws were written in 1790. Computers, photography, television, phonograph records, motion pictures, videodiscs, and advanced telecommunications have presented new challenges to legislators as to how to protect the rights of innovators and pioneers.

The latest major copyright laws revision was the 1976 Copyright Act. Under the new laws, a copyright is recognized and can be protected as soon as a literary or artistic work is created in any tangible medium of expression. This gives the copyright owner control over access to and publication of the work from the start. Copyright protection is available only to the person whose labor created the work (except in the case of a "work for hire"); however, it is also available for compilations (the assembly of preexisting materials) and derivative works (translations, re-creations, etc.).

A work for hire is essentially the exception to the general rule that the copyright in the work of authorship immediately becomes the property of the author who created the work. The Copyright Act defines a work for hire as being either a work prepared by an employee within the scope of his or her employment or a work ordered or commissioned if the parties expressly agree in a signed written instrument that the work shall be owned by a party other than the author as a work for hire. If the work has been previously prepared and not specially ordered or commissioned, then the written agreement should provide for an assignment of the copyright.

There are essentially two levels of copyright protection. The first level of protection is attained when the author places a copyright notice on the work when it is publicly distributed. The notice should include an encircled letter *c*, the name of the author, and the month or year when the work was first published. In most cases, this notice entitles the copyright owner to protection for the life of the author, plus 50 years. The owner of the copyright may then prohibit the unauthorized copying and distribution of the work by others. These rights can be a valuable tool in protecting market share, especially in service-oriented businesses, where training programs, recipes, operations manuals, and marketing materials may be the key documents that provide an edge over competitors.

At the second level, however, the author must register and deposit copies of the work in the Library of Congress depository in order to be able to enforce rights in court for copyright infringement. The Copyright Office examines the application for accuracy and to determine that the work submitted is copyrightable subject matter. The Copyright Office, unlike the USPTO, does not compare the works to those already registered, nor does it conduct interference or opposition proceedings. The copyright laws do provide remedies for private civil actions. Remedies for copyright infringement include injunctions against unauthorized use, attorney's fees, damages for lost profits, and certain statutory damages. These enforcement rights and remedies must be weighed against the fact that once a written work is registered, it may be viewed by the public, including competitors. Thus, it may make more sense to protect proprietary materials as trade secrets rather than expose them to the public through the Library of Congress.

A copyright generally is infringed by the unauthorized use or copying of the work; however, since it usually is difficult to prove copying, proof of "access" to the work and "substantial similarity" from the viewpoint of a reasonable person generally shifts to the alleged infringer the burden of proving that the work has been independently created. There are several limitations on the exclusive rights of a copyright owner, and there are several acts that are permissible without triggering an actionable remedy for infringement, such as use of the basic idea expressed in the work, the independent creation of an identical work without copying, and "fair use" of the work for purposes of criticism, comment, news reporting, teaching, scholarship, or research.

The federal copyright laws make willful copyright infringement for commercial profit a crime for which the court is required to order a fine of not more than $10,000, or imprisonment not exceeding one year, or both, as well as seizure, forfeiture, and destruction or other disposition of all infringing reproductions and all equipment used in their manufacture. The following civil remedies are among those also available to the holder of any exclusive rights in the copyrighted work under the federal law:

- An injunction against future infringement
- Impounding and destruction or other disposition of all infringing reproductions and articles used to make them
- The actual damages suffered by the copyright owner
- Any additional profits of the infringer
- Instead of actual damages and profits, at the copyright owner's election, statutory damages for all infringements of any one work from $250 to $10,000 (subject to reduction in some instances, or to increase to $50,000 for willful infringement)
- Full costs, including a reasonable attorney's fee

Trade Secrets

Owners and managers of growing companies whose success is due in part to the competitive advantage they enjoy by virtue of some confidential formula, method, design, or other type of proprietary know-how generally understand the importance of protecting trade secrets against unauthorized disclosure or use by a current or former employee, licensee, supplier, or competitor. Disclosure can cause severe and irreparable damage, especially to a smaller company where trade secrets may be the company's most valuable asset.

Courts have generally set forth three requirements for information to qualify for trade secret protection: The information must have some commercial value, the information must not be generally known or readily ascertainable by others, and the owner of the information must take all reasonable steps to maintain its confidentiality. Sweet-Tooth's recipe for the BagDough line of products falls within this definition. Other examples of trade secrets include business and strategic plans, research and testing data, customer lists, manufacturing processes, pricing methods, and marketing and distribution techniques. In order for Sweet-Tooth to maintain the status of the recipe as a trade secret, it must follow a reasonable and consistent program for ensuring that the confidentiality of the information is maintained.

There are many other factors, however, that courts have considered in deciding the extent to which protection should be afforded for trade secrets. Among those factors most often cited are

- The extent to which the information is known by others outside the company
- The measures employed inside the company to protect its secrets
- The value of the information, including the resources expended to develop the information
- The amount of effort required by others to duplicate the effort or reverse-engineer the technology
- The nature of the relationships between the alleged infringer and the owner of the trade secret

Smaller companies cannot generally afford a complicated security system to protect their trade secrets. With the mobile nature of today's work force, turnover caused by promotion within, and the openness and chaotic nature of most growing businesses, it is practically impossible to prevent a determined employee from gaining relatively easy access to the company's proprietary information. Often, and unfortunately, it is easier to ignore the problem. Nevertheless, there are some fundamental, affordable, and practical measures that growing companies can readily adopt to protect the data at the core of their competitive advantage.

Misappropriation of Trade Secrets

The first step in protecting trade secret rights is to establish a duty owed by those who come in contact with the information not to disclose or use the information in any way not in the best interest of the inventor. That duty must be breached before a cause of action will arise. The only exception to this rule is if wrongful misappropriation by improper means, such as theft or bribery, is established under applicable state criminal statutes.

The simplest way to create such a duty is by agreement. The owner of an emerging-growth business should have a written agreement with each employee who has access to the employer's trade secrets. The agreement should contain provisions regarding the nondisclosure of proprietary information, as well as covenants of nonexploitation and noncompetition applicable both during and after the term of employment. These covenants will be upheld and enforced by a court if they are reasonable, consistent with industry norms, and not overly restrictive.

Written agreements will go a long way toward proving to a court that the owner intended to and took reasonable steps to protect the trade secrets in the event of any subsequent litigation, but they are only the beginning of an ongoing program to make employees mindful of their continuing duty to protect their employer's trade secrets.

Employment is not the only context in which this duty of nondisclosure might arise. An entrepreneur submitting proposals or business plans to prospective investors, lenders, licensees, franchisees, joint venturers, lawyers, accountants, or other consultants should take steps to ensure confidentiality from the start of any such relationship where trade secrets may be disclosed in presentations, meetings, and documents.

The key elements of a cause of action for misappropriation of trade secrets are

1. *Existence* of a trade secret;
2. *Communication* to the defendant;
3. While defendant was in a *position of trust or confidence* (some duty not to disclose); and
4. Information constituting the trade secrets was *used* by defendant to the *injury of the plaintiff.*

In analyzing whether these essential elements are present, the court will consider the following factors:

1. Was there any relationship of trust and confidence by express agreement or implied that was breached?
2. How much time, value, money, and labor have been expended in developing the trade secret?
3. Had the trade secret reached the public domain? Through what channels?
4. Has the company maintained a conscious and continuing effort to maintain secrecy (agreements of nondisclosure, security measures, etc.)?
5. What were the mitigating circumstances surrounding the alleged breach or misappropriation?
6. What is the value of the secret to the growing company?

Implementing a Trade Secret Protection Program

Even in an effort to protect trade secrets, there is overkill. In fact, like the boy who cried wolf, if an emerging-growth business tries to protect every aspect of its operation by classifying everything in sight as a trade secret, it is likely that virtually nothing at all will be afforded protection when put to the test. Genuine trade secrets may be diluted if the owners and managers try to protect too much.

The process of establishing a trade secret protection and compliance program should start with a trade secret audit to identify which information is genuinely confidential and proprietary. Although each type of business has its own priorities, all companies should consider financial, technical, structural, marketing, engineering, and distribution documents as candidates for protection. The owner should next classify and develop security measures for protecting these documents. A separate office manual should be drafted for employees, written in basic terms to inform them of trade secret protection procedures. The importance of following procedures in the manual could be supported with timely interoffice memoranda, employee seminars, and incentive programs. Trade secret protection must be part of the orientation program for newly hired employees, and departing employees should be fully briefed on their continuing duty and legal obligation to protect the secrets of their former employer. Periodic reviews of the technical and creative staffs may identify new and existing trade secrets and reiterate the duty of nondisclosure. The following components are central to a compliance program:

- Ensure that adequate building security measures are taken—restricted access to highly sensitive areas, fences or gates to protect the premises, visitor control and log-in procedures, alarm systems, and locked desks, files, and vaults for proprietary documents. Post signs and notices in all appropriate places.
- Purchase stamps to be placed on documents that are trade secrets in order to give notice to users of their proprietary status.
- Designate a trade secret compliance officer who will be in charge of all aspects relating to the proper care and monitoring of trade secrets.
- Restrict employee access to trade secrets. Determine which employees need to know this information to do the job properly.
- Carefully review advertising and promotional materials and press releases to protect trade secrets. Restrict access for interviews by reporters and other members of the media. Everyone has one horror story about the wandering reporter who brought his camera along for the ride or about the company that was so proud of its new product that it inadvertently disclosed the proprietary features of the discovery in its promotional materials.
- Ensure that all key employees, marketing representatives, service providers, licensees, prospective investors or joint venturers, customers, suppliers, and anyone else who has access to the company's trade secrets have signed confidentiality and nondisclosure agreements.
- Police the activities of former employees, suppliers, and licensees. Include postterm obligations in agreements that impose a duty on the employee to keep the former employer aware of his or her whereabouts.
- If trade secrets are contained on computers, use passwords and data encryption to restrict access to terminals and telephone access through modems.
- Establish controlled routing procedures for the distribution and circulation of certain documents.
- Purchase a paper shredder and use where appropriate.
- Restrict the photocopying of documents. Use legends and maintain log-books on the location of original.
- Monitor the trade press and business journals for any news indicating a possible compromise and/or exploitation of your trade secrets by others.
- Provide employees with guidelines on the care and use of confidential documents. They should never be left unattended in the office, cars, airplanes, hotel rooms, trade shows, conventions, meetings, or conferences.

• Conduct exit interviews with all employees who have had access to the company's trade secrets. Remind them of their obligations not to use or disclose confidential and proprietary data and of the costs and penalties for doing so. Notify the future employer in writing of these obligations, especially if it is directly or indirectly competitive. Conversely, in order to avoid litigation as a defendant, remind new employees of the company's trade secret policies and that they are being hired for their skills and expertise, not for their knowledge of a former employer's trade secrets.

Remedies for Misappropriation

The most important and most immediate remedy available in any trade secret misappropriation case is the temporary restraining order and preliminary injunction. This remedy immediately restrains the unauthorized user from continuing to use the trade secret in any manner, pending a hearing on the owner's charge of misappropriation. Prompt action is necessary to protect the trade secret from further unauthorized disclosure. If the case is brought to trial, the court's decision will address the terms of the injunction and may award damages and profits resulting from the wrongful misappropriation of the trade secret.

There are certain risks to evaluate before instituting a trade secret suit. The company may face the risk that the trade secret at issue or collateral trade secrets may be disclosed during the course of the litigation, although certain federal and state rules of civil procedure and laws of evidence protect against this risk to a limited extent. The prospective plaintiff should consider that trade secret law is unsettled and often turns on the facts of each case. Establishing the paper trail needed to prove all of the elements of misappropriation may be virtually impossible in some cases, and lengthy litigation is likely to be cost prohibitive for the average small-business owner. This is all the more reason why preventive and protective measures are a far more attractive alternative than litigation.

Protective Measures Pertaining to Departing Employees

Growing companies must be aware of their rights and obligations when attempting to protect intellectual property in connection with a departing employee. Remember that Eatalot had threatened to leave Sweet-Tooth if franchising plans for BagDough were not implemented. Could he leave and take the intellectual property with him? No employer can prevent an enterprising employee from using his or her personal skills and experience in the launch of a new venture or in a new job. The law does not mandate nor will it enforce an agreement requiring employees to clean their mental slate upon departure. There is a fine line between what knowledge belongs to the employee and what belongs to the former employer. Courts have attempted, relatively unsuccessfully, to develop some objective standard for what an employee in that position would have learned regardless of where he might have been employed. Growing companies should note, however, that a few states, including Pennsylvania, have determined that an employee may use trade secrets that were created by the employee while still in the employ of the former employer. Another 12 or so states severely limit or even prohibit the nature and scope of noncompeting agreements.

In analyzing a claim against Eatalot were he to leave, Sweet-Tooth should consider: what information Eatalot was exposed to that truly constituted a trade secret; the terms of any employment or noncompetition agreements; steps Sweet-Tooth took to protect the secret; the extent to which this secret could have been discovered through reverse engineering; the extent to which Eatalot used any company assets or resources to form his own business; the extent to which Eatalot acquired this knowledge independent of Sweet-Tooth; the extent to which Eatalot contracted current vendors or customers of Sweet-Tooth during or after his employment with the company; the similarity of product or service to be offered; and the proximity of the new business to the former employer.

Overall the courts are hesitant to stifle competition and the entrepreneurial spirit absent some express agreement or foul play. However, clear breach of an agreement, a breach of a noncompete clause, or misappropriation of a customer list or proprietary data should be pursued.

14

Growth-Oriented Distribution Strategies

Drive along any country road on a hot summer weekend, and you will always find plenty of farm produce stands. These fresh fruit and vegetable outlets represent one extreme along the horizon of marketing channel decisions: There is no channel at all. Rather, the farmer harvests the produce from the fields and sells directly to consumers without the need for market intermediaries, agency costs, or sophisticated distribution strategies. Such a strategy, however, is rare in the typical distribution and marketing systems. Most producers of goods and services use various levels of market intermediaries to reach the targeted end users through a vertical channel of distribution.

The number of organizations represented in any given vertical channel of distribution varies from industry to industry. The choices range from direct marketing, where the manufacturer sells directly to the consumer, to multilevel marketing, where the product must flow through the hands of wholesalers, jobbers, and retailers before reaching consumers. The distribution decision depends on a variety of factors, such as:

- The nature of the product or service
- The structure of the market (e.g., nature of competitors, geographic location)
- The extent to which the industry is regulated by the government
- The ability to manage conflicts that may arise along the distribution channel
- The ability to motivate channel members
- The availability of real estate that may be required by each channel member (e.g., storage, manufacturing, or retail sites)
- The extent to which the distribution of the product or service is regulated by the federal, state, or local government
- The advertising and promotion required to develop consumer awareness and goodwill for the products and services

- The extent to which key elements of the products or services are proprietary
- The price at which the products or services will be offered to the consumer and the profit margins along the way
- The ongoing maintenance and service that will be required for the product or service
- The need for quality control as the product or service passes through the various levels of the distribution channel
- The extent to which customer, vendor, product, or territorial restrictions will be applied

The method of distribution that an emerging company selects has a direct effect on its ability to grow. For example, a manufacturer that determines that a fully integrated and internally owned system of distribution will be the most effective and efficient method of distribution runs the risk that its growth will be restricted by

- The cost and availability of capital required by the company-owned expansion
- The inability to attract and retain management personnel needed to operate the channel of distribution
- The unfamiliarity with the special issues affecting local markets
- The time delays that result from a strategy relying solely on internal growth as a method of expansion

Franchising, licensing, distributorships, and joint ventures represent contractual methods of coproduction and distribution that

- Obtain operating efficiencies and economies of scale;
- Achieve more rapid market penetration at a lower capital cost;
- Create cooperative advertising and promotion;
- Replace the need for internal personnel with motivated owner-operators; and
- Shift the primary responsibility for site selection, employee training and personnel management, local advertising, and other administrative concerns to the franchisee, licensee, or joint venture partner with the guidance or assistance of the franchisor.

Essentially the franchisee shares the risk of expanding the market share of the growing company by committing its capital and resources to the development of satellite locations. The risk of business failure of the franchisor or licensor is further reduced by the improvement in competitive position, reduced vulnerability to cyclical fluctuations, existence of a captive market for the franchisor's proprietary products and services due to the network of franchisees, and the reduced administrative and overhead costs.

The disadvantages of a contractual distribution system include the costs of compliance with federal and state regulation, the risk of exposure to vicarious liability for the acts or omissions of franchisees and licensees, management inflexibility caused by the franchise agreements that may make changes in the system difficult or expensive to implement, the challenge of meeting the expectations for ongoing support and financial reward expected by most franchisees, the difficulty of attracting an inventory of qualified and motivated franchisees, and the disclosure of valuable intellectual property to franchisees and their employees.

The Quality Control Challenge

The greatest concern of most companies considering a growth-oriented distribution strategy is the loss of quality control over the operation and management of the business. The concept of quality control, however, presents an interesting challenge for owners and managers of dynamic growth companies regardless of the actual marketing and distribution strategy selected. On the one hand, the development of production, distribution, and management systems to protect quality control is an integral part of any company's plan for successful growth. On the other hand, an inability to develop effective quality control systems could discourage and impede growth, usually because of fears that additional locations or market intermediaries will never be able to duplicate the level of quality offered by the prototype facility.

Management consultants, business professors, production managers, and entrepreneurs have labored for many years to develop systems to ensure that the key characteristics of a particular product or service are consistently maintained within a given range of value, however many times it is reproduced. At the heart of any such system is a method of analysis to reduce the production process to a set of steps that others can follow; a standard of measurement that defines the minimum acceptable level of quality; a monitoring and reporting process to ensure that quality control standards are being met; and economic sanctions for noncompliance.

Contractual Methods of Quality Control

An often overlooked and underestimated method of ensuring that quality control standards are met is by contract. A legally enforceable instrument, prepared in conjunction with a comprehensive Operations Manual, that sets forth quality control standards clearly and intelligibly and includes a system for monitoring and inspection, as well as penalties for failure to meet these standards, may be

the most effective tool available for ensuring that quality is maintained throughout the production and distribution system.

Among the many contractual ways to ensure and protect quality are provisions
addressing quality control in employment agreements that spell out performance
standards (based on sales, adherence to company policies, customer relations,
etc.); contracts of manufacture or sale (specifying whether the buyer is obligated
to purchase goods that do not meet certain quality standards); distribution contracts; and licensing and franchising agreements (setting forth the standards that
the licensee or franchisee must follow).

Licensing and Franchising as a Growth Strategy

A growing company should consider licensing and franchising as a strategy for
expanding its market share and distribution channels. Licensing has been defined
as the "controlled, selective transfer of intellectual property rights for value."
This may be a license of a trademark or character for production of merchandise,
or it may be a patent holder who licenses marketing and distribution rights to
another company, or even a license of trade secrets to expand a company's research efforts or market share. The licensor may, depending on the terms of the
license agreement, enjoy the following advantages:

- Royalty income
- Market expansion
- Shared development costs and greater access to wider (and often interna-
  tional) distribution channels
- Contributions toward further research and development
- Capital formation and supplementation, and availability of needed raw ma-
  terials
- Development of collateral markets and uses of the original intellectual prop-
  erty
- Reduction of risk in a start-up situation
- Ability to adapt to local markets and potential elimination of antitrust and
  related litigation

Franchising

Perhaps the most well-known type of contractual licensing arrangement is the
Franchise Agreement between a franchisor and franchisee. Under such an ar-

rangement, the franchisor grants a license to the franchisee for the limited right to establish and operate a proved business format, usually in exchange for an initial franchise fee and an ongoing royalty. Among the benefits the franchisor enjoys when this strategy for growth is adopted are: rapid market penetration at a lower cost than internal growth, a network of highly motivated franchisees who have greater familiarity with the trends and pitfalls of local markets, an ongoing royalty stream, economies of scale in purchasing and distributing products and services consumed and offered by the franchisees, and cooperative national advertising and promotion.

Building a Franchising Program

Over the last two decades, franchising has emerged as a popular expansion strategy for a variety of product and service companies, especially smaller businesses that cannot afford to finance internal growth. Recent Department of Commerce statistics demonstrate that retail sales from franchised outlets comprise nearly 40 percent of all retail sales in the United States and are estimated at over $640 billion. Franchises employed some 7.3 million people in 1988. Notwithstanding these impressive figures, franchising as a method of marketing and distributing products and services is appropriate for only a select few because a host of legal and business prerequisites must be satisfied.

Many companies prematurely select franchising as a growth alternative and then haphazardly assemble and launch their franchising program. Other companies are urged to franchise by unqualified consultants or advisers who may be more interested in professional fees than in the long-term success of the franchising program. Companies that prematurely or unadvisedly franchise may suffer financial distress or even failure.

The franchising community must take a responsible view toward the creation and development of their franchising programs; it will be the only way that franchisors and franchisees will be able to coexist harmoniously in the next century. Responsible franchising means that the franchisor must offer a secure foundation from which the franchising program is launched. For its part, any company or individual considering franchising as a method of getting into business must understand the components of this foundation. The key components of this foundation are listed in Exhibit 14-1.

Business Prerequisites to Launching a Franchising Program

The most important prerequisite for the success of any business format franchise system is a successful prototype. This prototype location is where all operating problems must be resolved; recipes and new products tested; equipment and design decisions made; management and marketing techniques tested; a trade identity and goodwill established; and financial viability proved. In short,

Exhibit 14-1. The foundation for franchising.

1. A proven prototype location (or chain of stores) that will serve as a basis for the franchising program. The store or stores must be successful and profitable but not too dependent on the physical presence or specific expertise of the founders.

2. A strong management team made up of internal officers and directors, as well as qualified consultants, who understand the industry in which the company operates and the legal and business aspects of franchising as a method of expansion.

3. Sufficient capitalization to launch and sustain the franchising program to ensure that capital is available for the franchisor to provide initial and ongoing support and assistance to franchisees.

4. A distinctive and protected trade identity, which includes federal- and state-registered trade names, as well as a uniform trade appearance and image.

5. Proprietary and proven methods of operation and management that can be reduced to writing in a comprehensive Operations Manual and enforced through clearly drafted and objective quality control standards.

6. A comprehensive training program for franchisees at the company's headquarters and on site at the franchisee's proposed location at the outset of the relationship and on an ongoing basis.

7. Field support staff who are available to visit and periodically assist franchisees, as well as monitor quality control standards.

8. A set of comprehensive legal documents that reflect the company's business strategies and policies. Offering documents must be in accordance with applicable federal and state disclosure laws, and Franchise Agreements should strike a delicate balance between the rights and obligations of franchisor and franchisee.

9. A demonstrated market demand for the products and services developed by the franchisor that will be distributed through the franchisees. Market research and analysis should be sensitive to trends in the economy and specific industry, the plans of direct and indirect competitors, and shifts in consumer preferences.

Exhibit 14-1.   (continued).

10. A set of carefully developed site selection criteria, based on market studies and demographic reports, that require sites that can be readily and affordably secured.

11. A genuine understanding of the competition (both direct and indirect) that the franchisor will face in marketing and selling franchises and that franchisees will face when marketing products and services.

12. Relationships with suppliers, lenders, real estate developers, and related key resources that will benefit the franchisees through group buying programs and discounts, financing and site preferences, and contributions toward national advertising.

13. A franchisee profile regarding the minimum financial qualifications, business acumen, and understanding of the industry that will be required to be successful.

14. Research and development capabilities for the ongoing introduction of new products and services.

the franchisor is selling a tested package to a franchisee, and the contents of that package must be clearly identified prior to sale.

The concept of a system or prescribed business format operated pursuant to a uniform and consistent trade identity and image is at the heart of franchising. A prospective franchisor must be able to reduce all aspects of running the business to be franchised into an Operations and Training Manual for use by franchisees in their day-to-day operation. If a company offers services that are highly personalized or a product that is difficult to reproduce, franchising may not be the most productive alternative for growth. Similarly, if all the kinks in the system have not been worked out, it is probably premature to consider franchising.

A number of other important business and planning factors must be considered before franchising. First, franchising should not be viewed as a solution to undercapitalization or as a get-rich-quick scheme. While it is true that franchising is less capital intensive than construction of additional company-owned sites, the initial start-up costs for legal, accounting, and consulting services can be extensive. Second, franchisors must view franchising as the establishment of a series of long-term relationships; the continued success of the company as a franchisor will depend on the harmony of these relationships. A field support staff must be built to provide ongoing services to the existing franchisees, as well as to maintain quality control and uniformity throughout the system. New products and services must be developed so that the franchisee can continue to compete with others in its local market. Innovative sales and marketing strategies must be continually developed to attract new customers and retain existing patrons. If the franchisor expects the franchisee to make its royalty payment on gross sales each week, an array of valuable support services must be regularly provided to meet the franchisee's changing needs.

Legal Definition of a Franchise

No single definition conclusively sets forth the exact elements that must be present in a business relationship in order for it to be characterized and legally defined as a franchise. The most logical place to begin the search for a working definition is the Federal Trade Commission's (FTC) trade regulation Rule 436, entitled "Disclosure Requirements and Prohibitions Concerning Franchising and Business Opportunity Ventures." Known as the FTC Rule, it applies to the sale of franchises in all states and requires disclosure of specified material information to prospective franchisees. Unlike certain states that have their own registration and disclosure regulations, the FTC Rule does not require registration or filing with the commission or any other federal agency.

The FTC Rule generally applies to a continuing commercial relationship between two or more parties that meets the statutory elements of a franchise. According to the rule, three central characteristics must be present in a relationship for a package or product franchise to exist:

1. Goods or services are distributed in connection with the franchisor's trade identity.
2. The franchisor provides significant assistance and/or exercises significant control over the franchisee.
3. The franchisee is required to pay at least $500 during the first six months of the operation of the franchised business.

Although a detailed discussion of these elements is beyond the scope of this chapter, it is safe to assume that if an offer is made under which a third party seeks to license the rights to operate a business in connection with another's identity and reputation and in reliance on training, assistance, and a marketing plan provided by the licensor, for a fee exceeding $500, then a franchise attorney should be consulted in order to evaluate whether the relationship will be subject to franchise laws.

Regulation of Franchise Offers and Sales

The offer and sale of a franchise is regulated by both the federal government and certain state governments. At the federal level, the FTC Rule specifies the minimum level of disclosure that must be made to a prospective franchisee in any state. In addition, over a dozen states have adopted their own rules and regulations for selling franchises within their borders. Known as the registration states, they include most of the nation's largest commercial marketplaces, such as California, New York, Illinois, Maryland, Virginia, and Wisconsin. These states generally follow a more detailed disclosure format, known as the Uniform Franchise Offering Circular (UFOC).

The UFOC was developed by the Midwest Securities Commissioners Association in 1975 in an attempt to streamline state regulation of franchising. The FTC has stated that compliance with the UFOC format will satisfy its rule, but the converse is true in only a handful of the registration states. Therefore the UFOC format makes the most sense for a franchisor planning to launch a nationwide sales program. The UFOC format consists of a prescribed cover page and 23 specific items of disclosure, including financial statements concerning the franchisor, a copy of the Franchise Agreement, and a detachable Acknowledgment of Receipt, which is signed by the prospective franchisee upon receipt of the disclosure documents.

The preparation of the necessary disclosure documents is typically time-consuming and expensive. Among other items, the history of the company and its principals, all aspects of the franchise relationship, procedures for termination and renewal of the relationship, quality control standards, fee structure, and a full set of financial statements must be disclosed in the prescribed federal or state format. In many ways, the disclosure document is a mirror image of the Franchise Agreement that the prospective franchisee must sign. The two documents should contain all of the information that a prospective franchisee and its counsel would need to conduct a thorough analysis of the offering and to make a fair and informed decision.

Assume that Sweet-Tooth Bakery Products Company establishes a retail location for the sale of its BagDough line of products. The products are well accepted by consumers, and the prototype store is profitable. A year and a half later, two sites are added in retail markets, which are also operated successfully. Convinced that a franchising program should be developed and launched, Sweet-Tooth retains a team of experienced advisers to develop a comprehensive franchising program. The key tasks to be accomplished are

- Prepare the UFOC.
- Prepare the Franchise Agreement.
- Prepare the Operations Manual for franchisees.
- Develop a franchising sales and marketing compliance program.
- Compile a full set of audited financial statements.
- Protect Sweet-Tooth's intellectual property.

Let us look at some of these key tasks in greater detail.

Preparing the UFOC

The UFOC is essentially a mirror image of the Franchise Agreement with certain historical and biographical information about Sweet-Tooth and its principals included in the early sections of the document. Each registration state has its own statutory version of the UFOC, and the regulations for each state should be carefully reviewed before filing for registration.

The specific disclosure items that must be included in Sweet-Tooth's UFOC are as follows:

1. *The franchisor and any predecessor.* Sweet-Tooth must provide a full and candid history of the company and any of its predecessors or affiliates. The address, state of incorporation, operating history, and a brief description of the franchise offered must be included.

2. *Identity and business experience of persons affiliated with franchisor; franchise brokers.* The name and exact position of each principal officer or key member of Sweet-Tooth's management team must be disclosed, including their principal occupation for the last 5 years and their experience as relevant to the management and operation of the franchise.

3. *Litigation.* A full litigation and arbitration history of Sweet-Tooth and its principal officers, directors, or franchise brokers must be provided for the 10-year period immediately preceding the date on which the offering circular is filed.

4. *Bankruptcy.* Any bankruptcy proceeding involving Sweet-Tooth, a predecessor, or any person listed in item number 2 during the 15-year period immediately preceding the date of the offering must be disclosed.

5. *Franchisee's initial fee or other initial payment.* The initial fee payable for the franchise must be disclosed. The terms of the payment, whether the fee is refundable in whole or in part, and the franchisor's use of the payment must be disclosed. Any other initial fees, such as site selection fees, referral fees, or sale of opening inventory, must be included.

6. *Other fees.* Any other monetary obligation of the franchisee to Sweet-Tooth or an affiliate must be disclosed and discussed, including, but not limited to, royalty payments, training fees, advertising contributions, mandatory insurance requirements, and any consulting fees payable to the franchisor or an affiliate for special services.

7. *Franchisee's initial investment.* All components of the franchisee's initial investment required in order to open the franchised business must be discussed in this section, usually in chart form, whether or not such payments are made directly to the franchisor. Real estate, equipment, fixtures, inventory, construction, and any other costs and expenditures are estimated. The disclosure specifies to whom such payments are made, under what general terms and conditions, and what portion, if any, is refundable.

8. *Obligations of the franchisee to purchase or lease from designated sources.* Any obligation of the franchisee to purchase services, supplies, fixtures, equipment, or inventory from a specific source designated by Sweet-Tooth is disclosed. If Sweet-Tooth will or may derive income based on these required purchases, the nature of the arrangement and payment must be able to withstand the scrutiny of the antitrust laws.

9. *Obligations of the franchisee to purchase or lease in accordance with specifications or from approved suppliers.* All quality control standards, equipment specifications, and approved supplier programs must be disclosed. The criteria Sweet-Tooth developed for becoming an approved supplier must be included. The standards and specifications need not be set forth in the UFOC; a summary discussion of these standards with reference to exhibits or confidential Operating Manuals is sufficient.

10. *Financing arrangements.* The terms and conditions of any financing arrangements offered directly or indirectly by Sweet-Tooth or an affiliate in connection with the establishment or operation of the franchise business must be disclosed.

11. *Obligations of the franchisor: other supervision, assistance, or services.* All preopening and postopening obligations of Sweet-Tooth in terms of support services and assistance to be provided to the franchisee should be disclosed.

12. *Exclusive area or territory.* The exact territory or exclusive area, if any, to be granted to the franchisee and the method by which it is computed must be disclosed, and any right of Sweet-Tooth to adjust the size of this territory if certain performance quotas are not met must be included.

13. *Trademarks, service marks, trade names, logotypes, and commercial symbols.* Aspects of Sweet-Tooth's trade identity (trademarks, logos, slogans, etc.) are disclosed, including whether these marks are registered at the federal and state level or whether there are any limitations or infringement disputes involving the marks or any related aspects of the trade identity.

14. *Patents and copyrights.* If Sweet-Tooth owns any rights in patents or copyrights that are material to the operation or management of the franchise, they must be described in the same detail as required by item 13.

15. *Obligation of the franchisee to participate in the actual operation of the franchised business.* Sweet-Tooth must disclose in this section whether absentee ownership and management will be permitted in connection with the operation of the franchise.

16. *Restrictions on goods and services offered by franchisee.* Any restrictions or conditions imposed by Sweet-Tooth on the goods and services that may be offered by the franchisee are disclosed.

17. *Renewal, termination, repurchase, modification, and assignment of the Franchise Agreement and related information.* All terms and conditions of re-

newal or transfer, rights of the franchisee upon death, grounds for termination of the franchise—such as definitions of the event of default, notice, and opportunity to cure—obligations upon termination, covenants against competition, and rights and remedies of the parties must be included in this item.

18. *Arrangements with public figures.* Any compensation or benefit given to a public figure in return for an endorsement of Sweet-Tooth or its products and services must be disclosed. The right of the franchisee to use the name of the public figure in its legal promotion and advertising must be included.

19. *Actual, average, projected, or forecasted franchise sales profits or earnings.* Sweet-Tooth must first disclose whether it will provide franchisees with financial forecasts predicting what they are likely to earn, usually referred to as "earnings claims." If it does not, a specific statement in accordance with statutory requirements must be included. If the franchisor does make earnings claims, the earnings claims disclosure must include a reasonable basis for the claim at the time it is made, a description of the factual basis for the claim, and an overview of any material assumptions supporting the claim.

20. *Information regarding franchises of the franchisor.* The number of franchises sold, units open for business, and company-owned stores must be broken down in this section, usually in tabular form, including a state-by-state estimate of franchise sales for the upcoming fiscal year.

21. *Financial statements.* Virtually all UFOC states require comprehensive and audited financial statements for the franchisor's last three years of operation. Failure to provide complete and accurate statements in accordance with the applicable regulations may result in escrow or security bond requirements or even complete prohibition from offering or selling franchises within that state's borders until such statements are provided.

22. *Franchise Agreement and all related contracts between franchisor and franchisee.* Copies of the Franchise Agreement and any other agreement the franchisee will be expected to sign must be included as exhibits to the UFOC.

23. *Acknowledgment of Receipt by a prospective franchisee.* A detachable receipt for the prospective franchisee to sign in order to confirm that Sweet-Tooth has provided a UFOC should be the last page.

Preparing the Franchise Agreement

The binding rights and obligations of each party to the franchise relationship are defined in the Franchise Agreement. These provisions will be binding on the parties for the life of their relationship and therefore must maintain a delicate balance of power. Sweet-Tooth must retain enough control to enforce uniformity and consistency throughout the system yet provide enough operational latitude to meet the special considerations or demands caused by the franchisee's local market conditions.

The Franchise Agreement reflects Sweet-Tooth's business philosophy and sets the tenor of the relationship. A well-drafted agreement reflects the culmination of thousands of business decisions and hundreds of hours of market research and testing. This foundation must be built well in advance of the sale of the first franchise. The time to discover problems in the Franchise Agreement is not when a conflict with a franchisee eventually erupts, which can be detrimental to the whole system, but rather during the planning stages when the agreement is still being built.

The key elements of Sweet-Tooth's Franchise Agreement are as follows:

1. *Recitals.* The recitals or preamble essentially sets the stage for the discussion of the contractual relationship. It provides the background information regarding the development and ownership of the proprietary rights of the franchisor that are being licensed. The preamble should always contain at least one recital specifying the obligation of the franchisee to operate the business format in strict conformity with the Operations Manual and quality control standards provided by Sweet-Tooth.

2. *Grant, term, and renewal.* The typical initial clause of the Franchise Agreement is the grant of a franchise for a specified term, influenced by market conditions, the franchisor's need to change certain material terms of the agreement periodically, the cost of the franchise and the franchisee's expectations in relation to start-up costs, the length of related agreements necessary to the franchisee's operations such as leases and bank loans, and anticipated consumer demand for the franchised goods and services. The renewal rights granted to a franchisee, if included at all, will usually be conditioned on the franchisee's being in good standing (e.g., no material defaults by franchisee) under the agreement. Other issues that must be addressed in any provisions regarding renewal are renewal fees, obligations to execute the then-current form of the Franchise Agreement, and any obligations of the franchisee to upgrade its facilities to the latest standards and design. Sweet-Tooth's right to relocate the franchisee, adjust the size of any exclusive territory granted, or change the fee structure should also be addressed.

3. *Territory.* The size of the geographic area granted to the franchisee must be specifically discussed in conjunction with any exclusive rights that will be granted to the franchisee with respect to this territory. These provisions address whether the size of the territory is a specific radius, city, or county and whether the franchisor will have a right to operate company-owned locations and/or grant additional franchises within the territory. Some franchisors specify a territory in which market research indicates that a given number of locations could be successful without market oversaturation and then sell that exact number of franchises, without regard to specific location selected within the geographic area. Any rights of first refusal for additional locations, advertising restrictions, performance quotas relating to territory, and policies of Sweet-Tooth with regard to territory are addressed in this part.

4. *Site selection*. The responsibility for finding the specific site for the operation of the franchised business will rest with either the franchisor or franchisee. If the franchisee may choose, the Franchise Agreement usually provides that the decision is subject to the franchisor's approval. Some franchisors provide significant assistance in site selection in terms of marketing and demographic studies, lease negotiations, and securing local permits and licenses, especially if a turnkey franchise is offered. Site selection, however, can be the most difficult aspect of being a successful franchisee, and as a result, most franchisors are reluctant to take on full responsibility for this task contractually. For additional protection and control, some franchisors insist on becoming the landlord to the franchisee through a mandatory sublease arrangement once an acceptable site has been selected. A somewhat less burdensome method of securing similar protection is to provide for an automatic assignment of the lease to the franchisor upon termination of the franchise.

5. *Services to be provided by the franchisor*. The Franchise Agreement should clearly delineate which products and services will be provided to the franchisee by Sweet-Tooth or its affiliates, in terms of both the initial establishment of the franchised business (preopening obligations) and any continuing assistance or support services provided throughout the term of the relationship (postopening services). Among the usual preopening obligations are a trade secret and copyright license for the use of the confidential Operations Manual, recruitment and training of personnel, standard accounting and bookkeeping systems, inventory and equipment specifications and volume discounts, standard construction, building and interior design plans, and grand opening promotion and advertising assistance. The quality and extent of the training program is the most crucial preopening service and should include classroom as well as on-site instruction. Postopening services provided on a continuing basis generally include field support and troubleshooting, research and development for new products and services, development of national advertising and promotional campaigns, and the arrangement of group purchasing programs and volume discounts.

6. *Franchise, royalty, and related fees payable to the franchisor*. The Franchise Agreement should set forth the nature and amount of fees payable to Sweet-Tooth by the franchisee, initially and on a continuing basis. The initial franchise fee is usually a nonrefundable lump sum payment due upon execution of the Franchise Agreement. This fee is compensation for the grant of the franchise, the trademark and trade secret license, preopening training and assistance, and the initial opening supply of materials, if any, to be provided by the franchisor to the franchisee.

A second category of fees is the continuing fee, usually as a royalty on gross sales. This percentage can be fixed or be based on a sliding scale for different ranges of sales achieved at a given location. Often a minimum royalty payment will be required, regardless of the franchisee's actual performance. These fees should be payable weekly and submitted to Sweet-Tooth together with some standardized reporting form for internal control and monitoring. A weekly payment schedule, as opposed to monthly or quarterly, generally allows the franchisee to budget for this payment from a cash flow perspective, as well as providing the franchisor with an early warning system if there is a problem, and to react before the past-due royalties accrue to a virtually uncollectible sum.

The third category is a recurring fee that is usually in the form of a national cooperative advertising and promotion fund. The promotional fund may be managed by Sweet-Tooth, an independent advertising agency, or even a franchisee association. Either way, Sweet-Tooth must build a certain amount of control over the fund into the Franchise Agreement in order to protect the company's trademarks and ensure consistency in marketing.

Other categories of fees payable to Sweet-Tooth may include the sale of proprietary goods and services to the franchisee, consulting fees, audit and inspection fees, lease management fees (where the franchisor is to serve as sublessor), renewal fees, and transfer or assignment fees.

7. *Quality control.* A well-drafted Franchise Agreement always includes a variety of provisions designed to ensure quality control and consistency throughout the franchise system. Such provisions often take the form of restrictions on the franchisee's sources of products, ingredients, supplies, and materials, as well as strict guidelines and specifications for operating procedures. These operating procedures usually specify standards of service, trade dress and uniform requirements, condition and appearance of the facility, hours of business, minimum insurance requirements, guidelines for trademark usage, advertising and promotional materials, accounting systems, and credit practices. Any restrictions on the ability of the franchisee to buy goods and services or requirements to purchase from a specific source should be carefully drafted within the perimeters of applicable antitrust laws. If Sweet-Tooth is to serve as the sole supplier or manufacturer of one or more products the franchisee uses in the day-to-day operation of the business, such as the batter for the BagDough products, the exclusivity must be justified by a product that is truly proprietary or unique.

8. *Protection of intellectual property and covenants against competition.* The Franchise Agreement should always address the obligations of the franchisee and its employees to protect the trademarks and trade secrets being licensed against misuse or disclosure. The franchisor should insist on a clause that clearly states that the trademarks and trade names being licensed are the exclusive property of the franchisor and that any goodwill established is to inure to the sole benefit of the franchisor. This section should also make clear that the confidential Operations Manual is on loan to the franchisee under a limited use license and that the franchisee or its agents are prohibited from the unauthorized use of the trade secrets during and after the term of the agreement. To the extent

that such provisions are enforceable in local jurisdictions, the Franchise Agreement should contain covenants against competition by a franchisee—during the term of the Franchise Agreement and following termination or cancellation.

9. *Termination of the Franchise Agreement.* The section of the Franchise Agreement discussing how a franchisee may lose its rights to operate the franchised business is very important. The various events of default should be carefully defined and tailored to meet the needs of the specific type of business being franchised. Grounds for termination can range from the bankruptcy of a franchisee to failure to meet specified performance quotas or strictly abide by quality control standards. This section should identify the procedures for notice and opportunity to cure, as well as the alternative actions that Sweet-Tooth may pursue to enforce its rights to terminate the Franchise Agreement. Such clauses must be drafted in the light of certain state regulations that limit franchise terminations to "good cause" and have minimum procedural requirements that must be followed. The obligations of the franchisee upon default and notice of termination must also be clearly spelled out, such as the duty to return all copies of the Operations Manual, pay all past-due royalty fees, and immediately cease the use of the franchisor's trademarks.

10. *Miscellaneous provisions.* Like any other well-prepared business agreement, the Franchise Agreement should contain a notice provision, a governing law clause, severability provisions, an integration clause, and a provision discussing the relationship of the parties. Some franchisors add an arbitration clause, a "hold-harmless" and indemnification provision, a reservation of the right to injunctions and other forms of equitable relief, specific representations and warranties of the franchisee, attorney's fees for the prevailing party in the event of dispute, and even a contractual provision acknowledging that the franchisee has reviewed the agreement with counsel and has conducted an independent investigation of the franchise and is not relying on any representations other than those expressly set forth in the agreement.

Establishing a Sales and Marketing Compliance Program

An effective sales and marketing program can be a franchisor's greatest asset—or its greatest liability. Clearly Sweet-Tooth will be unable to grow and prosper as a franchisor without an aggressive marketing and promotional campaign. On the other hand, the benefits of a few franchises sold will be quickly outweighed by the costs of disputes with federal regulators, state administrations, and disgruntled franchisees if sales and marketing practices are not kept within the bounds of the law. In short, advertising and sales practices must be designed to attract franchisees, not litigation.

The key members of the Sweet-Tooth franchising team should develop a sales and marketing compliance program well before the first franchise is sold. The compliance program will have comprehensive record-keeping requirements for all prospective, current, and former franchisees, procedures for answering inquiries from states where the franchisor is not registered to offer and sell franchises, a litigation and dispute-resolution system for existing franchisees, due diligence procedures for franchise sales staff, and initial and ongoing training for sales personnel.

Sweet-Tooth should establish a comprehensive file for each franchisee containing the following types of information:

- Date, place, and method of initial and subsequent meetings with prospective franchisee
- Name(s) of representative(s) of Sweet-Tooth who met with the franchisee and all material subjects discussed and questions addressed
- Internal screening or evaluation criteria for determining applicant's eligibility
- The date on which offering documents were delivered and copies of documents actually delivered, as well as copies of all executed agreements, riders, addenda, and exhibits between franchisor and franchisee
- Description of payments made to franchisor (copies of checks, promissory notes, etc.)
- Dates on which training was commenced, conducted, and completed (identify location, fees, documents provided, names of instructors, courses provided, list of attendees, etc.)
- A copy of the franchisee's lease (and any addenda or attachments) and the name of the lessor
- A detailed account of all preopening assistance provided by the franchisor and related correspondence
- All ongoing correspondence, records of visits and inspections, performance reviews or evaluations, customer or vendor complaints, royalty payment records, and all other material information governing the continuing relationship

Area Development Agreements and Subfranchising

Most franchises are sold to individual owner-operators who will be responsible for managing a single site in accordance with the franchisor's business format and quality control standards. A recent trend in franchising, however, has been the sale of master franchises to more aggressive entrepreneurs who will be responsible for the development of an entire geographic region.

There are two primary types of master franchises: *subfranchisors,* who act as independent selling organizations that are responsible for recruiting and ongoing support of franchisees within their given region, and *area developers,* who have no resale rights but are themselves responsible for meeting a mandatory development schedule for their region.

Generally the inclusion of master franchises in a franchisor's development strategy allows for even more rapid market penetration and fewer administrative burdens. Nevertheless, a wide range of legal and strategic issues must be addressed when master franchises are included in the overall franchising program.

Area development agreements typically involve issues similar to agreements used in the sale of a single-unit franchise. The key issues and negotiations usually center on the size of the territory and the mandatory timetable for development. The franchisor usually wants to reserve certain rights and remedies in case the franchisee defaults on its development obligations. The area developer must usually pay an umbrella development fee for the region, in addition to the individual initial fee, that is to be due and payable as each unit becomes operational within the territory. The development fee is essentially a payment to the franchisor that prevents the franchisor from offering any other franchises within that region (unless there is a default).

Subfranchise agreements present a myriad of issues that are not raised in the sale of an individual franchise, primarily because the rewards and responsibilities of the subfranchisor are much different from those of the area developer. In most subfranchising relationships, the franchisor shares a portion of the initial franchise fee and ongoing royalty with the subfranchisor in exchange for the subfranchisor's assuming responsibilities within the given region. The proportions in which fees are shared usually has a direct relationship to the exact responsibilities of the subfranchisor. In addition, the subfranchisor receives a comprehensive regional Operations Manual covering sales and promotions, training, and field support over and above the information contained in the Operations Manuals provided to individual franchisees. Some of the key issues that must be addressed in the subfranchise relationship follow:

- How will the initial and ongoing franchise fees be divided between franchisor and subfranchisor? Who will be responsible for collecting and processing franchise fees?

- Will the subfranchisor be a party to the individual Franchise Agreements? Or will the actual parties to the contract be limited to franchisor and individual franchisee?

- What is the exact nature of the subfranchisor's recruitment, site selection, franchising, training, and ongoing support to the individual franchisees within its region?

- Who will be responsible for preparing and filing the franchise offering documents in states where the subfranchisor must file separately?

- What mandatory development schedules and related performance quotas will be imposed on the subfranchisor?

- Will the subfranchisor be granted the rights to operate individual units within the territory? If yes, how will these units be priced?

- What will the subfranchisor be obligated to pay the franchisor initially for the exclusive rights to develop the territory?

- What rights of approval will the franchisor retain with respect to the sale of individual franchises (e.g., background of the candidate, any negotiated changes in the agreement, decision to terminate)?
- What rights does the franchisor reserve to modify the size of the territory or repurchase it from the subfranchisor?

Many of the other provisions in a Subfranchise Agreement regarding protection of intellectual property, maintenance of quality control standards, or remedies of the franchisor upon termination or default are similar to those contained in the individual Franchise Agreement.

Alternatives to Franchising

Not all growth businesses have systems or formats conducive to franchising, and many lack the foundational prerequisites. Nevertheless, there are many other contractual growth-oriented marketing strategies from which to choose—among them licensing, exclusive distributorships, joint ventures, limited partnerships (where the company managers operate the business on behalf of passive owner-investors), cooperative associations, and the sale of consulting services. I will examine three of these alternatives.

Distributors and Dealerships

Many growing product-oriented companies—commonly manufacturers of electronic and stereo equipment, computer hardware and software, sporting goods, medical equipment, and automobile parts and accessories—bring their wares to the marketplace through independent third-party distributors and dealerships. These dealers are generally more difficult to control than a licensee or franchisee because the agreements that govern this type of relationship are not nearly as comprehensive or complex; as a result, the agreement between the manufacturer and the distributor is much more informal than a franchise or license agreement.

In developing distributor and dealership agreements, growing companies must be careful to avoid being included within the broad definition of a franchise under the FTC's Rule 436, which requires the preparation of a disclosure document. To avoid such a classification, the agreement must impose minimal controls over the dealer, the products must be sold at bona fide wholesale prices without any form of initiation fee, and the manufacturer must provide minimal assistance or control in the marketing or management of the dealer's business. A well-drafted distributor agreement should address a number of key issues, which are listed in Exhibit 14-2.

Exhibit 14-2. Questions to consider in preparing and negotiating distributor agreements.

- What is the scope of the appointment? Which products is the dealer authorized to distribute and under what conditions? What is the scope, if any, of the exclusive territory to be granted to the distributor? To what extent will product, vendor, customer, or geographic restrictions be applicable?
- What activities will the distributor be expected to perform in terms of manufacturing, sales, marketing, display, billing, market research, maintenance of books and records, storage, training, installation, support, and servicing?
- What obligations will the distributor have to preserve and protect the intellectual property of the manufacturer?
- What right, if any, will the distributor have to modify or enhance the manufacturer's warranties, terms of sale, credit policies, or refund procedures?
- What advertising literature, technical and marketing support, training seminars, or special promotions will be provided by the manufacturer to enhance the performance of the distributor?
- What sales or performance quotas will be imposed on the dealer as a condition to its right to continue to distribute the manufacturer's products or services? What are the rights and remedies of the manufacturer if the dealer fails to meet these performance standards?
- What is the term of the agreement, and under what conditions can it be terminated? How will posttermination transactions be handled?

Licensing Proprietary Products and Services

Licensing is a contractual method of developing and exploiting intellectual property by transferring *rights of use* to third parties without the transfer of *ownership*. Virtually any proprietary product or service may be the subject of a license agreement, ranging from the licensing of the Mickey Mouse character by Walt Disney Studios in the 1930s to the licensing of computer software and high technology. From a legal perspective, licensing presents complex issues of contract, tax, antitrust, international, tort, and intellectual property law. From a business perspective, the advantages of licensing must be weighed against the disadvantages in comparison to alternative types of vertical distribution systems.

Many of the benefits that licensing provides closely parallel the advantages of franchising:

- To spread the risk and cost of development and distribution and to achieve more rapid market penetration
- To earn initial license fees and ongoing royalty income
- To build consumer loyalty and goodwill
- To preserve the capital that would otherwise be required for internal growth and expansion
- To test new applications for existing and proved technology
- To avoid or settle litigation regarding a dispute over ownership of the technology

The disadvantages of licensing are also similar in nature to the risks inherent in franchising:

- A diluted ability to enforce quality control standards and specifications
- A greater risk of another party's infringing upon the exploitation of the licensor's intellectual property
- A dependence on the skills, abilities, and resources of the licensee as a source of revenue
- Difficulty in recruiting, motivating, and retaining qualified and competent licensees
- The risk that the licensor's entire reputation and goodwill may be damaged or destroyed by the act or omission of a single licensee
- The administrative burden of monitoring and supporting the operations of the network of licensees

Failure to consider all of the costs and benefits of licensing could easily result in a regretful strategic decision or an unprofitable license agreement caused by the licensor's underestimation of the licensee's need for technical assistance and support or an overestimation of the market demand for the products and services. In order to avoid such problems, the licensor should conduct a certain amount of due diligence prior to engaging in any serious negotiations with a prospective licensee. This due diligence generally includes market research, legal steps to protect intellectual property, an internal financial analysis of the technology with respect to pricing, profit margins, and costs of production and distribution, and a more specific analysis of the prospective licensee with respect to its financial strength, research and manufacturing capabilities, and reputation in the industry.

Once the decision to enter into more formal negotiations has been made, the terms and conditions of the license agreement should be discussed. Naturally these provisions will vary, depending on whether the license is for merchandising an entertainment property, exploiting a technology, or distributing a particular product to an original equipment manufacturer or value-added reseller. As a general rule, any well-drafted license agreement should address the following topics:

1. *Scope of the grant*. The exact scope and subject matter of the license must be initially addressed and carefully defined. Any restrictions on the geographic scope, rights of use, permissible channels of trade, restrictions on sublicensing, limitations on assignability, or exclusion of improvements to the technology covered by the agreement should be clearly set forth.

2. *Term and renewal*. The commencement date, duration, renewals and extensions, conditions to renewal, procedures for providing notice of intent to renew, ground for termination, obligations upon termination, and licensor's reversionary rights in the technology should be contained in this section.

3. *Performance standards and quotas*. To the extent that the licensor's consideration will be dependent on royalty income calculated from the licensee's gross or net revenues, the licensor may want to impose certain minimum levels of performance in terms of sales, advertising and promotional expenditures, and human resources to be devoted to the exploitation of the technology. The licensee will argue for a best-efforts provision that is free from performance standards and quotas. In such cases, the licensor may want to insist on a minimum royalty level that will be paid regardless of the licensee's actual performance.

4. *Payments to the licensor*. Virtually every type of license agreement includes some form of initial payment and ongoing royalty to the licensor. Royalty formulas vary widely, however, and may be based on gross sales, net sales, net profits, a fixed sum per product sold, or a minimum payment to be made to the licensor over a given period of time, or it may include a sliding scale in order to provide some incentive to the licensee as a reward for performance.

5. *Quality control assurance and protection*. Quality control standards and specifications for the production, marketing, and distribution of the products and services covered by the license must be set forth by the licensor. In addition, procedures should be included in the agreement that allow the licensor an opportunity to enforce these standards and specifications, such as a right to inspect the licensee's premises; a right to review, approve, or reject samples produced by the licensee; and a right to review and approve any packaging, labeling, or advertising materials to be used in connection with the exploitation of the products and services that are within the scope of the license.

6. *Insurance and indemnification*. The licensor should take all necessary and reasonable steps to ensure that the licensee has an obligation to protect and indemnify the licensor against any claims or liabilities resulting from the licensee's exploitation of the products and services covered by the license.

7. *Accounting, reports, and audits*. The licensor must impose certain reporting and record-keeping procedures on the licensee in order to ensure an accurate accounting for periodic royalty payments. Further, the licensor should reserve

the right to audit the records of the licensee in the event of a dispute or discrepancy, along with provisions as to who will be responsible for the cost of the audit in the event of an understatement.

8. *Duties to preserve and protect intellectual property.* The obligations of the licensee, its agents, and employees to preserve and protect the confidential nature and acknowledge the ownership of the intellectual property being disclosed in connection with the license agreement must be carefully defined. Any required notices or legends that must be included on products or materials distributed in connection with the license agreement (such as to the status of the relationship or actual owner of the intellectual property) are also described in this section.

9. *Technical assistance, training, and support.* Any obligations of the licensor to assist the licensee in the development or exploitation of the subject matter being licensed are set out in this section. The assistance may take the form of personal services or documents and records. Any extra fees due to the licensor for such support services must also be specified.

10. *Warranties of the licensor.* A prospective licensee may demand that the licensor provide certain representations and warranties in the license agreement. These may include warranties regarding the ownership of the technology (such as absence of any known infringements of the technology or restrictions on the ability to license the technology) or that the technology has the features, capabilities, and characteristics previously represented in the negotiations.

11. *Infringements.* The license agreement should contain procedures under which the licensee must notify the licensor of any known or suspected direct or indirect infringements of the subject matter being licensed. The responsibilities for the cost of protecting and defending the technology should be specified.

Joint Ventures as a Growth Strategy

Other major alternatives to committing the capital and management resources necessary for internal expansion are joint venture and strategic partnering. Unlike franchising, distributorships, and licensing, which are usually vertical in nature, joint ventures and strategic partner relationships are structured at either horizontal or vertical levels of distribution. At the horizontal level, the joint venture is almost an alternative to a merger; two companies operating at the same level in the distribution channel join together (by means of a partnership-type agreement or by joint ownership of a specially created corporation) in order to achieve certain synergies or operating efficiencies. At the vertical level, a manufacturer and distributor join forces in a similar manner in order to create the equivalent of a fully or substantially vertical integrated company. Strategic partnering may be formally structured as a joint venture or may be more informal, such as an affiliation of two or more companies for a specific purpose or to achieve a shared objective.

Joint venture agreements, especially at the vertical level, must be carefully structured to avoid classification as a franchise under FTC Rule 436. (The FTC Rule provides an exemption for a bona fide joint venture, and state regulations also address the possible abuse of the joint venture structure by those wrongfully seeking to avoid registration and disclosure requirements under applicable franchise laws.) Joint venture agreements must be carefully structured, taking into consideration applicable principles for antitrust, partnership, corporate, tax, labor, intellectual property, and contract law.

From a business perspective, joint ventures are typically formed by growing companies that lack the capital or management talent required to undertake a specific project and as a result pool their resources with another company with complementary skills and talents that is willing to share in the risk of the venture. The particular project or venture may involve research and development, manufacturing, distribution, or even retailing of the product or service produced by the collaborative efforts of the two companies.

Before attempting to draft a formal joint venture or special corporate shareholders' agreement, the parties must address certain preliminary issues:

- What are the specific immediate and long-term objectives of both parties to the agreement? How compatible are the two entities from a financial and managerial perspective?

- How will the joint venture be structured (the basic four choices are a closely held corporation, a limited partnership, a general partnership, or a contractual joint venture or strategic partnering relationship)?

- How will the joint venture be capitalized and then financed on an ongoing basis? Will external financing be required? If so, to what extent will each party be responsible for capital contributions or repayment of loans?

- What types of tangible and intangible assets will each party contribute to the joint venture? Who will have ownership rights in the property contributed during the term of the joint venture and thereafter? Who will own property developed as a result of joint development efforts?

- What covenants of nondisclosure or noncompetition will be expected of each joint venturer during the term of the agreement and thereafter?

- What timetables or performance quotas for completion of the projects contemplated by the joint venture will be included in the agreement? What are the rights and remedies of each party if these performance standards are not met?

- How will issues of management and control be addressed in the agreement? What will be the respective voting rights of each party? What are the procedures in the event of a major disagreement or deadlock? What is the fallback plan?

Once all of these preliminary issues have been discussed by the joint venturers, a formal joint venture agreement or corporate shareholders' agreement should be prepared. If the joint venture is structured as a partnership, the following topics must be addressed in the agreement:

- Nature, purpose, and trade name for the joint venture
- Status of the respective joint venturers
- Representations and warranties of each joint venturer
- Mutual covenants governing the joint venturers (e.g., covenants of confidentiality)
- Capital contributions of each joint venturer
- Allocation and distribution of profits and losses among the joint venturers
- Management, control, and voting rights of each joint venturer
- Books, records, bank accounts, inspections, and audits
- Insurance and cross-indemnification obligations for each joint venturer
- Rights in joint venture property
- Responsibility for administrative and overhead expenses of the joint venture
- Restrictions on the transferability of ownership interest in the joint venture
- Default, dissolution, and termination of the joint venture
- Obligations and distributions upon termination of the joint venture
- Dispute-resolution procedures
- Miscellaneous topics (governing law, force majeure, notices and consents, modifications and waivers, severability, etc.)

15

Legal Regulation of Marketing Practices

The legal consequences of many of the sales and marketing decisions made as a company grows must be carefully considered before these actual plans and strategies are implemented. Failure to understand legal requirements will disrupt implementation and could subject the growing company and its officers, directors, and managers to substantial civil and even criminal penalties. Owners and managers of growing companies should have a working knowledge of federal and state antitrust laws, consumer protection (advertising, packaging, labeling, and warranty) laws established by federal regulatory agencies such as the Federal Trade Commission (FTC) and U.S. Food and Drug Administration (FDA), and state and common-law principles of unfair competition and related business torts.

Antitrust Laws

The federal antitrust laws, beginning with the Sherman Act of 1890, the Clayton Act of 1914, the Robinson-Patman Act of 1936, and the Federal Trade Commission Act of 1914, have been designed to promote a free-market system and protect against restraints of trade. Conflicts have arisen, however, between these two themes, which are at the heart of antitrust policy. On one hand, political theory supported a body of law that promoted equality and fair play among businesses. Under this view, the interests of the smaller-business owner are paramount, even if the result is economic inefficiency. This view essentially states that the interests of the small-business owner are paramount to the interests of the consumer. On the other hand, antitrust laws have also been developed based on economic theory. Economists viewed antitrust as a body of law designed to protect competition and production efficiency, with the emphasis on the consumer, not the interests of individual competitors. No matter which theory is currently at the forefront, owners and managers of growing companies adopting aggressive strategies in order to expand market share must be aware of the pricing, customer relations, marketing practices, and distribution methods that will not be tolerated.

Essentially two general categories of restraints are prohibited by antitrust laws. Vertical restraints are those placed by a manufacturer on a distributor or by a wholesaler on a retailer. These are restraints on trade that develop between firms at different levels in the production and distribution network, such as if Impasse, the electronics manufacturer, attempts to impose overly burdensome restrictions on a particular chain of retail stereo centers as part of its turnaround strategy. Examples include *resale price maintenance*, such as an attempt by Impasse to fix the prices at which the stereo outlets could offer its products; *geographic and customer limitations*, such as limiting a distributor to an exclusive territory; *exclusive dealing arrangements*, such as forcing a distributor to sell only Impasse-manufactured products; *tying*, which forces a distributor to buy products A and B when all he really wants is B; and *price discrimination*, such as selling to one wholesaler in a given area under terms and conditions designed primarily to drive out regional competition. In certain cases, these arrangements are contractual and voluntary, such as in a Franchise Agreement, or are necessary to protect against free riders, who threaten product quality and pricing formulas. However, if it is determined that a company is implementing these restraints merely to protect and expand its market share in bad faith, antitrust violations are likely to be triggered.

The second category of practices of antitrust concern are horizontal restraints. Here the law is concerned with practices by firms operating at the same level in the distribution chain and doing business in generally the same markets. The laws are designed to protect against large portions of market strength and market share being concentrated in one or only a few firms. Monopolistic practices, such as predatory pricing (underselling rivals in order to acquire or preserve market share) or refusals to deal, price fixing among market leaders (in order to squeeze out smaller firms and create greater barriers to market entry), production and output agreements, and other forms of collusion among market leaders and restrictions on mergers and acquisitions generally fall within the category of horizontal restraints. Antitrust laws should be strongly considered before Impasse enters into any of the joint ventures or acquisitions proposed by Phyllis Compactdisc & Associates, its consulting firm. For example, the transaction may require that Impasse file certain premerger notification documents with the FTC.

The penalties for failure to obey the federal antitrust laws can be severe and in the past have included criminal sanctions, injunctive relief, damages for lost profits, and in some cases treble damages. The following discussion of specific marketing practices that run afoul of the antitrust laws should be of interest not

only to the growing company seeking to avoid these sanctions but also to entrepreneurs who feel that they may have been injured by such practices by a competitor.

Specific Marketing Practices Scrutinized Under
Federal and State Antitrust Laws

A wide variety of specific marketing, distribution, and pricing practices are
closely scrutinized by federal and state antitrust laws. For example, suppose that
Impasse adopted a marketing strategy calling for entry into new geographic markets by means of acquisition of other consumer electronics product manufacturers or by developing a below-cost pricing structure in new territories. Although
such a strategy appears to be legitimate, it may trigger horizontal restraint problems under the Sherman Act or predatory pricing problems (if an anticompetitive
intent is proven) under the Robinson-Patman Act; both carry civil and even criminal penalties. Impasse's marketing department must develop strategies and objectives that comply with applicable antitrust laws and must recognize when to
consult legal counsel.

The following specific practices have been deemed to be anticompetitive or in
restraint of trade under federal and state antitrust laws:

1. *Monopolistic practices.* It may seem ironic that a capitalistic society that
fosters entrepreneurship and business growth also has laws that penalize companies that manage to acquire substantial market power. Nonetheless, the antitrust laws have struggled over the last century to draw a line between those
practices permissible because market power was achieved due to a superior product or business skill as opposed to practices that must be condemned as being
anticompetitive and harmful to economy and society because market power was
achieved due to a conscious effort by a growing company to reduce output and
raise prices. The current approach for striking this balance involves the application of a rule-of-reason test to the conduct in question. The test examines all
relevant facts and circumstances in an attempt to determine whether a particular
act was exclusionary and harmful to competition or whether it should be permitted as fostering and promoting competition.

A wide variety of acts could be deemed to be monopolistic in nature: price
discrimination, refusals to deal, certain customer and territorial restrictions,
mergers of rivals, tying arrangements, and conspiracies among competitors.

Courts have consistently stated that size and growth alone, even at the expense
of competitors, is not enough to determine guilt under the antitrust laws; rather,
there must be some wrongful intent or illegal conduct by which the company
seeks to obtain or sustain market power.

2. *Price fixing.* The Sherman Act specifically prohibits "contracts, combinations or conspiracies" in restraint of trade. Under §1 of the Sherman Act, if
two or more competitors conspire to fix prices or methods of price computation

(e.g., base-point pricing) at a certain level, such conduct is per se illegal. This means that such practices will not be tolerated by the courts regardless of the facts and circumstances, even if prices are fair, reasonable, and in the best interests of all competitors within the industry or geographic area. This per se approach not only affects any agreements among competitors as to price but also covers any term and condition of sale, such as credit terms, shipping policies, or trade-in allowances.

Another practice closely related to horizontal price fixing is known as conscious parallelism: Companies follow the acts of a dominant market leader, such as a change in price or sales terms, even in the absence of a formal agreement to fix prices among competitors.

Similar legal principles apply to price-fixing attempts in the vertical chain of distribution, generally known as resale price maintenance (RPM). Attempts by a company to impose RPM policies on its distributors and retailers are also per se illegal, with a few limited exceptions for nonprice vertical restraints, such as unilateral refusals to deal, customer restraints, and the designation of exclusive territories. Perhaps the most noted exception to the per se illegality of vertical price fixing is the unilateral refusal-to-deal rule, which allows an objective decision by a manufacturer that it will not deal with distributors who cut prices below suggested levels, provided that the decision to refuse to deal is both truly unilateral (e.g., not at the urging of another distributor) and not the result of threats or intimidation.

The only other well-recognized exception to the per se rule against RPM occurs when a manufacturer essentially retains ownership of the product by distributing on a consignment basis. These consignment arrangements make the reseller a mere agent of the manufacturer and thus create a legal and business justification for controlling prices.

3. *Price discrimination.* Most price discrimination issues arise under the Robinson-Patman Act when a seller offers its otherwise uniform products at different prices based on the buyer's size or geographic location. The Robinson-Patman law is designed to ensure fair pricing among the various buyers of the seller's products and to protect against pricing strategies intended to drive out local competition.

Here again the antitrust laws attempt to draw a line between competitive practices that will be encouraged and anticompetitive practices that will be prohibited. For example, Robinson-Patman does not expressly prohibit a seller from charging a lower price to a customer if its actual costs of the sale are lower due to the quantities purchased by the buyer or the geographic proximity of the buyer. Similarly, a seller is permitted to drop its prices under certain circumstances if necessary to meet changing market conditions—for example, in order to compete with a rival's equally low price—as long as products are not sold below cost. As with certain related monopolistic practices, Robinson-Patman issues must be considered not only for direct pricing issues but also for nonprice considerations, such as promotional allowances and credit terms.

4. *Vertical nonprice restraints.* Manufacturers may attempt to implement a variety of restraints affecting distribution channels that trigger antitrust considerations. The three most common forms are tying, exclusive dealing, and territorial and customer restrictions.

Tying is an arrangement where the sale or lease of product X (which the buyer wants) is conditioned on the buyer's also purchasing product Y (which the buyer does not necessarily want). Recent cases have set forth a clear test for distinguishing when a tie-in arrangement will be permitted and when it will be prohibited, although the exact elements of the test vary among jurisdictions. A threshold condition to finding an illegal tying arrangement has always been that the seller have sufficient market power and exercise enough coercion to force the buyer to purchase product Y as a condition to getting product X.

Exclusive dealing involves a situation where a buyer contracts to purchase all of its requirements of a given product exclusively from a particular seller. Where the buyer is entering into such an arrangement merely to protect its requirements for a given product in a period of market supply uncertainty, it would clearly be wrong to classify such an agreement as anticompetitive. If, however, the exclusive dealing contract is designed to suppress competition, the exclusive dealing contract will be examined by the court in the light of all relevant facts and circumstances under the rule-of-reason test.

Territorial and customer restrictions usually involve attempts by sellers to divide the targeted market into distinct territorial segments and grant geographic or customer exclusivity to a buyer. Courts have struggled with the antitrust implications of such arrangements primarily because of the dual effect on competition that territorial and customer restraints tend to have: that interbrand competition (competition among different manufacturers) is generally increased at the same time that intrabrand competition (competition among different retailers of the same manufacturer) is generally adversely affected. The courts have attempted to balance this conflicting effect on competition by analyzing all of the surrounding facts and circumstances in the analysis of a territorial or customer restraint under the rule-of-reason test.

State Antitrust Statutes

State antitrust statutes closely parallel the principles codified in the federal antitrust laws, although specific rules and regulations often vary widely among states. Nevertheless, certain trends have emerged recently at state levels that owners and managers of growing companies should consider when developing marketing and distribution strategies.

First, as federal enforcement of the antitrust laws becomes more relaxed, many state attorney generals have become more vigilant in enforcing civil and criminal state antitrust statutes. These statutes are being used as vehicles to enforce economic and political positions regarding antitrust enforcement policies within the state's jurisdiction, as well as to pursue white-collar and organized criminals whose business practices may be in restraint of trade. A second important trend has been the willingness of state courts and juries to interpret the state antitrust statutes more broadly and the exceptions to antitrust violations more narrowly. For example, arguments concerning economic efficiency may not be very effective in persuading a jury in a case where a large local employer is being adversely affected by the trade practices of an unknown out-of-town conglomerate. Finally, many recent state antitakeover statutes designed to protect local business have fostered an environment where proposed mergers are being challenged on anticompetitive grounds by state antitrust enforcement officials more often than in the past.

Developing an Antitrust Compliance Program

As a company's growth leads it into new product lines, expanded geographic territories, and increased market share, it needs to establish and maintain a formal antitrust compliance program to avoid antitrust problems and penalties. Such a program should begin with an antitrust audit, which consists primarily of the circulation of a questionnaire to all key employees responsible for marketing, distribution, and pricing within the organization (see Exhibit 15-1). The purpose of the questionnaire is to identify existing company policies, objectives, activities, contracts, practices, or even attitudes that could create problems under the antitrust laws if not promptly corrected. Legal counsel should review the answers provided by the managers of the company to determine whether a change in policy or practice should be implemented.

The other key component of the initial antitrust audit is document review. Legal counsel should review all customer sales contracts, licensing agreements, distributorship contracts, joint venture agreements, prior litigation documents, employment agreements, trade association by-laws, minutes of board and shareholder meetings, merger and acquisition agreements, customer lists, sales representative agreements, marketing and business plans, internal memoranda, correspondence with competitors and suppliers, customer leasing agreements and service contracts, invoices, and any other document used in connection with the company's dealings with suppliers, consumers, or competitors.

Once all the operating policies and marketing strategies of the company have been developed, legal counsel should review them and then proceed to prepare an antitrust Compliance Manual. The Compliance Manual should provide an overview of federal and state antitrust laws, as well as a more detailed discussion of areas of law that directly or indirectly regulate or otherwise affect the company's business practices. The company's policies regarding antitrust compliance should be widely disseminated to all employees through distribution of the manual, bulletins, antitrust compliance seminars, new employee orientation meetings, and small group workshops.

Exhibit 15-1. Antitrust audit questionnaire.

---

1. Does the company have an oral or written understanding with any direct or indirect competitor with respect to pricing, warranties, discounts, shipping and credit terms, promotional contributions, or service policies in connection with any of the company's products?
2. What are the exact product and geographic markets in which the company competes? What is the respective market share of the company in each of these markets?
3. Has the company experienced any actual or threatened antitrust litigation or investigation in the past? What were the specific company practices upon which these claims were based? What steps, if any, have been taken to resolve any of the problems previously identified?
4. How are the company's pricing policies developed? Is the same product ever sold to different customers at different prices? What is the rationale or justification for such a price disparity?
5. What distribution channels have been selected for marketing the company's products and services? What oral or written agreements have been developed with wholesalers and retailers? Do any of these agreements include specific provisions or understandings as to price, territory, or customer restrictions? Does the company engage in dual distribution? Are any buyers of the company's products or services forced to purchase unwanted products and services as a condition to dealing with the company?
6. To what trade associations does the company belong? What type of information is exchanged among members? Why?

An effective compliance program is especially important in the antitrust law area, where the actual intent of the company and its personnel will be closely examined in connection with its conduct. Effective antitrust compliance will also require careful record keeping when sales and marketing personnel interact with customers, suppliers, and competitors. Top management must be committed to implementation and enforcement of the antitrust compliance program. The time and resources invested in it usually far outweigh the costs of civil and criminal penalties that the company, and even its individual officers and directors, may face in the event of an antitrust violation.

Consumer Protection Laws

Countless federal, state, and local consumer protection laws directly and indirectly affect marketing and distribution planning and decision making. Owners and managers of emerging-growth companies must carefully review legal restrictions on product manufacturing, packaging and labeling, false advertising, and related consumer protection laws when developing marketing strategies. In addition to laws of general applicability, a wide variety of industry-specific regulations in businesses such as textiles, pharmaceutical, and food products have been developed by the FTC, FDA, and other federal and state regulatory agencies.

The consumer protection laws of general applicability to growing companies generally fall into one of two categories: laws affecting design and production and those affecting sales and advertising.

Laws Affecting Design and Production

Companies of all sizes and in all industries that manufacture consumer or industrial products have a legal as well as a social responsibility to offer products that are safe for their intended use. A commitment to product safety must begin with the design of the product by the research and development department; it then becomes the responsibility of the manufacturing department, which must ensure that products are produced without defects or hazardous parts; finally the marketing department has the responsibility for ensuring that the product is packaged in a manner that is not misleading in terms of its range of capabilities and instructions for use.

Consumer product safety laws have attracted significant attention in the last decade as a result of increases in litigation (resulting in excessive damages awards to plaintiffs) and in the rising costs of insurance (resulting in excessive and even inaccessible insurance rates for small companies).

At the state and local levels, the laws governing product liability, negligence, and personal injury determine the manufacturer's responsibility to produce safe products and the penalties for failure to do so. Liability may be imposed due to an act of negligence by the company, a breach of a warranty, or even as a result of strict liability, a theory that forces a manufacturer to pay damages even if there was neither the intent to produce a faulty product nor a breach of the duty of reasonable care, which is at the heart of all negligence law. Because the scope and limitation of these state laws are constantly changing, manufacturers of products, especially at the small-business level, should attend to the state product liability laws in all the jurisdictions where their products are manufactured and distributed.

At the federal level, most consumer product safety laws are developed by the Consumer Product Safety Commission (CPSC), the FDA, and the FTC. The CPSC was created in the early 1970s as part of the Consumer Products Safety Act in order to develop federal regulations designed to reduce the hazards posed to consumers by unsafe products. CPSC regulations now affect the design, manufacture, and marketing of a wide variety of consumer products offered by small and growing companies. CPSC has the power and authority to

1. Inspect a company's manufacturing facilities.
2. Publicize information about companies and products it determines are in violation of its regulations.
3. Force a manufacturer to order a recall, pay a refund, or offer the replacement of a hazardous product.
4. Establish regulations for minimum standards of safety and quality control for specific products.
5. Impose a complete ban on a given hazardous product from the marketplace.

A second major federal regulator in this area is the FDA, which enforces the Federal Food, Drug and Cosmetic Act (FFDCA). The Act is intended to ensure the following:

1. Food products are pure and wholesome, safe to eat, and produced under sanitary conditions.
2. Drugs and medical devices are safe and effective for their intended uses.
3. Cosmetic and beauty aid products are safe and made from appropriate ingredients.
4. Packaging and labeling of all types of food, drug, and cosmetic products are truthful, informative, and not deceptive.

In addition, the Fair Packaging and Labeling Act regulates the contents and placement of information required on the packaging of all consumer and industrial products. The FDA is also charged with the regulation of manufacturing and distribution of certain biological products and electronic devices. Many new products must obtain premarket approval (PMA) pursuant to the FFDCA prior to being offered and sold in the United States. The PMA process is often lengthy, complex, and very expensive.

The FFDCA prohibits interstate distribution or international importation of adulterated or misbranded products. An adulterated product is defined by the statute as one that is defective, unsafe, filthy, or produced under unsanitary conditions. A misbranded product is defined by the statute as one that includes false, misleading, or incomplete packaging or labeling. A number of federal regulations and court cases have attempted to interpret the scope of these two broad prohibitions as applied to the facts and circumstances surrounding each alleged violation of the statute.

The FFDCA also sets forth certain penalties for the refusal or failure of a company to provide the FDA with reports as well as for a refusal by a manufacturer to allow FDA officials to inspect a facility that is regulated by the statute.

Laws Affecting Sales and Advertising

Sales and advertising campaigns are usually developed by emerging-growth companies in order to introduce the marketplace to the company's products and services, build goodwill and consumer loyalty, and increase the company's revenues and profits once a market is developed.

Advertising must communicate the benefits, features, and competitive advantages of the company's products and services clearly, concisely, and accurately. Companies that use false or misleading information in their advertising materials are likely to lose market share, consumer goodwill, and the cooperation of their distribution network. In addition, it is likely that suppliers, creditors, consultants, shareholders, and lenders will become disenchanted with the credibility of a company that uses deceptive practices.

The costs of false and deceptive practices go beyond problems affecting the operation and management of the company from a business perspective. These types of practices also trigger legal problems at federal and state levels because of consumer protection laws that regulate advertising and sales strategies.

At the heart of the legal regulation of sales and marketing practices is the FTC, which, through §5 of the Federal Trade Commission Act, has the authority to prohibit all unfair or deceptive acts or practices in interstate commerce. The FTC can bring a formal enforcement action against a company for a deceptive act if three elements are present: (1) there is a representation, omission, or practice that is likely to mislead the consumer; (2) the specific act will be analyzed from the perspective of the consumer acting reasonably under the circumstances; and (3) the act in question must be material. The broad nature of these elements vests the FTC with considerable discretion in determining whether an unfair or deceptive act or practice has occurred.

The primary safe harbor available to a growing company in developing aggressive sales and marketing strategies is known as puffing, which has been referred to as "a seller's privilege to lie his head off, so long as he says nothing specific, on the theory that no reasonable man would be influenced by such talk." In order to fall within the parameters of this safe harbor, the contents of the specific advertisement should discuss the company's products and services using only subjective opinions, superlatives, or exaggerations and not claim to be based upon any specific facts, unless such facts have been reasonably substantiated.

To avoid a claim for false or deceptive advertising under federal or the various state laws, the following general guidelines should be followed:

- Accuracy, full disclosure, and the ability to substantiate claims are placed at a premium by federal and state regulators. Claims that are made about the company's products or services, regardless of whether they are made in a radio advertisement or a written brochure, must be backed up with facts, test results, opinion letters, market surveys, and customer testimonials supporting and substantiating the representations made to the general public.

- An informed sales staff not only builds customer loyalty but also helps to avoid claims for misrepresentation or deception. Regular sales training meetings, manuals, and marketing information systems keep sales staff up to date on product developments and capabilities.

- Avoid sales gimmicks. Very few successful growth companies were ever built on bait-and-switch techniques, liquidation sales, or cheap gifts or prizes.

- A material omission can be just as damaging as an affirmative misrepresentation. Leaving important information out of an advertisement or brochure concerning the side effects of a product, a disclaimer of warranty as to a particular service, or a condition to obtaining a particular benefit can trigger a claim by regulators or consumers for deception.

Unfair Competition Law and Related Business Torts

A broad and growing body of state and local unfair competition laws must also be considered in developing marketing plans and strategies. Although the nature and scope of the law of unfair competition vary among the states, most jurisdictions recognize some form of the following business torts that usually fall under the unfair competition umbrella: trade libel, product disparagement, interference with existing or prospective contractual relations, misappropriation and infringement of intellectual property (as discussed in chapter 13), passing off, invasion of privacy, commercial bribery, price fixing, price discrimination, and the enforceability of equitable servitudes and covenants.

Owners and managers of growing companies should be aware of the following general principles when developing marketing plans and strategies:

1. *Trade libel and product disparagement.* A company that makes a false and malicious statement to the public regarding the reputation or products of one of its competitors may be liable for any pecuniary losses the competitor suffers as a result. Therefore, although comparative advertising is permitted and even encouraged by federal and state regulations, statements about a competitor should

be very carefully substantiated or fall within the safe harbor of puffery in order to avoid the risk of a disparagement or libel action.

2. *Interference with contractual relations.* Although the antitrust laws are designed to foster competition, excessive competitive zeal in approaching the customers and suppliers of competitors will not be tolerated by state courts. Solicitations of a competitor's customers or suppliers that are designed to encourage a breach of an existing or even prospective contract are generally improper under the law and could result in a civil cause of action by the competitor. In determining whether the alleged act or practice was improper, most courts consider the nature of the actor's conduct, the proximity of the actor's conduct to the alleged interference, the current status of the relationship that was interfered with, and the interests of the third-party supplier or consumer that dealt with the competitor. The bottom line is that there is a large gray area separating a legitimate effort to take business away from a competitor and an improper attempt to induce a breach of contract. Marketing and advertising strategies must attempt to strike this delicate balance, and sales staff must be provided with guidelines as to what conduct is acceptable and what is not. Recently the tort of interference has become part of the growing body of labor and employment law for cases when an employer attempts to recruit the employees of a competitor.

3. *Passing off.* This common-law business tort is closely related to trademark infringement and trade secret misappropriation in that it attempts to penalize a company that copies the packaging, design, name, shape, appearance, taste, color scheme, or general physical characteristics of the products or services offered by a competitor where the intent is to confuse the consumer as to source of origin. Therefore, although competitors are all equally entitled to ensure that their products and services offer attractive features and are presented attractively, no competitor is entitled to confuse the public by posing as another company.

4. *Equitable servitudes and covenants.* An attempt by a seller to restrict the use of a product following the sale may constitute equitable servitude and is generally unenforceable as an illegal restraint of trade. An example of such an attempt would be a manufacturer's telling a wholesaler which retailers it can resell to. Similarly, an unreasonable covenant against competition following the termination of an employment or franchise relationship will not be tolerated by most state courts. A company with a legitimate business justification for the use of such covenants or servitudes bears the burden of proving the reasonableness of the provision when challenged.

Staying One Step Ahead

A s a company grows, its ability to remain one step ahead of its competitors, as well as continue to prosper, depends in large part on how effectively it manages economic distress and business conflicts. Accordingly, the last three chapters of this book are devoted to the legal identification and management of these types of challenges.

At various crossroads in the company's growth, conflict and distress are inevitable. If the problems caused by these occurrences are well managed, growth will continue. Chapter 16 helps to identify legal issues well before they mature into problems and conflicts through the use of legal audits. This preventive law technique has increasingly been recognized by growing companies as a cost-effective means of managing legal problems caused by the changes that growth brings. Chapter 17 takes the reader through the intricacies of litigation and alternative dispute resolution. Finally, chapter 18 discusses bankruptcy and its alternatives.

16

Legal Audits for Growing Companies

Preventive law is a method under which company owners and managers are taught to work with their attorneys in order to recognize legal issues well before they mature into serious problems or conflicts. If steps are taken periodically, legal counsel can assess the legal health of the company and prescribe a set of strategies and solutions for any problems identified. This legal checkup is often referred to as a *legal audit*.

In a legal audit, the company's management team periodically meets with corporate counsel in order to discuss strategic plans and objectives, review key documents and records, and analyze and identify current and projected legal needs of the entity. The audit also lays the groundwork for the establishment of an ongoing legal compliance and prevention program in order to ensure that the company's goals, structure, and ongoing operations are consistent with the latest developments in business law. Finally, the audit helps managers identify the legal issues triggered by changes in strategies, goals, or objectives and plan for the legal tasks that must be accomplished as a result of the issues identified.

A comprehensive legal audit examines a wide range of issues; they may be as mundane as whether the company is qualified to do business in foreign jurisdictions or as complex as an analysis of the company's executive compensation and retirement plans in order to ensure consistency with current tax and employment law regulations. The topics that must be addressed include:

- Choice and structure of the entity
- Recent acts of the board of directors and documentation (or lack thereof) relating to those decisions
- Protection of intellectual property
- Forms and methods of distribution and marketing
- Pending and threatened litigation
- Hiring and firing practices

- Employment agreements
- Securities law compliance
- Antitrust and related trade regulations
- Product liability and environmental law
- Review of sales and collection practices

A legal audit may be performed as part of an ongoing compliance program, in connection with a specific event, such as a financial audit, or in connection with a specific transaction, such as an acquisition or securities offering. Suppose that Jim Cleansoil and Barbara Pureair, the principals of CleanWorld Consulting Company, determined to secure legal counsel in order to conduct a legal audit in connection with the anticipated private placement of CleanWorld's preferred stock. The mechanics of the legal audit and a sample questionnaire are shown below.

Mechanics of the Legal Audit

Step 1: Preliminary Questionnaire. The legal audit should begin with a comprehensive questionnaire prepared by audit counsel for Cleansoil, Pureair, and the rest of CleanWorld's management team to review and complete prior to the arrival of the team of attorneys who are to conduct the legal audit.

Step 2: Initial Conference. Once the documents and related materials requested in the questionnaire have been assembled and problem areas preliminarily identified, audit counsel and the designated officers of CleanWorld who are well versed in the company's operations will schedule a meeting. Other members of the management team, such as the company's outside accountant and other professionals who play key advisory roles to the company, should be present during at the least the portion of the audit that relates to their area of expertise. This initial series of conferences is basically an information-gathering exercise designed to familiarize the legal auditor with all aspects of CleanWorld and to review the completed questionnaires and materials. In addition to these conferences with key personnel, the audit team should perform some on-site observations of the day-to-day operations of the company.

Step 3: Implementation of the Postaudit Recommendations. Once the legal audit team has completed its review and issued its postaudit evaluation, CleanWorld's management team should consider the implementation of specific recommendations contained in the report. The steps it takes will vary depending on the growth planned by the company, as well as the specific findings of the report. At a minimum, meetings with key personnel should be scheduled to review and discuss the postaudit recommendations; internal memoranda prepared on specific topics to educate rank-and-file employees; employee seminars scheduled to educate employees about proper procedures and compliance; and in certain cases, handbooks and Operations Manuals developed for continued and readily available guidance of the company's staff. In addition, a "tickler system" for periodic reporting and key dates/deadlines should be established, as well as a time set for the next legal audit.

Sample Legal Audit Questionnaire

Corporate Matters

- Under what form of ownership is the company operated? When was this decision made? Does it still make sense? Why or why not? Have all annual filings and related actions (such as state corporate annual reports or required director and shareholder meetings) been satisfied?
- What are the company's capital requirements in the next 12 months? How will this money be raised? What alternatives are being considered? What issues are triggered by these strategies? Have applicable federal and state securities laws been considered in connection with these proposed offerings?
- Will key employees be offered equity in the enterprise as an incentive for performance and loyalty? Is such equity available? Has the adoption of such plans been properly authorized? Up to what point? Have all necessary stock option plans and employment agreements been prepared and approved by the shareholders and directors of the corporation? Will any of the founders of the company be retiring or moving on to other projects? How will these changes affect the current structure?
- If the company is a corporation, was an election under Subchapter S ever made? Why or why not? If the entity is an S corporation, does it still qualify? Is such a choice unduly restrictive as the company grows (e.g., ability to attract foreign investment, taxation of undistributed earnings)? If the entity is not a Subchapter S corporation, could it still qualify? Is this a more sensible entity under the new tax laws?
- Have by-laws been prepared and carefully followed in the operation and management of the corporation? Have annual meetings of shareholders and directors been properly held and conducted? Have the minutes of these

meetings been properly and promptly entered into the corporate record book? Have transactions outside the regular course of business been approved or ratified by directors (or, where required, by shareholder agreements or by-laws) and resolutions been recorded and entered into the corporate records? Have quorum, notice, proxy, and voting requirements been met in each case under applicable state laws?

Business Planning Matters

* Has a business and management plan been prepared? Does it include information about the company's key personnel; strategic objectives; realistic and well-documented financial statements; current and planned products and services; market data, strategy, and evaluation of competition; capital structure and allocation of proceeds; capital formation needs; customer base; distribution network; sales and advertising strategies; facility and labor needs; risk factors; and realistic milestones and strategies for the achievement of these plans and objectives?

* How and when was the business plan prepared? Has it been reviewed and revised on a periodic basis, or is it merely collecting dust on a bookshelf? Has it been changed or supplemented to reflect any changes in the company's strategies, plans, or objectives?

* To whom has the plan been shown? For what purposes? Have steps been taken to preserve the confidential nature of the document? To what extent have federal and state securities laws been reviewed to prevent violations due to the misuse of the business plan as a disclosure document?

Compliance With Government Regulations

* Have all required federal and state tax forms been filed (i.e., employer's quarterly and annual returns, federal and state unemployment tax contributions, etc.)? Are federal and state record-keeping requirements being met for tax purposes? Have all payroll and unemployment tax accounts been established?

* Has the company been qualified to do business in each state where such filing is required? Have all required local business permits and licenses been obtained? Are the company's operational policies in compliance with federal and zoning requirements? Has the company developed smoking, maternity leave, or child care policies and programs that are in compliance with federal, state, and local laws? When is the last time the company consulted these statutes to ensure that current practices are consistent with applicable laws?

Employee Benefit Plans

* Has the company adopted a medical reimbursement plan? Group life insurance? Retirement plans? Disability plans? If not, should they be adopted?

If yes, have all amendments to the structure and ongoing management of these plans been made to maintain qualification? Have annual reports been filed with the U.S. Department of Treasury and U.S. Department of Labor for pension and profit-sharing plans?

- Have there been any changes in the administration of these plans? Have there been any recent transactions between the plan and the company, its trustees, or its officers and directors?

Contractual Matters

- On which material contracts is the company directly or indirectly bound? Were these agreements drafted in compliance with applicable laws, such as the state's version of the Uniform Commercial Code? Is the company still able to meet its obligations under these agreements? Is any party to these agreements in default? Why? What steps have been taken to enforce the company's rights and/or mitigate damages?

- To what extent are contractual forms used when selling company products and services? When were these forms updated? What problems have these forms triggered? What steps have been taken to resolve these problems?

- Are employees who possess special skills and experience under an employment agreement with the company? When was the agreement reviewed and revised? Are sales representatives under a written agreement and commission schedule? Has the scope of their authority been clearly defined and communicated to the third parties with whom they deal?

- To what extent does the company hire independent contractors? Have agreements been prepared with these parties? Have intellectual property law issues, such as work-for-hire provisions, been included in these agreements?

Protection of Intellectual Property

- To what extent are trademarks, patents, copyrights, and trade secrets among the intangible assets of the business? What are the internal company procedures for these key assets? What agreements (such as ownership of inventions, nondisclosure, and noncompete) have been struck with key employees who are exposed to the company's intellectual property? What procedures are in place for receiving new ideas and proposals from employees and other parties?

- Have trademarks, patents, and copyrights been registered? What monitoring programs are in place to detect infringement and ensure proper usage by third parties? Are documents properly stamped with copyright and confidentiality notices? Has counsel been contacted to determine whether the new discovery is eligible for registration? Does the company license any of its intellectual property to third parties? Has experienced licensing and franchising counsel prepared the agreements and disclosure documents?

Relationships With Competitors

- To what professional and trade associations does the company belong? What types of information are exchanged? Does the company engage in any type of communication or have any cooperative agreement with a competitor regarding price, geographic territories, or distribution channels that might constitute an antitrust violation or an act of unfair competition? Has the company established an in-house program in order to educate employees about the mechanics and pitfalls of antitrust violations? Has an antitrust action ever been brought or threatened by or against the company? What were the surrounding facts? What was the outcome?

- Has a former employee of a competitor been hired recently? How was he or she recruited? Does this employee use skills or knowledge gained from the prior employer? To what extent has the prior employer been notified? What steps are being taken to avoid a lawsuit involving misappropriation of trade secrets and/or interference with contractual regulations?

- Does the company engage in comparative advertising? How are the products and services of the competitor generally treated? Are any trademarks or trade names similar to those of competitors? Has the company been involved in any prior litigation with a competitor? Threatened litigation?

Marketing and Distribution Issues

- Has the company clearly defined the market for its products and services? Who are the key competitors? What are their respective market shares, strengths, weaknesses, strategies, and objectives? What new players are entering this market? What barriers exist to new entry? What is the saturation point of this market? What are the key distribution channels for bringing these products to the market? Have all necessary agreements and regulations affecting these channels been adequately addressed (i.e., labeling and warranty laws, distributorship agreements, etc.)?

- Is the company considering franchising as a method of marketing and distribution to expand market share? To what extent can all key aspects of the company's success be reduced to an Operations Manual and taught to others in a training program? To what extent are competitors engaged in franchising?

- If franchising is appropriate for distribution of the company's products or business, have all necessary offering documents and agreements been prepared by experienced franchise legal counsel? What initial franchise fee will be charged? Ongoing royalties? Are these fees competitive? What ongoing programs and support are given to franchisees? What products and services must the franchisee buy from the company? Under what conditions may one franchise be terminated or transferred?

CHAPTER

17

Managing Business Conflicts

As a company grows, the number of vendors, customers, employees, consultants, investors, and competitors it comes into contact with also grows. This increase in the number of relationships the company must effectively manage also increases the chances that business conflicts will arise. The management and disposition of business conflicts is a time-consuming and expensive process that can hamper a growing company. A rule of thumb is that in litigation, there are really no winners—only successful or unsuccessful litigants.

Most owners and managers of growing companies prefer to engage in battle in the marketplace or in the boardroom rather than in the courtroom. Nevertheless, there will be situations where an amicable settlement or resolution of the conflict seems impossible. If a business dispute matures into a courtroom battle, owners and managers must understand the basic rules of litigation and arbitration.

Avoiding Litigation

Most disputes and conflicts among companies are the result of a misunderstanding over the rights and obligations of the parties to a particular agreement or in a particular situation. The failure to provide acceptable products or services, pay the bills of a trade creditor on a timely basis, meet the expectations of an investor, comply with the covenants imposed by a lender, adequately compensate an employee or consultant, complete a proposed transaction or investment, or consider the antitrust laws in dealing with competitors are all situations likely to lead to litigation.

A good relationship with counsel and a well-managed legal compliance program will contribute to reducing the risk of litigation. Other steps, such as those listed below, will help growing companies stay out of the courtroom.

1. *Management, management, management.* A well-managed company is far less likely to get entangled in a legal dispute with an employee, investor, creditor, or competitor than is a haphazardly managed one. A well-run company is far more likely to meet its contractual obligations on a timely basis; deal with its employees, shareholders, and competitors more fairly; manage and monitor the activities of its staff and authorized agents; apply quality control standards to the production of goods and services; and regularly communicate with legal counsel to identify and solve risks and problems well before they mature into a formal dispute.

2. *Undercapitalization is the kiss of death.* An undercapitalized company is much more likely to experience financial problems that will lead to litigation. Ironically, when the company is undercapitalized, it will tend to avoid the use of professionals at a time when they are needed the most. A lack of capital translates into corners being cut as to quality of product and service, bills being paid late, legal documents and procedures not being prepared or followed in connection with the issuance of securities, and covenants with lenders and investors being broken. These acts of desperation, caused by financial distress, will lead only to conflicts and problems.

3. *Get it in writing and get it right.* Many business disputes that end in litigation begin because there is no written agreement setting forth the respective rights and obligations of the parties in a given transaction. If there is a written document, it may be unclear or ambiguous, or perhaps it fails to anticipate the facts the parties are now disputing. Owners and managers of growing companies who wish to avoid litigation should ensure that each significant transaction is evidenced by an agreement or series of agreements and that these documents clearly reflect both the spirit and intent of the transactions and the respective rights and obligations of each party.

4. *Understand the big picture.* An emerging-growth company negotiating a contract, hiring an employee, or dealing with a competitor can easily get too caught up in the narrow objectives of the transaction. When this happens, owners and managers often fail to see the big picture; they take legal risks or overlook or ignore warning signals. Each contemplated transaction must be analyzed with more than tunnel vision. The broader risks and potential problems, both short term and long term, must be taken into account and discussed with counsel well before the documents are executed.

5. *It is cheaper to be a skeptic than a plaintiff.* A growing company will take risks and seize opportunities, and both will present costs and benefits. A financial intermediary who promises to raise an unlimited amount of capital within 30 days, or the sales representative who promises to deliver more customers than the company can handle, are a dime a dozen. That same dime probably represents a fair price for the value of such boisterous claims. Rather than trying to build a company on shallow representations and then spending valuable time and money in court trying to enforce these worthless promises, it is far better to

be skeptical at the outset and either force the party on the other side of the table to document his or her claims or forgo the opportunity.

6. *Establish a legal compliance program.* All employees within the growing company must be made aware of the legal risks of their actions. Legal compliance programs, developed with the assistance of counsel, should include periodic legal audits, legal Compliance Manuals and employee seminars, form letters and checklists for routine transactions, and established procedures for record keeping and file management.

Litigation Planning and Strategy

If and when a growing company determines that litigation is the most sensible and efficient way to resolve a business dispute, or when an adversary brings suit, the company must develop plans and strategies in light of the following principles:

1. It must develop goals and objectives and communicate them to legal counsel. A broad strategy statement such as "sue the bastards and get everything they've got" is not sufficient. Rather, counsel must be made aware of any budgetary limitations or time constraints that affect the company well before the complaint or answer is filed.

2. It must gather all documents relevant to the dispute and organize them well before the opponent serves the first discovery request.

3. It should explore alternative methods of dispute resolution, clearly define parameters for settlement, and communicate them to legal counsel.

4. It should discuss with legal counsel the risks, costs, and benefits of entering into litigation.

5. It should review with counsel the terms of payment of legal fees (as well as those of any experts needed).

6. It should develop a litigation management system for monitoring and controlling costs.

7. It should maintain clear lines of communication with legal counsel throughout all phases of the litigation.

The decision to resolve a dispute through litigation must be based on a genuine understanding of the legal rights, remedies, and defenses available. For example, suppose that goods ordered from a supplier by Far East Imports Company are of a significantly lesser quality than David Decor had anticipated. Decor reviews the contract and decides that the quality control specifications seem to be clear; however, a material difference of opinion has developed because the supplier refuses to replace the merchandise. Before filing a complaint for breach of contract, Decor should carefully review

- Alternative methods for resolving the dispute
- The elements of a legal breach of contract in the jurisdiction that governs the agreement
- The various defenses that may be available to the supplier
- The direct and indirect costs of litigation
- The range of damages that may be recovered if a breach is successfully established

Only after Decor is satisfied that the answers to these questions indicate that litigation is a viable alternative should formal action be pursued. Similarly, if Far East Imports is sued by a creditor or landlord, it should attempt to resolve these disputes before responding with a formal answer.

The Mechanics of Litigation

Suppose that Lisa Paymerent, the property manager for a large regional mall, institutes legal action against Far East Imports for nonpayment of rent. Her first step is to prepare and file a Complaint, which must set forth her claim against Far East Imports. Each allegation should be set forth in a separate paragraph and written clearly and concisely, with any necessary exhibits attached to the end of the Complaint. Each allegation should relate to a claim upon which Paymerent is entitled to relief and to make a demand for judgment.

If the Complaint meets all statutory and procedural requirements, the clerk of the court prepares a summons, which is served with the Complaint on Far East Imports. The summons directs Far East Imports to serve an Answer upon Paymerent's lawyer, usually within 20 days after service of process is made.

Far East Imports may file certain preliminary motions before delivering an Answer or they are waived. These motions, essentially specific requests for the court to act, include those to dismiss (due to a lack of jurisdiction, improper service or process, etc.), to dismiss due to failure to state a claim upon which relief can be granted, to strike, or to request a more definite statement.

Once the Answer is filed, it must contain three principal components:

1. Admit the allegations contained in the complaint that are true;
2. Deny the allegations that the defendant believes are not true; and
3. Allege any affirmative defenses to the causes of action raised by the plaintiff.

Far East Imports must also file any counterclaim it may have against Paymerent that may have arisen out of the same transaction or occurrence. Failure to raise such claims results in a waiver by the defendant. The Complaint, Answer, and any counterclaims and answers to counterclaims are usually collectively referred to as the pleadings.

Once all of the pleadings and preliminary motions are filed, the parties are permitted to begin the process of discovery, a pretrial procedure for obtaining information necessary for the disposition of the dispute. Discovery serves a number of important purposes. It

- Narrows the issues actually in dispute
- Prevents surprise by allowing each party to find out what testimony and other evidence is available for each issue in dispute
- Preserves information that may not be available at the actual trial, such as the statement of a very ill witness
- Encourages resolution of the dispute prior to trial

Despite these many benefits, discovery tends to increase significantly the legal fees and related expenses of the company in connection with the litigation, as well as the amount of time necessary to resolve the dispute.

One of the key issues to consider is the permissible scope of the discovery. The general rule is that virtually any information is discoverable, provided that it is relevant and not subject to any category of evidentiary privilege, which refers to communications that have been exchanged during the course of relationships, such as those between a doctor and patient, attorney and client, priest and penitent, or husband and wife. The five principal discovery devices that are available to litigants are depositions, written interrogatories, requests for production of documents, physical and mental examinations, and requests for admissions (see Exhibit 17-1).

Once the parties have completed the discovery process, the litigation proceeds to the pretrial conference, the actual trial, the appeal, and any posttrial proceedings. Although a comprehensive discussion of the mechanics of a trial is beyond the scope of this book, it is safe to say that this process consumes two of the most important resources to an emerging-growth business: time and money. Alternatives to litigation, which are likely to be less expensive and less time-consuming, should be considered in resolving disputes.

Alternatives to Litigation

A broad range of methods and procedures generally expedite the resolution of disputes without litigation. These processes are broadly referred to as alternative dispute-resolution (ADR) methods. The most commonly known ADR method is arbitration: A neutral third party is selected by the disputants to hear the case

Exhibit 17-1.   Five discovery devices.

1. Deposition. A deposition generally involves the pretrial examination and cross-examination of a witness by counsel of any person who has information relevant to the case, whether or not the person is a party to the action. The written record of the deposition may be admitted at trial as substantive evidence and may be used to impeach a witness whose testimony at trial is inconsistent with the testimony given during the deposition.

2. Written Interrogatories. An interrogatory is a written question one party may pose to another party; it must be answered in writing, under oath, within 30 days. Unlike depositions, interrogatories may only be served upon parties to the litigation. Most courts limit the number of interrogatories that may be filed and the scope of the questions so that they are not overly burdensome and to prevent parties from engaging in a mere fishing expedition. If a party objects to an interrogatory, it must specify its grounds for refusing to answer; at this time the burden shifts to the proponent of the question to convince the court why an answer should be compelled. An answer to an interrogatory may also include a reference to a particular business document or set of records provided that the other party is given an opportunity to inspect the documents.

3. Requests for Production of Documents or Inspection of Land. A party may request another party to produce and permit inspection, copying, testing, or photographing business documents, tangible assets, financial books, and records or anything else that may be relevant to the litigation. Similarly, a party may request entry to the business premises of another party for the purposes of inspection, photographing, surveying, or any other purpose that is relevant and not subject to an evidentiary privilege. These requests are limited to parties to the litigation, with the exception of a *subpoena duces tecum*, which is a demand to produce certain documents and records in connection with the deposition of a nonparty.

Exhibit 17-1. (continued).

4. <u>Physical and Mental Examinations</u>. A party may request that another party submit to a mental or physical examination by a physician or psychiatrist. The mental or physical condition of the party, however, must be relevant to the issues in dispute. The court grants such a request only if good cause is shown and usually limits the scope of the examination to the actual issues in controversy.

5. <u>Requests for Admissions.</u> A party may serve a request for admission on another party for the purposes of ascertaining the genuineness of specific documents, obtaining the admission or denial of a specific matter, or confirming the application of certain law to a given set of facts. Failure to respond to a request will be deemed to be an admittance. Therefore the party on which a request has been served must deny the request, explain why it is unable to admit or deny, or file an objection to the request as improper within 30 days.

and render an opinion, which may or may not be binding on the parties depending on the terms of the arbitration clause or agreement.

There are many forms of arbitration. However, each involves a process for the parties in dispute to submit arguments and evidence in an information fashion to a neutral person or persons for the purpose of adjudicating the differences between the parties. The evidentiary and procedural rules are not nearly as formal as in litigation, and there tends to be far greater flexibility in the timing of the proceeding and the selection of the actual decision makers.

An arbitration may be a voluntary proceeding that the parties have selected in advance of any dispute, such as in a contract or by mutual agreement, or it may be a compulsory, court-annexed procedure prerequisite to full-blown litigation. Owners and managers of growing companies who wish to avoid the cost and delay of litigation should ensure that arbitration clauses appear in all key contracts. The clause should specify

- That the parties agree to submit any controversy or claim arising from the agreement or contract to a binding (or nonbinding) arbitration;
- The place of the arbitration;
- The method for selecting the parties who will hear the dispute;
- Any limitations on the award that may be rendered by the arbitrator;
- Which party shall be responsible for the costs of the proceeding; and
- Any special procedural rules that will govern the arbitration.

A key factor is whether the decision of the arbitrator will be binding or non-binding. If the parties agree that the award will be binding, both must live with the results. Binding arbitration awards are usually enforceable by the local court unless there has been a defect in the arbitration procedures. The opinion rendered in a nonbinding arbitration is advisory only; the parties may accept it or reject it and proceed to litigation. In a court-annexed arbitration, the court will order the arbitration as a nonbinding proceeding that is intended to work out the differences between the parties without the need for litigation.

Unless the parties have specific rules and procedures in mind that will govern the arbitration, I recommend that the Commercial Arbitration Rules of the American Arbitration Association be closely followed. The association provides a copy of its rules and fees to interested parties who write or call its national office: 140 West 51st Street, New York, New York 10020–1203; (212) 484-4000.

Various forms of mediation, private judging, minitrials, and moderated settlement conferences are also available to companies that are unable to resolve their disputes and wish to avoid the expense and delay of a trial. Each method offers certain advantages and disadvantages that may make one process far more appropriate for resolving a particular dispute than another. The procedures, costs, and benefits of each should be carefully reviewed with experienced legal counsel.

CHAPTER

18

Managing Economic Distress

B usiness problems and financial distress are the inevitable result of the various changes that emerging-growth companies experience. Although effective strategic planning helps mitigate the risk of business failure, nothing guarantees against economic distress or even bankruptcy. Most of the reasons that growth companies experience financial distress or complete failure stem from ineffective management or adverse economic conditions. The owners and managers of a growing company must learn how to manage and adapt to the more positive aspects of growth but also how to anticipate the financial problems that can be caused by growth, manage the costs and risks caused by these economic problems, and understand the methods available for resolving financial problems, including the bankruptcy process and its alternatives.

Risk Management and Control

Risk management is a term generally referred to in the insurance industry as the process of identifying and analyzing a company's exposure to risk (see Exhibit 18-1) and then selecting alternatives for protecting against these risks. Various forms of business insurance policies are designed to provide financial protection to a company when the losses caused by these risks actually come to fruition. The cost of this protection varies depending on the extent to which risks can be managed and controlled.

Certain types of economic and financial risks are predictable and can be managed once identified; others are beyond the control of even the best management team. Similarly, certain types of risks can be mitigated with insurance, and others, such as hostile acts by suppliers or competitors, are not insurable.

Effective risk management for a rapidly growing company goes far beyond the installation of smoke detectors and a periodic safety check for all company-owned vehicles. From a management perspective, it means establishing internal

241

Exhibit 18-1. Conducting a risk assessment.

- What aspects of the company's operations could directly or indirectly cause an economic loss?
- What is the likelihood that such a loss will actually occur?
- If the potential loss identified actually does occur, what are the tangible and intangible costs to the company?
- To what extent are the potential losses insurable? Does the cost of the insurance policies outweigh the cost of potential conflict or loss?
- To what extent can the company implement internal financial controls in order to prevent or reduce the exposure to financial distress?

financial and managerial controls designed to ensure ongoing compliance with the company's strategies, policies, and procedures. From an accounting perspective, it means maintaining accurate and comprehensive financial records so that periodic financial statements are produced on a timely basis in accordance with generally accepted accounting principles. From a legal perspective, it means compliance with corporate law formalities, labor and employment laws, and antitrust and trade regulations; maintenance of all necessary business licenses and permits; and upholding of material contractual obligations (such as vendor agreements, leases, and loan documents), obligations to protect intellectual property, and any other laws and regulations that may be applicable to the operation and management of the company. Periodic legal audits are one effective method of ensuring that a growing company remains in compliance with its legal obligations, the nature and extent of which are likely to change as the company grows and develops.

Anticipating Financial Distress

The primary role of a risk management and control system is to provide early warning signs of financial distress. Early detection of business problems is vital to the continued growth of the company and to the management of situations likely to cause economic distress. Once a problem or risk has been identified, strategies must be developed promptly to remedy the situation in a cost-effective manner.

Business problems rarely occur suddenly. Most fester a long time as a result of a series of financial, legal, operational, and strategic mistakes or miscalculations that went largely undetected by the company's management team. The following red flags should be strongly considered in determining whether a company's rapid growth has put it on a course leading to disaster:

1. *Lack of depth in the management team.* A growing company's risk of business failure increases if it depends on an overly centralized management team comprised of a limited number of individuals who founded the business. Although key-man life insurance may satisfy the concerns of an investor, the long-term health of the growing company depends on the founders' ability to recruit and retain qualified personnel capable of guiding the company to its next phase of growth. A middle level of management must be trained as replacements who can handle certain tasks performed by the founders of the company at its earlier stages, especially in anticipation of death, retirement, disability, or other departure from the company.

2. *Operating in an industry with rapidly changing technology.* A company operating in a marketplace where rapidly changing technology could render its products and services suddenly obsolete has a high chance of business failure. Management must stay abreast of technological developments, attempt to establish product diversification, and ensure adequate capitalization for ongoing research and modernization of equipment.

3. *Dependence on a key customer, supplier, lender, or contract.* Many companies are built and continue to flourish as a result of a single critical customer, source of supply, or special relationship with a lender or investor. Effective growth planning dictates that plans be developed to avoid the company's becoming a hostage to any third party that cannot be completely controlled. For example, if a rapidly growing company relies on a major customer for 35 to 60 percent of its revenues and the customer is lost to a competitor, what will be the effect on the company? Worse, if the key customer is aware of the company's dependence, how many demands will the company grant to preserve the account? Diversification of product lines, geographic trading areas, targeted markets, and distribution channels will help mitigate this risk of dependence. Similarly, an excessive dependence on patents, licenses, franchise agreements, concessions, and related contractual advantages that may be terminated or expire significantly increases the chance of business failure.

4. *Undercapitalization for specific projects.* Many rapidly growing companies try to take advantage of market opportunities even if they lack the capital necessary to complete the components of the project. Perhaps a company has the funds to manufacture a product but no capital to market it. Under such circumstances, it could sell or license the technology to another company and then use the proceeds or licensing royalties to exploit an existing product or service it offers.

5. *Defective information and monitoring systems.* A growing company with an inadequate or defective management information system is likely to have difficulty monitoring its competition, internal costs and budgets, changes in the

economic and political environment, inventory controls, management problems and internal conflicts, cash flow, and sales growth. If it lacks this information, it is likely to experience difficulty in making informed day-to-day decisions or engaging in meaningful long-term strategic planning—problems that typically lead to economic distress. Top management must insist on weekly, monthly, and quarterly sales, production, and profits reports so that it can identify financial problems well before they mature into a crisis.

6. *Retaining nonproductive divisions, assets, and people for no good reason.* Most companies that are growing quickly have some operating division, asset, or person(s) that is unproductive and is putting a strain on the overall profitability of the company. Get rid of the deadwood. Especially dangerous are projects or people that remain in the company for paternalistic or egotistical reasons. Chances are that such a division of assets is a hemorrhage that is bleeding precious cash. Similarly, obsolete or idle equipment, unused real estate, and unnecessary employee benefits (e.g., the company car, boat, condominium, or plane) should be candidates for disposal when cash is at a premium.

7. *Accounts receivable management problems.* There is nothing more frustrating to an emerging-growth company than to experience a tremendous increase in sales with an equally growing accounts receivable management problem. Customers must be carefully monitored; those seriously overdue should be provided with no further goods or services. As soon as a customer shows signs of difficulty in paying, the company should obtain collateral to secure the obligation. Collection agencies and attorneys should be used for larger problematic accounts. If cash flow becomes a real problem, consider discounting the accounts receivable at a commercial bank, obtaining the services of a factoring company, or obtaining credit insurance to protect against excessive bad debt losses.

The Costs of Financial Distress

Financial distress affects a company's employees, customers, stockholders, creditors, and suppliers. Customers and vendors often avoid dealing with a troubled company, which will then suffer greater financial problems and have more trouble raising capital. Vendors, to the extent that they are still willing to sell to a distressed firm at all, usually demand unreasonable sales terms in order to protect their risk. Key employees, fearful for their jobs, may flee to a more stable competitor, usually taking their enthusiasm, ideas, and expertise with them. The distressed company will face problems in attracting and retaining the skilled personnel it desperately needs to keep the company alive. Stockholders often seek to dispose of their securities, driving down the market price per share of the company. Creditors may seek to accelerate obligations in order to protect against the risk of default.

During this difficult period, it is likely that inventory is becoming obsolete, building and machinery are deteriorating, and equipment is not being maintained because the company lacks the resources to commit to servicing or replacement. Finally, even competitors are likely to become more aggressive in order to take advantage of the window of opportunity created by the company's financial distress.

Understanding Bankruptcy and Its Alternatives

If the management team of the company is unable to anticipate and plan for potential problems, develop effective strategies and solutions for such problems, and avoid the direct and indirect costs of financial distress, bankruptcy and its alternatives should be considered.

Bankruptcy does not carry quite the same stigma that it did 20 years ago. The Bankruptcy Reform Act of 1978 placed an even greater emphasis on business rehabilitation and restructuring than on the liquidation of a financially distressed company. In fact, reorganization under the federal bankruptcy laws has emerged as an integral part of the long-term strategic planning process and as a viable alternative for a troubled project, subsidiary, or even an entire company.

Nevertheless, bankruptcy is far from a panacea as a solution to problems caused by economic distress. The process can be extremely time-consuming and disruptive to the responsibilities and morale of the company's management, result in extensive negative publicity and loss of goodwill, involve substantial legal fees, and cause a significantly weakened bargaining position with creditors and competitors. A formal bankruptcy proceeding can and often will result in a transfer of the control of the company to a group representing the creditors, the need to terminate a large percentage of the company's work force, a significantly reduced ability to raise capital, and difficulty in attracting qualified employees and service providers. These costs and risks should be carefully weighed when considering bankruptcy and its alternatives.

Remember that David Decor and Sarah Thinkbig of Far East Imports Company have been threatened by many of its creditors. The company's hasty growth has made bankruptcy a realistic alternative strategy to ensure long-term survival. Far East Imports has several alternatives available under the federal bankruptcy laws and informally with major creditors. A determination as to which alternative is most sensible usually depends on whether the principal cause of the failure is temporary, which tends to favor formal or informal reorganization, or permanent, which would favor liquidation of the company's assets because it will ultimately be worth more to creditors and stockholders dead than it is alive.

Many companies initially explore the several organizational alternatives before considering liquidation:

1. *Informal negotiations with creditors.* In almost all cases, an informal "work-out" with creditors will be more efficient and less disruptive than a formal Chapter 11 proceeding. In an informal work-out, Far East Imports will seek to renegotiate the terms of its obligations to lenders and trade creditors. It may ask for an extension of the time in which the obligations will become due, a reduction in the overall cost or terms of the capital or credit, a composition agreement (under which all known creditors accept partial payment on a pro rata basis in full satisfaction of the obligation), a partial transfer of control of the company to major creditors, or even an exchange of all or part of the debt for equity in the debtor. If Far East Imports chooses this route, it must have the cooperation of all known creditors because there is usually no way to force dissenting creditors to become parties to a composition or settlement agreement. (This would not be the case in a formal Chapter 11 proceeding, where the judge can force a creditor to accept the terms of whatever the court deems to be a generally fair and equitable plan of reorganization.)

2. *Informal reorganization.* Far East Imports could also seek voluntarily to reorganize or restructure the corporation in order to achieve more efficient and more profitable operations. For example, it could choose to merge or be acquired by another company, which could make more effective use of the larger inventories it purchased for wholesale operations. Alternatively, the company could separate the profitable retailing division from the unprofitable wholesale division and create two subsidiaries. Capital formation efforts could then be placed on the profitable subsidiary with plans to rebuild the unprofitable subsidiary at a later date. Finally, Far East Imports could simply spin off certain assets to third parties and then use the proceeds of the sale to repay debts and concentrate on the growth and development of the remaining operations. Each of these methods of informal reorganization usually can be implemented more quickly and inexpensively than a formal proceeding under Chapter 11, provided that the company has the cooperation and support of its stockholders and creditors.

The benefits of implementing an informal work-out or reorganization plan as an alternative to formal bankruptcy proceedings must not be underestimated. This is especially true for owners and managers of closely held companies, where the list of trade creditors and lenders is likely to be far shorter than for a larger, publicly traded corporation. Smaller companies are much more likely to be able to round up their creditors for the purposes of negotiating a composition agreement than would a multinational corporation with thousands of creditors.

3. *Petition for formal reorganization under Chapter 11 of the Bankruptcy Act.* Far East Imports may voluntarily petition for relief under Chapter 11 or be involuntarily forced into reorganization by at least three of its creditors (unless the company has fewer than 12 creditors, in which case even a single creditor can force a reorganization).

In a typical Chapter 11 proceeding, the debtor is essentially reclassified as a debtor-in-possession and is either permitted to continue to operate and manage its business, subject to certain restrictions imposed by the court and the federal bankruptcy statutes, or the court may determine that the company's management is so incompetent that a trustee or management committee must be appointed to full or partial control and operate the company during the period that the plan of reorganization is being developed and approved.

Once Far East Imports has been reclassified as a debtor-in-possession, it has a fiduciary duty to protect the assets of the business on behalf of Far East Imports' secured and unsecured creditors. As a result, its ability to borrow and raise capital, enter into new contracts, hire new employees, implement management strategies, and conduct certain business operations will be restricted. The direct and indirect costs of these restrictions are high in terms of professional fees and management resources. It is likely that Decor and Thinkbig will spend more time at court appearances, meetings with creditors, and preparing financial statements and schedules than they will operating and managing the business.

To be weighed against these costs, however, are the benefits the company will enjoy after the petition has been filed and once the formal plan of reorganization has been approved. For example, upon the filing of the petition for reorganization, all actions against the company and its assets are subject to an automatic stay, which has the effect of delaying almost all immediate obligations and proceedings until the formal plan has been approved. Creditors who attempt to violate the automatic stay provisions may be held in contempt of court. Once the statutory requirements of the formal plan have been met and all necessary consents obtained, the plan is ready to be confirmed by the presiding bankruptcy judge. The confirmation of the plan has the following legal ramifications:

1. The plan has a binding effect on Far East Imports and its creditors.
2. All property of the bankruptcy estate is vested in the reorganized debtor, free and clear of all liens and encumbrances unless otherwise stated in the plan.
3. All prior debts of Far East are discharged except as may be provided in the plan.
4. The debtor company commences its operations pursuant to the terms of the plan.

The benefits accruing to a troubled company by the development and approval of a formal plan of reorganization are significant. Approval, however, marks the beginning, not the end, of a successful turnaround. If the company has been reorganized properly, it may emerge and prosper. But it might not. Many emerging-growth companies that survive the bankruptcy process are subsequently unable to flourish under the terms and conditions of the approved reorganization plan. The change in control, management policies, and operational freedom caused by the reorganization plan could result in an eventual collapse of the company, leading to another reorganization or even liquidation proceedings under Chapter 7.

Chapter 7: When Things Aren't Getting Better

If Far East Imports cannot be formally reorganized or if the plan of reorganization proves to be unsuccessful, a formal liquidation under Chapter 7 of the Bankruptcy Act must be considered. The proceedings under Chapter 7 begin with the filing of a voluntary or involuntary petition for liquidation. The court then issues to Far East Imports an order for relief, which triggers the automatic stay provisions. At the same time, a trustee is appointed to manage the company's assets, referred to as the bankruptcy estate. Creditors must file a Proof of Claim within 90 days of the first meeting between the debtor, trustee, and creditors. The appointed trustee must

- Gather all available assets into the bankruptcy estate for liquidation.
- Set aside any fraudulent transfers.
- Review the validity of all Proofs of Claim submitted by creditors.
- Separate the interests of secured and unsecured creditors.
- Determine if any assets collected are exempt from liquidation.
- Arrange for the sale of the assets in the bankruptcy estate in a manner and on terms most advantageous to the creditors.

Once the assets have been gathered, inventoried, appraised, and sold, the proceeds are distributed to the creditors according to the terms of the plan of liquidation by the trustee, and virtually all obligations of the debtor are discharged.

Index